TIGER WOODS STUNS THE GOLF WORLD!

"The odds of a golfer winning the modern Grand Slam have always been roughly equivalent to a baseball player hitting 70 home runs, a running back gaining 2,500 yards or a basketball player averaging 60 points per game. In other words, possible, imaginable, but highly unlikely . . .

"But that was before Tiger Woods and his otherworldly performance [in the Masters] . . ."
—*The New York Times*, Tuesday, April 15, 1997

The click of the camera was a blessing: it sent Tiger into the maw of his gallery, allowed him to make that walk up the 18th through a tunnel. He thought of many things after he hit that second shot on the 72nd hole. He thought of his father up there at the 18th green waiting for him; his father who just had a triple bypass, his father who put him through the basic training, who dedicated his life to his son's career. He thought of his mother, and the talks she used to give him about sportsmanship and Buddhism. He thought of Jackie Robinson and Charlie Sifford and Lee Elder, and the swath they cut through racism. He thought about the dream he had as a kid, the dream where he won the Masters tournament, and now, almost fifty years to the day after Robinson played his first major league game for the Brooklyn Dodgers, here Tiger Woods was, doing just that.

—From *Tiger Woods: The Makings of a Champion*

ALSO BY TIM ROSAFORTE:

Heartbreak Hill

TIGER WOODS

THE MAKINGS OF A CHAMPION

TIM ROSAFORTE

St. Martin's Paperbacks

To Genevieve, Genna and Molly

TIGER WOODS: THE MAKINGS OF A CHAMPION

Copyright © 1997 by Tim Rosaforte.

Cover photograph by Michael Lloyd/*The Oregonian*/Sygma.

ISBN: 0-312-96437-4

Printed in the United States of America

St. Martin's Press hardcover edition/January 1997
St. Martin's Paperbacks edition/July 1997

10 9 8 7 6 5 4 3 2 1

ACKNOWLEDGMENTS

Is any 20-year-old kid worth a 70,000-word biography? Probably not, but Tiger Woods is not just any 20-year-old kid. Contracts have already been signed for six Tiger-related books, and I can guarantee you this is just a start to the media parade. Eventually, there will be Tiger in audio, video, compact disc, CD-ROM, and don't be surprised if International Management Group (IMG) negotiates the rights to a Tiger comic strip and a Tiger movie.

Back in September, St. Martin's Press, my editor, Neal Bascomb, and my agent, Scott Waxman of Literary Group International, wanted *Tiger Woods: The Makings of a Champion*, to hit the bookstores before Christmas 1996. Thanks to Tiger, my job was easy. He was in the news basically every day from the Amateur in late August until the Tour Championship in late October. It was a whirlwind ten weeks, with enough material and public attention that demanded this book be written.

By the time you finish these pages, you should know how Tiger arrived at where he is today: how he dominated junior golf, won the U.S. Junior Amateur three times, won the U.S. Amateur three times, signed a $40 million contract with Nike, won the Las Vegas Invitational and Disney World Classic, and became a bigger "box office" draw than Greg Norman. I'll try to take you inside the ropes, like I did in *Heartbreak Hill: The Anatomy of a Ryder Cup*, to give you a better sense of this Tiger Woods phenomenon.

Since this book is unauthorized, Tiger and IMG initially tried to stonewall me. Hughes Norton actually sat in the press tent at the Buick Challenge, making phone calls around the country, telling people not to cooperate with me. It was a waste of time. Ultimately Hughes and Team Tiger realized I was trying to be honest, objective and accurate—and to do that, it was in their best interests to cooperate. Sure there might be a few things in this book they might not like, but that's the difference between journalism and autobiography. Overall, Tiger Woods is a positive story, and that's what I wanted to tell. You want dirt, you're probably reading the wrong book. You want a comprehensive look at the most important golfer of our time, then you've invested your money wisely.

First, I'd also like to thank Jaime Diaz of *Sports Illustrated* and Larry Dorman of the *New York Times* and *Golf Digest* for their guidance and counsel. Everybody in the golf writing world knows they're my two best friends, and you can't do any better than Jaime or Larry for honest feedback. They'll tell it to you square, either in person or in print.

I'd also like to list some of the journalists who have been chasing Tiger along with me, a group of men and women who have contributed to the reporting and background of this book. They are, in alphabetical order: Jim Achenbach, Dave Anderson, Michael Arkush, Jeff Babineau, Michael Bamberger, Thomas Bonk, Jayne Custred, Tim Crothers, Mick Elliott, John Feinstein, Bill Fields, John Garrity, Don Greenberg, Larry Guest, Reid Hanley, Bob Harig, Melanie Hauser, John Hawkins, Lynn Henning, Steve Hershey, Robinson Holloway, Rick Lipsey, Michael Mayo, Pete McDaniel, Chris Millard, Mark Purdy, Rick Reilly, Phil Rogers, T.R. Reinman, Lorne Rubenstein, Jimmy Roberts, Jeff Rude, Geoff Russell, Dave Seanor, Len Shapiro, Glenn

Sheeley, Dave Sheinin, Ron Sirak, Garry Smits, Mark Soltau, John Strege, Greg Stoda, Jerry Tarde, Gary Van Sickle, Jeff Williams and Guy Yocom. If I left anybody out, I apologize.

Sports Illustrated also came up big, which is noteworthy because they're publishing their own Tiger Woods book. They took the high road, but I didn't expect anything less from Mark Mulvoy, Peter Carry and Bill Colson. They have treated me honorably, and although I am leaving *SI* on Jan. 1, I can look back on my three years under that famous masthead and say with all honesty that I wouldn't be on the bookshelves for St. Martin's Press if it wasn't for Mark, Peter, Bill and Jim Herre, the senior editor for *SI*'s golf coverage. Thanks, guys.

Bev Norwood (IMG), Ed Markey (NBC), Glenn Greenspan (Masters), Andrea Solomita and Craig Smith (USGA), Julius Mason (PGA) and the PGA Tour's media relations department (Lee Patterson, Wes Seeley, James Cramer and Mark Mitchell) all played vital roles in either sparking ideas, clarifying information or providing material that you'll read in the pages of this book.

Finally, I'd like to thank a young man who I think will be a superstar in the very near future. His name is Matt Rudy, and he works in the *Sports Illustrated* "bullpen" as a reporter. Matt helped me in the editing process. Remember his name. You'll be seeing his byline soon.

PREFACE

Tiger Woods was not happy, but I didn't expect him to be. We were in the locker room at En-Joie Golf Club in Endicott, N.Y., on Thursday, September 19, and I had just told him about this book. His face dropped and his body language changed.

Only thirty minutes before, we were on the ninth tee, where Tiger was completing the opening round of the 1996 B.C. Open. He was three under par in his 12th round as a professional golfer, grinding hard to get his PGA Tour card. Sitting on a bench behind the tee, I tried not to make eye contact or disrupt his concentration. I was writing something on my notepad when I felt somebody tap me on the knee.

It was Tiger, acknowledging me, saying *What's up?* I'd known the kid for six years, going back to my days covering golf for the *Palm Beach Post*. Tiger was playing the 1990 PGA Juniors Championship at PGA National when we first met. He was 14, and just as precocious then as now. The second paragraph of my article read:

"Eldrick 'Tiger' Woods, 14, doesn't wasn't to be the next great black golfer. He wants to be the next dominant player. Period. Regardless or race, color or creed. 'I want to tear it up on the Tour,' he said with great conviction."

Imagine a 14-year-old kid saying that? But, after seeing him play, I had no doubt that he *would* "tear up" the Tour one day. Yes, he was *that good.*

The next time I covered Tiger was the 1993 Honda Classic, again for the *Palm Beach Post*, and again he had a self-assured attitude and little time for the local media. Away from the interviews, he exuded charm. In the press room, he was a different person. At 17, he had a noticeable chip on his shoulder and little time for small talk. The only concern was that he was taking on too much, too soon, that he would either burn out mentally or fall apart physically. "By the time he's 21, he's either going to be out of the game or he's going to be one of the best players in the game," Jack Nicklaus predicted. "There'll be no in between."

Only at the 1994 U.S. Amateur did Tiger and I actually begin to develop what I interpreted as a trust. Editors hate when writers use that word—trust—but it's essential to get the type of inside information they want. By then I was working for *Sports Illustrated* and we had a policy of filing early Sunday morning and then "topping" the story with what happened the following day of competition. Dan Jenkins used to work this way when he was at *SI*. That way, if they need to "save" your copy, they have the extra time.

I based my story on Tiger's comeback in the second round against Buddy Alexander, the University of Florida golf coach and a former Amateur champion. The lead was the scene from the back nine at the Tournament Players Club at Sawgrass Stadium course. Tiger's father, Earl, was sitting on his walking stick and listening to jazz tapes on his headphones as his son came from having one foot in the grave to winning his match and advancing into the finals against Trip Kuehne of Oklahoma State. "This isn't over yet," Earl said. "Tiger will make another run." Sure enough, he did. Three up with five holes to play, Tiger won the 15th, 16th, 17th and 18th holes, and Alexander was sent packing back to Gainesville. "I was about to pass out,"

Woods said afterward. Pretty good material, right? I thought so and sent it to the *SI* news bureau in New York early Sunday morning. By the time I showed up at the TPC press room it was the lunch break, and Tiger was four down. I started writing again, and this time I constructed a story with Kuehne winning. I sent it to *SI* just as Tiger was in the middle of a comeback, playing the par-five 16th hole. At that point, you hate to root against a player of Tiger's enormous talent, but if you're human, the last thing you want to do is rewrite again.

I got out on the course just in time to see Tiger win the 16th hole and walk to the 17th tee. This hole, and this shot, although just 132 yards, is one of the scariest in the world. I was right behind the tee, within hearing distance of Tiger, as he talked with his caddy, Jay Brunza. He was pumped up and had two clubs in his hand—a pitching wedge and a sand wedge. I've covered enough TPCs and Players Championships to know what club the pros hit here: usually a nine-iron although I've seen some grip down and cut a soft eight and if the wind is blowing, a knockdown seven. Tiger threw down the pitching wedge and went with the sand wedge. Yes, the sand wedge. I thought the kid was crazy, that he'd come up short, *doink it* off the railroad ties, the match would be over, and with just a little bit of work, my second story would be "saved" back in New York.

Wrong. Tiger hit one of his towering shots that go up into the cumulus clouds and paint the sky like a tracer. The sand wedge from 132 yards didn't come down *short*, as I feared. It flew the flag, took one bounce, and checked up in the fringe, just long and right of the hole, maybe one yard from being wet. Later I called Tida Woods at the family home in Cypress, Calif. She told me she had fallen off the bed. "My son," she said. "He try to kill me."

I was up on the bank, next to *Sports Illustrated* photographer Mike O'Bryon, when Tiger made the putt. He was wearing a straw hat, shorts, and the look Michael Jordan wears when there's 10 seconds left and he's just hung in the air, driven the paint, and dunked on Shaquille O'Neal. Tiger started pumping, and pumping, and pumping, hitting that thick Jacksonville air with upper cut after upper cut after upper cut. O'Bryon got every frame of the sequence. The only thing Tiger didn't do was stick his tongue out.

I called New York, and my editor told me what I already knew: For the third time in less than 12 hours, I wrote the story of 94th U.S. Amateur for *Sports Illustrated*. I had all the material and the right lead, but the story was a mess—a mishmash of Tiger winning, then losing, then winning the Amateur. I had an editor "save it," and the story led the magazine. If it hadn't been the NFL Preview issue, it probably would have been a cover.

I took the readers right behind the tee with me, let them see, hear and feel that moment when Tiger threw down the pitching wedge and took the sand wedge at that hole. I'd seen a lot of shots hit in a lot of golf tournaments, but that shot, that moment, was the gutsiest I'd seen.

I covered the Amateur again the following year at Newport Country Club, across the bridges from my alma mater, the University of Rhode Island. There was no dramatic comeback this time, but there was a marvelous contrast between Woods and his opponent in the finals, Buddy Marucci of Berwyn, Pa. Buddy was a club champion at Pine Valley and was part of a mid-amateur fraternity that included guys like Davis Sezna, Barry Van Gerbig and Walker Cup captains Vinny Giles and Downing Gray. They play Seminole in the winter, Pine Valley in the summer, and just about anywhere they want to in between. They're all good guys who love and respect the game, and when someone like Tiger Woods comes along, they realize what a special moment it is in golf history—even if it does come at the expense of their best friend Buddy. And for 34 holes at Newport Country Club, George "Buddy" Marucci—career amateur, rich kid from Mainline Philadelphia—had Eldrick "Tiger" Woods—a professional in training—on the ropes. That's when Tiger threw it in another gear, and of course nearly holed out at the 18th to win the match and win his second consecutive Amateur.

I didn't know what I was going to lead with. Nothing new and dramatic really hit me the way Tiger's sand wedge did at the TPC-Sawgrass. So I was still poking around Newport CC, hustling to get a scene or a quote no one else in the press tent had, when I found Tiger, his father, Earl, and Tiger's teacher, Claude "Butch" Harmon, celebrating in the merchandise tent. Butch's brother, Billy, is the head professional at Newport, and he had a big week. They were all partying and it was a great scene, especially when Earl started toasting his son with some expensive champagne that had been produced from the clubhouse.

The money quote that I used was Earl predicting that Tiger would one day win 14 major championships. I remember when he said it, the embarrassment that came over Tiger's face. But Earl also said some other things, and I felt it was in his best interests, and Tiger's best interests, that they go unwritten. I went back to the Newport Marriott that night to write. I only had something like 120 lines, which is one page in *SI*. This time I was working with Mark Godich, a good friend and a guy I think is one of the world's best copy editors. I obviously wrote the story trying to soften Earl's predictions, but Godich saw right through that and moved the quotes up high. That's OK, I thought. Earl said it. I wasn't the only person in that tent who heard it. And, after the story came out, Butch Harmon thanked me for protecting Earl and Tiger.

Later, I discovered at the B.C. Open the Woods family didn't feel the same way. They felt that all quotes in the merchandise tent at Newport should have been off the record, that I used poor judgment in using them because it created a standard Tiger would have to live up to. It didn't matter that Jack Nicklaus would one day predict that Tiger would win more Masters titles than he and Arnold Palmer combined. Or that Earl would make with some ridiculous "black gunslinger" stuff. What mattered was that I used Earl drinking champagne from the Havemeyer Trophy and predicting 14 major championships for his son.

Tiger laid this guilt trip on me in the locker room at En-Joie the day after I told him about this book. He said it was a terrible thing to do, that his father had been drinking, that I should have known better, and that he couldn't trust me anymore. I told him *my* side of the story, that I thought I was going out of my way to protect *his* interests, that if any other writer was in that tent they would have printed *everything*, and that Earl *really* would have looked bad.

I walked away from his locker. Then I said, "Wait a second," and regrouped. I went back and got in Tiger's face, looked Tiger in the eyes, and told him: Look, man, this is the way it is. I have never done anything deliberately to hurt you or your family. I respect you for being a polite and intelligent young man who is good for the game of golf. All I can promise you is that I'll be fair to you in writing this book, just as I was that day in Newport. I can't do anything about the way you feel, but maybe in time you'll come to respect me, and trust me, as an honest journalist.

Later that night I called Earl at his home in Cypress and

told him what happened. I admire him for his response. He said he couldn't control the free-enterprise system. All he asked was me to be honest and forthright. He asked if I had an axe to grind, which I didn't. We cleared the air about Newport. He then gave me material that you will read later in this book.

Tiger obviously didn't like the fact that somebody was going to cash in on his fame. The International Management Group didn't like it because they weren't getting their 20 percent. At Mark McCormack's insistence, IMG had been taking bids on Tiger's book contracts. The offers for the package were reportedly as high as $1.5 million (Warner Books eventually paid $2.2 million for a two-book deal.). Tiger, however, didn't want any part of an autobiography, not at age 20, because of the perception it would give. I could see where he was coming from, but that wasn't going to stop me from doing, in Tiger's words, what I had to do.

I quickly found out that Team Tiger and IMG were not going to help me in any way. I never let that affect me. Maybe Tiger didn't sit down and give me a one-on-one, but I was around him enough, and talked to enough people, that I ended up with too much material. I worked to find scenes like the one I had behind the tee at the TPC, and in that tent at Newport. I used what I thought was fair because I'm in this for the long haul, and so is Tiger. I need him, and someday, even with the $40 million from his Nike contract in the bank, he may come to learn that he needs me, and the rest of the media, too.

At Walt Disney World, Tiger was asked by Larry Guest of the *Orlando Sentinel* about his relationship with the people who cover golf, why he felt uncomfortable in the fishbowl. "The reason being," he said, "is because I know a few guys I can trust in the media, and I know a few guys I can't trust. And I'm learning all the time."

It disturbs me that Tiger thinks I'm one of the guys whom he can't trust, but maybe he'll realize some day that he's got it wrong.

What was it that Earl said in Newport?

Sorry.

If you expect me to tell you, you've got the wrong guy.

And, the wrong book.

TIGER WOODS

INTRODUCTION

t was definitely one of the weak moments in Earl Woods's life. His son had just won the Las Vegas Invitational, and here he was at home watching it on TV, alone except for the dogs, Joey and Penny. Earl had been crying. Tiger makes Earl cry a lot. He cried after the three Junior Amateurs and after the three U.S. Amateurs. Now, he was crying after Vegas. It won't be the last time Earl Woods cries after his son wins a golf tournament.

What's it going to be like when Tiger wins his first green jacket, or raises that U.S. Open trophy over his head for the first time? Will Earl have any tears left after Tiger fulfills the Golden Bear's prediction and wins more Masters titles than Jack Nicklaus and Arnold Palmer did *combined?* And what about the British Open? You don't think the kid's going to win a bunch of those? Tiger shot 66 this past year at Royal Lytham. Sixty-six and he wasn't even playing his best golf. That was the round that told Tiger he was ready, the one that made up his mind about turning pro, the one that Nike later copied when he said, "Are you ready for me?" It was only Tiger's second British Open, and he finished 22nd. You don't think St. Andrews sets up for the kid? Muirfield? Turnberry? Troon? The Claret Jug's got Tiger's name on it.

"He had done everything correctly," Earl was saying now, about 90 minutes after the final putt fell in the cup at the TPC-Summerlin in Vegas. "And he's done it time and time before. He did it the same way he and I talked about it. For hours and hours and hours we talked about it. And it all happened right here in front of my eyes."

Earl, who grew up a Presbyterian in Manhattan, Kansas, believes that Tiger is a chosen one. So does Tiger's mom, Tida. They believe their son was put on this Earth with a greater purpose than just winning golf tournaments. Earl and Tida Woods also believe that some of the people who cross Tiger's path are also part of a divine fate. Says Earl, "A divine power has put him here for a purpose. This isn't just my analysis and my idea. There are other people who have been blessed to be a part of this, who have in retrospect gone back and reviewed their lives and come to the same conclusions . . . that they were individually prepared for the moment that their life intersected with Tiger's life. It has happened over and over again, and it will happen in the future. Other people will also be prepared, and they will interface with his life when it is time."

Earl was at Quad City when Tiger blew the three-shot lead on Sunday. He was outside the gallery ropes when Tiger double-crossed a tee ball and made the quadruple bogey eight. He was there when Tiger four-putted another green, shot 72, and finished fifth. Everybody was bummed out. Not Earl. He knew it wasn't Tiger's time. "I saw that power allow Tiger to take the lead, experience it, and then take it away from him, because the time wasn't right," Earl Woods said on the phone that night from Cypress. "It happened right in front of my eyes. Quad City was not the right venue, so when I got home, I told people, 'Vegas. Vegas will be it.' And that's what happened."

It was October 6, 1996, a day that will serve as a milestone in golf history. Tiger Woods didn't just capture his first professional golf tournament that day, leaving Las Vegas with a $297,000 first-place check and a sudden-death playoff win against one of the best golfers in the world. Tiger flat-out took over. He shot 64 on Sunday and looked like a young man who was playing to win. Davis Love III, winner of 10 PGA Tour events and a candidate to win the PGA Tour's money title in 1996, was so nervous that more than one person flat-out said he looked like a golfer playing not to lose. Tiger Woods, age 20 and in his fifth pro event, turned Davis Love into another road kill, placed him in the box next to Steve Scott, Buddy Marucci and Trip Kuehne. Afterward, Butch Harmon told Davis that he was sorry to see it happen to *him*. Davis just shrugged. ''Hey Butch,'' he said. ''It won't be the last time.''

Every putt Tiger missed that Sunday at Summerlin was past the hole, every shot he didn't hit close flew over the stick, every stride he took was forward, every move he made exuded confidence. At the 341-yard, par-four 15th hole, Tiger Woods hit three-wood *over* the green and into the back bunker. At the 560-yard 16th, he laced a bullet draw down the left side of the fairway, then flagged a 216-yard six-iron. For someone only 150 pounds, it was ungodly that he was hitting the ball that far. Earlier in the week, Paul Azinger was unable to explain the kid's ability to compress a 90-compression Titleist. ''He has something in his genetic makeup that allows him in a normal-sized body to hit the ball 50 yards farther than most people his size,'' Azinger said. But it was not just power that set the Tiger apart, it was his poise and maturity. Not since Jack Nicklaus had a golfer had the type of sudden impact on the game that Tiger Woods had in Vegas. He thought his way around the golf course better than anybody. He out-willed everybody. The kid whipped his game into the fast lane and never looked back. He said good-bye to all the critics saying he was overrated. He really was shouting, "Hello, World!"

Andy North, the former two-time U.S. Open champion who is now working as an on-course commentator for ESPN, called it the biggest thing to happen in American golf since Nicklaus's victory at the 1986 Masters. From a societal view, Tiger's win at Vegas had greater implications. The record gallery following Tiger on Sunday at Summerlin was by far the most ethnically diverse in the history of the PGA Tour, and for many of them tailing Tiger, it was their first time at a golf tournament. One month on the job and Tiger Woods was already transcending the game of golf, turning people on to it who always felt shut out by its prejudices and traditions. Tiger was taking it to the people, showing them in ghettos and barrios all over America that anybody can make it. In just his fifth pro tournament, he had taken over Vegas, the way Michael Jordan takes over Game 7, slam dunking birdie putts on the 11th, 13th, 14th and 16th holes coming in, beating a field that included not only Love, but Freddie Couples, Phil Mickelson and six of the top eight money winners on the PGA Tour. The kid always said he wanted to be the Michael Jordan of golf. Well, he had done it already.

Earl was right. It was better Tiger Woods won in Vegas, better than if he had won in Quad City or the B.C. Open. If he beat Ed Fiori or Fred Funk before four million viewers on The Golf Channel, so what? People would have said the fields were weak, and Tiger still had something to prove. Vegas was a big-money tournament that attracted a big-time field. It was televised on ESPN, with sixty million people watching it. And Tiger won it after opening with a one under 70, which in the Vegas tournament is like drawing 14 on the blackjack table at The Mirage when the dealer's got a face card showing. In other words, you're busted, son. Basically Tiger spotted the field one round, but after that 70, which placed him tied for 83rd out of 144 players, he shot 63-68-67 and that closing 64—26 under par in the last four rounds. The PGA Tour scoring record for a 72-hole tournament is 27 under, set by Mike Souchak in 1955. In only his fifth tournament as a professional, Tiger Woods was one stroke off the all-time record.

But even in that moment when he walked off the 18th green to sign his scorecard, Tiger had the poise that told him, "Don't celebrate." He went straight to the range, blew off ESPN's request for an interview, and striped three-wood after three-wood, first a high cut, then a low draw, gripping down one swing, letting out the shaft another swing, hitting the club he would use off the 18th tee on the first playoff hole, getting a picture in his mind what the shot would look like, mentally preparing himself for sudden death. This was not Kenny Perry in the PGA, spending that precious time in the TV Tower. This was Tiger Woods, staying loose and sharp, acting as if he had been in this situation all his life. Because in a way, he had.

When Love arrived in a golf cart on the 18th tee, Tiger Woods was there waiting for him, ready to go, focused on winning, and playing it cool. "Great playing, Tiger," Love said. "Thanks, Stud," said the kid. He was a little tense, but not the type of nervous you'd expect from a 20-year-old on the tee of his first professional playoff with $297,000 waiting at the clubhouse. Tiger Woods played it like he was on autopilot.

When Love cut a driver into Position A, about 280 yards down the fairway's sprinkler line, Woods took out his

15-degree three-wood and busted his drive right in Love's shadow. And when Love took out the eight-iron after he ripped nine-iron onto the green, the kid knew it was a mental mistake, he knew you take less club in that situation and rip it, you don't try to finesse a shot in the heat because you'll decelerate and the ball will invariably go left—which is exactly what Love's did—left and in the bunker. And when his 25-foot par putt went 2½ feet past the hole, Tiger didn't mark and wait, he putted out, to put the pressure on Love. Here was this 20-year-old kid, in his fifth tournament on the PGA Tour, in his first playoff, controlling the situation, dictating the mood and the terms of the deal. If Ryder Cup captain Tom Kite wasn't watching, he should have been.

The rest was a blur for Tiger. He barely remembered shaking Love's hand, hearing him say, "You deserved it," or seeing his name on the jumbo cardboard check with $297 and three zeroes behind it, or having the master of ceremonies call him "the richest college dropout in America." There were a couple of Vegas showgirls there on the 18th green, wearing plumage on their heads, tons of makeup, and not much else. There was his buddy Pete McDaniel from *Golf World*, his caddy Mike "Fluff" Cowan, his coach Butch Harmon, his sports psychologist Jay Brunza, and his pals Bryon Bell and Jerry Chang—all standing in the crowd, watching him raise that trophy over his head. And finally, there was his mother, Tida, coming out for a hug. He was calling her over, into his arms. It seemed like slow-motion.

"Come here, Mom."

"I am so proud of you," she said.

Earl Woods watched these scenes unfold on his wide screen, babysitting his dogs, flashing back through the moments in Tiger's life, and even before that, to when Tiger was just a premonition in the jungles of Southeast Asia. He thought about the chart Tiger drew and put up on his bed-room wall, a time line marking his progress compared to Nicklaus's. He recounted those three U.S. Amateurs, each one being so special. The first because it was the first, and because of the way Tiger came back, first in the semis—three down with five holes to play against former Amateur champion Buddy Alexander, the former University of Flor-ida golf coach—then in the finals against his junior golf buddy Trip Kuehne. The second because it was the repeat, and Nicklaus had never won two straight. And finally the third, because no amateur, not even the great Bobby Jones, had won three straight.

Earl kept going back in time. There were the three straight Junior Amateur titles, all of them coming down to the final holes, the playoff win in 1991 and the birdie-birdie finish in 1993. Earl Woods thought about all those miles he traveled with Tiger, those tight connections and lonely hotel rooms, and about the sacrifices he made to make sure his son had the same opportunities as those country club kids. He remembered that first L.A. Open when Tiger was 16, and his son shot on the Navy course at Los Alamitos, and of course that moment when Tiger slid out of the high chair when he was three years old, picked up his dad's putter and started swinging it.

It was all there as Earl Woods watched his son win the Las Vegas Invitational, tears streaming down his cheeks, the dogs to keep him company, the phone ringing and ringing, friends calling, the guys he plays golf with on the weekends, his regular game. . . .

Somewhere, somehow, Nguyen Phong had to be watching this, too. He just had to.

I

WONDER CHILD

*"God gave me a gift.
And He trusted me
to take care of it."*
—EARL WOODS

1

PHONG

It has been almost 30 years since Lt. Col. Earl Woods of the United States Green Berets bid his farewell to Nguyen Phong. Almost three decades since the fall of Saigon and the United States pullout of Vietnam. Phong, a lieutenant colonel in the South Vietnamese army, was probably MIA, captured, tortured and killed by the North Vietnamese Army. Yet, Earl Woods still had the hope—he'll always have the hope—that his buddy, the guy he named Tiger, made it out alive.

"That guy was so brave, such a bitch in the field, I decided my son's nickname would be Tiger," Earl has said. There was a time when they were inseparable, the eyes in the back of each other's heads, as tight as two men could be, tighter than blood brothers. If it wasn't for Phong, Earl Woods would probably have been killed in Vietnam. If it wasn't for Phong, Earl Woods sure as hell would have been sent home to Kansas in a body bag. How in creation did those bullets keep missing, anyway? Like the time they stormed that VC-held village, Phong leading the way, and they got out without a scratch. Had to be fate. Had to be some higher power looking after him, protecting him for some reason. Had to be. The connection between Earl Woods and Nguyen Phong was the first cosmic intersection in the life of a kid that hadn't been born yet, a kid who would touch the world.

Good old Woody and Tiger. One minute they'd be playing tennis at Than Thiet, the next they'd be in a helicopter flying to a drop zone. One minute it would be deuce in the third game of the second set, the next they'd be flying on the top of a jungle, dodging enemy fire, maybe on the last mission of their lives. Earl Woods had a bounty on his head and the Vietnamese Star on his breast pocket. He had to thank Nguyen Phong for both. "We'd be playing and they'd run in and say, 'Contact!' and he'd say, 'Meet you at the helicopter pad,'" Earl remembers. "They'd fly us in, we'd fight all day, then they'd come back at night and lift us out."

There is a matter-of-factness when Earl looks back on those days in the Special Services, his second tour of duty in a senseless war against an enemy that looked the same as his South Vietnamese allies. Earl made a vow. If he ever got out alive, if he ever had a family, his first son would be named in honor of Nguyen Phong. He would name him Tiger, knowing that son would be famous and maybe half a world away his war buddy would see the name and realize, "Hey, that's Woody's kid."

He still had that hope.

2

EARL AND TIDA

Kultida Punsawad worked as a secretary in the U.S. Army Office in Bangkok, Thailand. She lived with her wealthy parents, went to the Buddhist temple, and figured that when Earl asked her out for an eight o'clock date he meant a.m. not p.m., because, as is custom, proper Thai girls do not go out at night. Their first date was nearly a bust, but she found Big Earl the next day, boots up on the desk in his office. She took him to the temple of the Reclining Buddha on a holy day in Thailand. Tida brought a girlfriend with her, as a chaperone. That was Thai custom. Earl grunted and went along. They became husband and wife in 1969.

After the war, Earl and Tida moved to Brooklyn, N.Y. Earl was based at Fort Hamilton, and at age 42, played his first round of golf. It was at an Army base course in Fort Dix, N.J. He was talked into it by a fellow officer, who took not only his friend's money, but his pride. Earl shot 91 for 17 holes, and immediately declared his revenge. Four months later, just before his retirement from the service, he came back and shot 81, whipping his buddy by four strokes and winning back all his money. It was another of those intersections with good karma.

He later told Pete McDaniel of *Golf World*, "I got hooked

on that round of golf. I realized just what I'd been missing my whole life. I said if I ever have another son I'm starting him out at a young age."

Woody was an athlete. Before Vietnam, he was a catcher for Kansas State, the first man of color to play baseball in the Big Seven Conference, which is now the Big Eight. Earl had a little Native American in him, a little Chinese, even a little Caucasian blood, but mostly he was black and proud of it. Of course, Earl wasn't allowed to eat in the same restaurants as the K-State team, and found himself subjected to the same racism that most black men and women endured in the '50s and '60s. But Earl learned to deal with it, and he was reminded of it years later when he would walk in a golf club with his son, Tiger, and the room would go deathly silent and they'd get what Earl would call "The Look."

Why golf then? Was it spite? Was it because it epitomized the social injustice of this country? Was it because the white man played golf and the black man didn't? It was all of the above. Earl always said there are two colors in this country: white and not white. Golf was Woody's way to make a statement. It was his way to prove that a black man could play golf, too, that he wasn't just the caddy or the bus boy, that he could be the guy who walked in the front door of the clubhouse, changed his shoes in the locker room, and walked out on the first tee at a place like Shoal Creek with his head held high. But beyond those motives, Woody was quite simply an old college jock from Kansas who could swing a golf club like a machete and knock down six-footers with a vengeance. Within five years, he was playing off a 1 handicap. "I was known as the best six-hole player out there," he said. "The first three holes was getting rid of the stress, and then, watch out."

After the service, Earl took Tida and moved to Orange

County, Calif. He took a job negotiating contracts for materials for the McDonnell Douglas rocket program. It wasn't exciting, but did make for a decent living. On December 30, 1975, at a Long Beach Hospital, Earl and Tida had their first and only child, a boy they officially named Eldrick. Actually, it was Tida's name. "Mothers stick kids with names," Earl said. "Fathers just have to follow along."

Before Tiger could walk, Earl would take the kid out to the garage, strap him in a high chair, set up a net and beat balls. The kid would take his meals out there, and sit there for hours, mesmerized, as Earl pounded chewed-up X-outs into that net. Martin Luther King had his dream. Earl's was to produce a champion golfer. "I was a black kid, and golf was played at the country club—end of story," he has said. "But I told myself that somehow my son would get a chance to play golf early in life." Ten months was pretty early. When Earl unstrapped Tiger from the high chair, he took the old man's putter and swung it like a seasoned pro. Earl raced in the house and summoned Tida. The kid was still sucking on a bottle and eating mashed-up vegetables, but he had the whole routine down, even the pre-shot waggle.

Eighteen summers later, Jack Nicklaus would get crucified for saying that more black children didn't play golf because they had different muscles than white children, but what Nicklaus was trying to say was that black children never developed golfing muscles because they were never exposed to the game with proper training at a young age; instead, they were out playing playground sports like basketball, football and baseball. Essentially, Earl was proving that Jack Nicklaus would one day be correct, that if he gave his son a golf club while he was in the high chair, he would be hitting high fades with a three-iron by the time he was five. Yes, Earl knew that golf was a white man's game because of bigotry and racism, because of unspoken rules like Hall Thompson's at Shoal Creek. But he also believed that more black children would play golf if they had the same opportunities as white children, that they would inherently adopt the moves if they lived it and breathed it—the same way they lived and breathed basketball, football and baseball on the playgrounds. His son swinging that club proved there was truth to the theory of "assimilation through visualization." He couldn't wait to show Tida. "I used to tell people that the next generation of great golfers are going to be those who were introduced to the game between six months and a year," he'd say. "See, this is the first black intuitive golfer ever raised in the United States. Before, black kids grew up with basketball or football or baseball from the time they could walk. The game became part of them from the beginning. But they always learned golf too late. Not Tiger. Tiger knew how to swing a golf club before he could walk."

Earl had great vision. When Tida tried to throw out the rusty high chair, she was admonished by Earl. "You can't throw it away," he said. "That's going to be in the Hall of Fame someday." And so the chair is buried in the garage of their home, under the boxes of trophies Tiger started winning before he entered kindergarten. Maybe Earl didn't know his son would win three straight Junior Amateurs and three straight U.S. Amateur titles, but he knew that Tiger Woods, the kid he named after the South Vietnamese lieutenant colonel, had the makings of a champion. It would be Earl Woods's mission in life to see that his son had every opportunity to fulfill those dreams. It was his "Master Plan."

You want to know why Tiger has such great balance in his golf swing today? Look back 19 years and you'll find out. It wasn't anything Butch Harmon taught him. It started when he was barely able to walk.

Tiger was playing the Navy golf course in Los Alamitos when he was still in Pampers. Tida remembers the day Tiger pulled down his pants in a sand trap, "went pee-pee" in the sand, pulled his pants back up, and hit a shot. One day before his fourth birthday, he shot 48 from the red tees on the old back nine of the Navy Course in Cypress. Didn't matter that the old man teed up his shots from the fairway. The kid putted everything out. At age three, he won a Pitch, Putt and Drive competition against 10- and 11-year-olds. Word spread about this black kid from Cypress who had a golf swing. Jim Hill, the L.A. sportscaster, came out to the house and did a feature. He concluded the report by saying, "This young man is going to be to golf what Jimmy Connors and Chris Evert are to tennis."

The producers at the *Mike Douglas Show* saw the feature. They put three-year-old Tiger Woods on the air with Bob Hope and Jimmy Stewart. There was no stage fright. He putted a few against Hope, hit some balls off a mat just like his dad did in the garage, and it wasn't long before *That's Incredible* picked up on it and put Tiger on their show with host Fran Tarkenton. "When I get big," he said, "I'm going to beat Jack Nicklaus and Tom Watson." After *That's Incredible*, the kids at his school would ask for an autograph and Tiger would have to print it because he was too young to write in script.

"When most kids are in those circular walkers, you give them a rattle," Earl said. "He had a putter."

On August 27, 1980, Tiger Woods made his first birdie, a two on the 91-yard third hole at Heartwell Park Golf Club. The old man kept pushing. At age 6, Tiger was listening to subliminal tapes. He tacked the messages to the desk in his room, corny stuff like MY DECISIONS ARE STRONG! I DO IT ALL WITH MY HEART! and I FOCUS AND GIVE IT MY ALL! He'd go out in the garage and hit off the mat into that net, just like his father did, listening to that tape playing in the back of his head.

The old man wouldn't let up. He put the kid through golf's basic training when he was seven. They'd go out and play golf on the par-three course at Presidio Hills and he'd play mind games with the kid, employing psychological techniques he learned during prisoner interrogation. He wasn't trying to create a monster. He was just trying to toughen Tiger up.

Earl would do stuff like rip the Velcro on his glove when Tiger was at the top of his backswing. He'd roll balls in the kid's line while Tiger stood over a three-footer. He'd say "Better not hook it," when there were out-of-bound stakes down the left side of the fairway. Some parents would call it cruel, but Earl called it "psychological warfare." It was his customized version of tough love. The kid got stronger mentally. Nothing could distract him. Nothing. Sometimes it would make him mad, but he knew it was for his own good. He could stand over 80 straight four-foot putts and drill 'em all, center cut.

"There's a dark side to me," Earl says. "I pulled every nasty, dirty, ungodly trick on him. He'll tell you today it was one of the toughest periods of his life. After two months I finally told him, 'You're ready.' "

The old man talked about his equipment as if it were combat gear, making sure the kid's lies and lofts were in tiptop shape, that he understood the mission. Afterward, they wouldn't just go over the round. They had debriefings and the kid developed what Earl called eerily ". . . a coldness." The old man just had his kid's best interests at heart. He wanted to make sure that nobody was mentally tougher than his son.

Nobody.

3

LESSONS IN LIFE

Tiger Woods started asking mature questions when he was 10 years old, questions that his father couldn't answer.

"Daddy," he said. "Do you think when I turn pro you could live off $100,000 a year?"

Earl Woods knew what the kid was saying. He had five floating credit cards and two mortgages on the house. Tiger's schedule that year took them across the United States and to Mexico, France, Canada and Thailand.

"Let me think about it," he said. "The tab is going up every week."

Earl was still employed at McDonnell Douglas, trying to support the family and put in 10 years to get his pension. Tida stayed at home, making sure the homework was done, driving Tiger to tournaments sponsored by the Southern California Junior Golf Association. If they were invited to a party, Earl would go and she would stay home with the child. No baby-sitter for her Tiger. She made sure he prayed to Buddha and wouldn't allow him to throw clubs like some of the kids did. She'd tell him that golf was a gentleman's game, and used the example of John McEnroe and Jimmy Connors as examples of spoiled children whose behavior was unacceptable. "I tell him not to do it, because it will ruin my reputation as a parent," she used to say. "I will not have a spoiled child."

But she also implored Tiger to win. "I tell Tiger, 'When you are ahead, don't take it easy, kill them,'" she said. "'After the finish, then be a sportsman.'"

They were the only interracial family in an all-white neighborhood. Their home was pelted by limes and BB-gun fire while Tida was carrying Tiger. He was the only black child in his kindergarten class. The older white children once tied him to a tree. Tida remained the rock. "I see my husband cry and I think, 'Tida, god, why you not show some emotion?' But in my culture we don't show that. It not proper. You lose face."

Tiger wasn't losing much of anything on the golf course. At age eight, Eldrick Woods won his first Junior World Championship, shooting five under par 51 at Presidio Hills. Earl had taken him to see Rudy Duran, a golf pro at Heartwell Park in Long Beach. Duran coached him, but mostly he just watched in amazement. He thought he was seeing a Magic Johnson or a Wolfgang Amadeus Mozart, a kid with talent oozing from his fingertips. "It was mind-boggling to see a 4½-year-old swinging like a refined touring pro," Duran told the *Los Angeles Times*. "It was like watching a PGA player shrunk to 50 pounds. What would Jack Nicklaus shoot if he was 3'7"?"

One day, Tiger was given a set of sawed-off clubs. He looked in the bag and noticed there wasn't a one-iron. He told Duran that he wanted a one-iron, the hardest club to hit in the bag. Duran told him, "A one-iron? You're not gonna generate enough clubhead speed to get a one-iron airborne. You'll just hit it into the ground."

Later that day, Duran saw Tiger on the range. He had his father's one-iron in his hands and a ball teed up. The club was almost as tall as he was, but he took a swing and ripped it into the air. "So we went out and bought him a one-iron," said Duran.

Tiger learned more than just the golf swing at Heartwell Park. He learned how to gamble, too. He'd come home every day with his pockets stuffed with quarters, money from the skins he'd win on the putting green. Tida didn't like the idea of her son gambling, but Earl knew it was part of golf's basic training. He told Tiger it was bad, but in his heart, Earl knew it was a necessary evil.

Winning golf tournaments and shooting low scores became an obsession. Earl tried to tell Tiger to stop and smell the roses. Tiger told him, "Daddy, this is how I have fun, shooting low scores." Earl shut up and never said that again. Tida had to intervene. She had to explain that Jack Nicklaus and Tom Watson didn't win every tournament they played. Tiger still tried. Oh, how he tried.

There was never any pressure on him to play golf. All Earl cared about was raising a "meaningful, articulate citizen." They didn't care if Tiger grew up to be a professional golfer. "If tomorrow he said, 'Pop, I'm tired of golf,' I'd say, 'that's fine with me,' " Earl would say. "You make your own decisions. You have the freedom to make your own decisions."

But at the same time, Earl recognized that the ability was there, that Tiger was an artist. If he was content to do character sketches, it would be a waste, a flat waste of talent. Tiger never let Earl down. It took him eight years to beat his dad. Earl knew it was inevitable. His son was destined for greatness.

Heartwell Park and Presidio Hills soon weren't long enough for Tiger. At age 10, he was barely 4'9" and weighed 81 pounds. He had already won two Junior World 10-and-under championships in San Diego, but he wanted to play the big course, where he could tee off with woods. His father started taking him to the Navy course, but some of the members didn't like it. They enforced a rule that children under 10 were not allowed to play. Tiger now thinks it was because his skin was darker than theirs. It was his second perceived brush with racism.

"They don't like me at my home course," he said at the PGA Juniors in 1990. "They try to shut me out. I think it's my skin color. My dad outranks them all, and he happens to have a son who plays golf. The pro let me play when I was four, but all the members got mad because I was beating them."

At age 11 he came home from school and spent an afternoon making a chart to mount on his bedroom wall. Down the left-hand column he wrote the names of all the major golf tournaments. He then cut out a photograph of Jack Nicklaus and placed it at the top of another column. Carefully, he wrote Nicklaus's age each time he won a major championship for the first time. Finally he made a third column, with his name on top. "I wanted to be the youngest player ever to win the majors," he told Tim Crothers of *Sports Illustrated*. "Nicklaus was my hero, and I thought it would be great to accomplish all the things he did even earlier than he accomplished them."

4

ZONING

The old man retired from McDonnell Douglas in 1988 to travel the country with his son. Tiger was 12. Earl was 56. They stayed in low-rent hotels, flew red-eyes, showed up for practice rounds half asleep. One day Tiger asked Earl if they could get to sites early enough for a practice round. Earl thought about it and apologized. He promised his son from that day forward to give him "as good a chance as any of these country club kids." Even if it broke him, he'd stay at the fancy hotels and pay the extra day on the car rental so Tiger could play on a level field with his competition. From that point on, Earl says, Tiger "kicked butt and took names."

That summer he started working with John Anselmo, a teaching pro at Meadowlark Golf Course in Huntington Beach. At one point, Tiger looked disheartened.

"What's wrong?" Anselmo said.

"I'm hitting the ball at the flag, and it keeps sucking back. How do I get rid of the backspin?"

Anselmo shook his head.

"People spend their entire lives trying to get backspin on the ball," he said in an interview with the *L.A. Times*. "And here was this kid trying to get rid of it."

Tiger learned all the shots, how to hit it left-to-right, right-to-left, high, low, with or without backspin. The 21st Insurance Golf Classic was played at Texarkana Country Club in August 1989. All the big guns of junior golf were there, and Tiger was just 13, about to enter the eighth grade, playing his first national tournament. After the cut, the format was for professionals to be paired with the juniors, and in the third round, Woods drew the two-time Arkansas Player of the Year, a wild thing by the name of John Daly. At the turn, Tiger was three under and the future British Open and PGA champion was one over after an all-night drive from his home in Blytheville.

On the fifth tee, Daly told some friends, "I can't let this 13-year-old beat me." He had to birdie three of the last four holes to nip Tiger Woods by two strokes (72 to 70). "That kid is great," Daly said. "Everbody was applauding him and nobody applauding me. Of course I didn't do much to applaud. I had heard a lot of good things about him, but he's better than I heard."

Woods was 5′6″, 107 pounds. He beat eight of the pros that day, and ended up the tournament in second place, five strokes back of Justin Leonard. One of the juniors Woods beat that week was 18-year-old David Duval, who had made the cut in the previous week's U.S. Open at Medinah. "It's spectacular he's that young and is able to play on this level," said Leonard, who was 17.

Afterward, Woods told a reporter from the *Arkansas Democrat-Gazette*, "I like to play with better people and better competition. One thing I learned today is it doesn't matter how long you hit it. You've got to be accurate."

That summer he won his fourth Optimist Junior World title, one more than any of the previous champions—and the list included Corey Pavin, Scott Simpson, Craig Stadler and Nick Price. He shot even-par for 54 holes at Balboa Park in San Diego. He birdied the first three holes to open the final round, and coasted to a three-stroke victory over Scott Richardson of Laguna Niguel. "I gambled the first three holes. After that, I just played to the center of the greens," he said, sounding like a voice track from a PGA Tour interview tent.

Mechanically, Duran thought he was already on that level. "In my opinion he doesn't even have to get better," the pro at Heartwell Park said. "He's going to shoot lower scores because he'll continue to hit farther until he is completely developed. The unique thing about Tiger is he was really such a fine golfer when he was so young. He was a polished golfer at five and six. It was amazing to watch."

Duran was thoroughly convinced that Woods could be the next Nicklaus, or even better than Nicklaus. At 13, he felt like Woods could give Greg Norman and Nick Faldo a game. "On his good days and his bad days," Duran said, "Tiger could easily beat some of the best players in the world."

This was a pivotal time for Tiger, a time when Jay Brunza entered Tiger Woods's life. Brunza was a San Diego–based sports psychologist and a captain in the U.S. Navy. One Saturday night when Tiger was 13, he came to Woods's house in Cypress and worked with the kid for the first time. It was nothing serious that first night, just a series of mind tricks, and the next day, Woods joined Brunza's golf group at the Navy course. Through the first seven holes, Tiger had made five birdies. One of Brunza's buddies drove back in a cart. "What kind of monster have you created?" he wanted to know.

Hypnotism was next. Brunza could put Woods into a trance in less than a minute. "Tiger," he'd say. "Hold your arm out straight." When Tiger did, Brunza would tell Earl to bend it. Earl tried everything, even hanging on it. With all his weight, he couldn't bend it.

It was just an added edge Tiger had in his arsenal. He had the body. He had the mind. He had the heart. He had the game. And he had the name.

Earl had it all mapped out.

"In the United States, Tiger is black," he would tell reporters. "But in Thailand, he's Thai, so he'll have marketing value in the Far East as well. You can imagine a golfer of Norman's and Nicklaus's stature being from Bangkok."

By age 14, Tiger had grown to 5'9", 120 pounds. He was playing to a plus-two handicap at the Navy course, his average score a 68 on the par-70 track that measured 6,820 yards from the back tees, had a course rating of 73.5, a slope of 129, and water hazards on 14 of the 18 holes. The pro there, Dave Smith, would shake his head every time the little kid turned in his scorecard. "What Tiger has done is remarkable, truly remarkable," he would say. "What set him apart is his mental approach to the game. I have been a PGA professional for 13 years, almost as long as he has been alive, and he knows more about the game then I do. I have never known anyone who was so naturally adaptable mentally to the game as Tiger. He had all the knowledge to play golf when he was much younger. All he needed was to grow a little taller, and now he's done that."

His game matured beyond his years. It was almost Zen-like. "In golf you have to concentrate like this," he would say, snapping his fingers. "My father and my friends call it zoning. If you mishit a shot, hit it out of bounds, put it in the water, you have to get your focus back. You've got to start thinking ahead. Don't look behind." That summer he shot 63 in the La Mirada (Calif.) City Junior Championship, recorded a three-stroke victory in the Big I Insurance Youth Classic in Fort Worth, and won the Optimist Junior World for a record fifth time. He made it to the semifinals of the USGA Juniors, and traveled to Paris to play in the Southern California/France Junior Cup.

In Fort Worth he shot 69 in the pro-junior event, beating or tying 18 of the touring pros, including Scott Verplank, Billy Mayfair and his playing partner, Tommy Moore. Tiger was a basket case before that one; in fact, the night before the final round, he went through the buffet line at a steak house five times, returned to his hotel room, and was so nervous, he took a shower and couldn't even pick up a bar of soap. The next day he was clearly choking, scraping it around for six holes and then shanking a four-iron right-of-right at the seventh. But after a recovery to the green, Woods stood over a par putt of eight feet and told himself, "If you make this putt, you win." He made it and it changed his entire mindset. He stood up on the next tee, smashed his drive, and went on to beat Stanford freshman Notah Begay and every one but three of the pros. "I wish I could have played like that at 14," Moore said. "Heck, I wish I could play like that at 27."

Earl figured that in some ways, Tiger *was* 27 years old. "He isn't 14 out there," he would say. "A transformation takes place when he steps on a golf course. When he was two or three, he'd hit the ball like a 10-year-old. Then he'd return to two years old, pick up flowers and give them to his mother. When it was time to hit, he was 10 years old again."

Mentally, Tiger simply loved the competition. "I like the feeling of trying my hardest under pressure," he said. "But it's so intense, it's hard to describe. It feels like a lion is tearing at my heart." Physically, Tiger had developed golf muscles that would allow him to drive the ball over 300 yards. At an American Junior Golf Association event in Texas, he won a long-drive contest with a ball that measured 310 yards.

The legend was growing.

"I get lots of leverage," Tiger would explain. "I have flat muscles like a fighter. In a few years, when I fill out, I expect to average 300 yards and hit it like Greg Norman."

5

IMG'S FIRST OVERTURE

arl Woods carried the picture around in his wallet. It is a snapshot of Tiger, age one, standing in front of his refrigerator, in a followthrough pose, holding a vacuum cleaner attachment. "He just knocked a tennis ball down the hall out the back door without touching the walls," Earl would say. "And he didn't think anything of it."

It was August 22, 1990, and Earl Woods was walking with his son during the opening round of the United Van Lines PGA Junior Championship at PGA National Golf Club in Palm Beach Gardens, Fla. Attempting to become the youngest winner in tournament history, his 14-year-old son was off to a roller coaster start—an eagle, three birdies, three bogeys and a triple bogey for an opening-round 73 put him five shots off the lead held by 17-year-old Chris Couch.

Tiger was not happy. He lost his temper and took a swipe at his bag. He was one under, but it wasn't good enough. He claimed it was a horrible round. He gave short answers to the media. Earl didn't attempt to apologize.

What upset Tiger the most was a decision that led to a triple bogey on his 17th hole. From the woods, he tried to hit a four-iron through trees, over water and onto the eighth green at the Champion course. It wasn't a good play. The ball skipped across the pond four times, hit the bank on the far side of the water hazard, and disappeared. Tiger compounded the bad course management by three-putting for a seven.

"He let his desire to make par interfere with common sense," Earl said. "But that's when I realized he's 14 years old."

On Sunday in Palm Beach Gardens, it came down to Couch and Woods. There was a big crowd following them, bigger than some of the galleries that attended the 1987 PGA Championship at PGA National. They came to watch Tiger, but it was Couch who put on the show, shooting 63 to Woods's 72 to win by 10 strokes. Afterward, Tiger admitted he was outclassed. "I was playing good, but I was just getting hammered," Woods said. "I hate to lose, but in golf everybody loses because it's so hard mentally."

After the PGA Juniors, Woods traveled up the Florida Turnpike to Orlando for the Canon Cup. Earl and Tiger did their debriefing in the car, analyzing how humble Tiger felt when Couch ripped seven straight birdies on the first 13 holes. This wasn't a loss that they could really dwell on. It was time to look ahead and move on, to do his summer school work (he was taking an advanced course that required him to read three Edgar Allan Poe short stories and write an essay in the author's voice) and get ready for the next tournament. A game had been arranged at Arnold Palmer's Bay Hill Club & Lodge. Earl and Tiger were already being courted by the International Management Group, and Palmer was IMG's flagship client. Tiger teed it up with Jim Bell, tournament director for Palmer's Nestle Invitational. They played the tournament tees and Bell called George White, then of the *Orlando Sentinel*, to tell him the Tiger Tale.

"I've never seen anything like this young man," Bell said. "We played from the back tees and he starts with birdies at one, three and four. He bogeyed number six but parred in the rest of the way for a 70. Remember, now, we're talking about a 14-year-old here. At 17, the 214-yard par-three, he hits a four-iron pin high. At No. 18, where Robert Gamez won the tournament with a seven-iron shot from the fairway, Tiger hit a high hook off the tee and had only 151 yards to the pin. He hit an eight-iron to put it by the pin. Most of the pros used driver and six-iron there in the tournament. He used driver-eight!"

That fall he went back to his middle school class in Anaheim, where he maintained a 3.75 grade point average. Imagine what it must have been like when the teacher said, "OK, Tiger, what did you do this summer?"

Tiger was too modest to tell them that he had met Hughes Norton, vice president of the International Management Group's golf division, and that his father had told Mr. Norton, "The first black superstar on the tour is going to make himself and somebody else a whole lot of money."

He didn't dare tell his classmates Norton's response: "That's why we're here, Mr. Woods."

6

COACH GOODWIN

There he was, in *Sports Illustrated* for the first time. September 24, 1990: page 109, a Face in the Crowd, next to Ryan Lusk of Hilton Head, S.C., Michele DeGennaro of Secaucus, N.J., and Tracey Day Selden of New York. "TIGER WOODS, CYPRESS, CALIF. Tiger, 14, shot a two under 286 for 72 holes to win a national junior golf tournament at Ridglea Country Club in Fort Worth. He has also won five Junior World Titles, including the Optimist International in San Diego last July."

At Stanford University in Palo Alto, Calif., Wally Goodwin saw the picture and the achievements and took a chance, writing a letter to Tiger Woods. "If you ever want to take a shot at Stanford, drop me a line," Goodwin said. To Goodwin's surprise, Woods wrote back immediately, saying that he was carefully planning his life and wanting to know exactly what it took to get into Stanford.

Goodwin kept Woods's letter. It was early in his career at Stanford, and he had a team that was brilliant academically but mediocre athletically, a team that would sometimes challenge the coach's authority. One day in the golf office, the Cardinal golfers were giving Goodwin a hard time, and Goodwin wanted to know why they couldn't be like this minority kid from L.A. The kid had perfect penmanship, diction and grammar. And most importantly, he already knew what he wanted in life. "He writes a letter better than anybody in this room," Goodwin told them. "He capitalizes correctly, he punctuates correctly, every one of his sentences has a verb. You guys can't come close."

To prove it, Goodwin went to a photocopy machine and handed out copies of the letter Tiger Woods wrote, dated April 23, 1989:

> Dear Coach Goodwin:
> Thank you for your recent letter expressing Stanford's interest in me as a future student and golfer. At first it was hard for me to understand why a university like Stanford was interested in a thirteen-year-old seventh grader and after talking with my father I have come to understand and appreciate the honor you have given me. I further appreciate Mr. Sargant's interest in my future development by recommending me to you.
> I became interested in Stanford's academics while watching the Olympics and Debbie Thomas. My goal is to obtain a quality business eduction. Your guidelines will be most helpful in preparing me for college life. My GPA this year is 3.86 and I plan to keep it there or higher when I enter high school.
> I am working on an exercise program to increase my strength. By April, my NCGA handicap is one and I plan to play in SCGA and maybe some AJGA tournaments this summer. My goal is to win the Junior World in July for the fourth time and to become the first player to win each age

bracket. Ultimately I would like to be a PGA professional. Next February I plan to go to Thailand
and play in the Thai Open as an amateur.

I've heard a lot about your golf course and I
would like to play it with my dad some time in
the future.

Hope to hear from you again.
Sincerely,
Tiger Woods 5-5/100

There was dead silence in the golf office at Stanford
University.

Wally Goodwin had made his point on Don Christen-
sen, Brad Greer and the others. They would graduate and
become doctors and attorneys and overseas executives, but
in the fall of 1989, they were just free-thinking college kids
trying to get under the golf coach's skin until Wally Goodwin showed them the Tiger Woods letter.

He was not just a face in the crowd.

II

BRAVE NEW WORLD

"I want to be the
Michael Jordan of golf . . .
I want to be the best ever."
—TIGER WOODS

7

ALMOST

Standing in the 16th fairway at Los Cerranos Country Club in Chino, Calif., Brad Gallagher of the Ben Hogan Tour and Ron Hinds, the head professional at Westlake Village (Calif.) Golf Course, were a good 40 yards behind the golf ball driven by Tiger Woods. It was February 1991, a local qualifier for the Nissan Los Angeles Open, and the kid needed to make some birdies coming in. He had just celebrated his 15th birthday, but becoming the youngest player in history to qualify for a PGA Tour event wasn't on his mind; shooting a score was. His drive on the 504-yard hole measured 344 yards and he had a nine-iron into the par-five green.

Behind him, Gallagher turned to Hinds and said, "This kid is mean." He didn't mean *mean* in the sense that Tiger was a mean-spirited kid. Gallagher meant that Tiger Woods had the type of competitive meanness not usually associated with a high school freshman.

Tiger pitched onto the green and two-putted for birdie. That put him five under for the day, just below the bubble. He birdied 17 and was at six under. Coming off the green, Tiger and his father heard that Mac O'Grady was in the clubhouse at eight under. There was one golfer at seven

under. Only two players in the field of 132 would qualify
for L.A. Tiger came to 18, another par-five, figuring his
needed eagle.

His drive landed in a tight lie, slightly downhill, more
dirt than grass under the ball. He had 250 yards to clear the
water hazard, and another 30 yards to make the green. Earl
wanted him to lay up, play the smart shot, make his four
with a wedge and go into a playoff with the guy at seven
under. "Son," he whispered, "you've got to make birdie."

The kid was too stubborn to listen. Earl was caddying
that day and figured his son needed to learn his lesson the
hard way. Tiger took out his fairway wood and took his rip.
The ball sounded awful coming off the clubface and never
had a chance, diving into the water, and with it, taking
Tiger Woods out of the Los Angeles Open. It was his only
bogey of the day, and he finished with a 69, three strokes
behind O'Grady. Afterward, Hinds admitted that Tiger
Woods was already in another league. "You try to avoid
envy in golf," he said, "but that kid humbled all of us."

In the front seat of his father's Mustang, Tiger Woods
buried his face in his hands. It turned out he did need eagle
at 18, that in one of the final groups, John Burckle, the leading money winner on the Golden State Tour, shot eight-
under 66 to tie O'Grady. Tiger Woods in the L.A. Open
would have to wait for a year.

"Honestly, I felt myself rooting for him," Hinds said.
"I was hoping he would get into the tournament so I could
watch this awesome kid play against Kite and Crenshaw
and those other guys. After seeing Tiger play, you can't help
but wonder what might have been."

8

BEL AIR

ddie Merrins, the distinguished head professional at Bel
Air Country Club in Los Angeles, has hosted the Friends
of Golf tournament at his club since 1980. The list of hon-
orees includes Lee Trevino, Byron Nelson, Arnold Palmer,
Greg Norman, Ben Crenshaw, Hale Irwin, Raymond Floyd
and in 1991, Jack Nicklaus. The event raises over $200,000
annually, and the money is donated to junior golf, high
school golf and college golf programs in the L.A. area.

Phil Mickelson, the reigning Amateur champion and
winner of the Northern Telcom Open as an Arizona State
sophomore, was scheduled to be there and take part in a
clinic with Nicklaus. Terry Jastrow, the ABC golf producer
as well as a Bel Air member and president of Jack Nicklaus
Productions, was all fired up. He saw it as a chance to get
Nicklaus and Mickelson, who at the time was being called
"The Next Nicklaus" on tape for the first time. A production
crew was sent to Bel Air, and set up on the first tee.

But Mickelson couldn't make it and Jastrow was crest-
fallen. Merrins told him not to worry. He had somebody
waiting in the wings who might turn out to be better.

There was this kid from Cypress who had been tearing
up junior golf and high school golf in California, a kid by

the name of Tiger Woods. Merrins got his phone number and had talked to Earl, explaining what the day was all about. Since it was for such a good cause, Tiger received permission to miss school. So instead of getting a chance to tape Mickelson and Nicklaus, Terry Jastrow was there to produce the first meeting of the Tiger and the Bear.

In the gallery that day were some of L.A.'s leading men, a collection of movie and television stars, doctors, attorneys, advertising executives, developers, investors and retired moguls. Bel Air has by far the least pretentious membership among the most prestigious golf clubs in the world, and they welcomed Tiger and Earl as they do all their guests—with open arms.

Merrins introduced Tiger as the best junior golfer in the United States and a star of tomorrow. Tiger was shy and soft-spoken as he stepped onto the tee, but once he started unleashing shots that flew into the skyline of Westwood, the kid from Cypress enjoyed putting on a show.

"I'm not sure if Terry was aware of the magnitude of Tiger," Merrins said. "Nicklaus was quite aware, through his sons and the media. Knowing Jack as I do, I'm always suspicious as to who the heir apparent might be. I've seen a lot come and go like comets in the sky, and I think Jack was just as curious as I was. But I watched him as Tiger hit balls, and he was visibly impressed. He was all eyes as Tiger stepped forward and hit his shots. He truly amazed one and all, including Jack Nicklaus. In retrospect, it was a historic meeting."

Nicklaus truly *was* amazed. He thanked Merrins for the introduction, and complimented Tiger. "When I grow up," he said to the phenom, "I hope my swing is as pretty as yours."

In the afternoon pro-am, Woods did the undoable,

reaching the 14th green, 575 yards away, in two shots. Nobody reaches that par-five at Bel Air in two, but Woods did it with an iron. That was the buzz among the members that night at dinner, but the players in Tiger's group confirmed it, and the kid immediately became part of Bel Air's lore. Tiger and Earl were introduced, and they respectfully hung around to listen to Nicklaus's speech before driving the 35 miles home to Cypress. The next day Tiger Woods returned to his classmates at Western High School and his teammates on the Pioneers golf team. Jack Nicklaus and Bel Air in one day was definitely pretty sweet.

9

NATIONAL CHAMP

n the coming months, Tiger would win the CIF–SCGA High
School Invitational Championship, the Southern California Junior Championship, the Ping Phoenix Junior, the
Edgewood Tahoe Junior Classic, the Los Angeles City Junior
Championship, the Orange Bowl Junior International and
for the sixth time, the Optimist International Junior World.
The living room at his home in Cypress was starting to look
like a shrine, but the one trophy that took its place in front
of the others was the one Tiger won at Bay Hill in Orlando
on July 28.

That was the day Tiger won his first national title, the
United States Junior Amateur Championship.

The victory had historic implications. At 15 years and
seven months, Woods became the youngest winner in the
Junior Am. He was also only the third African American to
win a USGA title, joining 1982 Senior Amateur champion
Alton Duhon and 1959 U.S. Amateur Public Links winner
William A. Wright.

The moment was not lost on Woods, but he had
grander plans. "I want to become the Michael Jordan of
golf," he told the *New York Times*. "I want to be the best
ever."

The practice round Tiger played at Bay Hill the summer before with Jim Bell of the Nestle Invitational paid off. He was medalist qualifier, shooting four under 140, and the first five matches were a breeze as he coasted into the final against Brad Zwetschke of Kankakee, Ill. It didn't figure to be much of a match, but Zwetschke decided to make it one.

He came out of the blocks with birdies on three of the first six holes to go three up. Tiger halved the seventh and won the next five holes. At the 13th, Tiger gave ground by hitting his tee shot out of bounds, and he lost the 14th as well. The match was all square until the par-five 16th, when Woods nearly holed his third shot for a conceded birdie and a one up lead going to the 18th. Again Tiger faltered off the tee, hooking driver O.B. to lose the hole and square the match.

During the break, Woods huddled with Brunza, who was carrying his bag. He decided to settle down and do like he said: go into that instant zone and leave the past behind. "It was just the pressure," Woods would later say. "I never dreamed that the pressure would be that great."

The playoff would start on Bay Hill's first hole, a long dogleg par-four with a driving range down the left side bordered by out-of-bounds stakes. Zwetschke hit first and drove into the rough. Woods found the rough, too. They both missed the green with their second shots, but Zwetschke left himself with an awkward stance and a bad lie. He was unable to get his wedge shot on the green and ended up making double bogey. Tiger tapped in for bogey, and the title.

One week later, playing a junior team championship in Santee, Calif., he was still wiped out. "I haven't really had time to think about what it means," he said. "The pressure is so awesome, and I was so tired, I couldn't talk afterward."

What it meant was that Tiger automatically qualified for his first United States Amateur, which began a month later at the Honors Course in Ooltewah, Tenn. There, he would face off against the other golfing prodigy, 21-year-old Phil Mickelson of Arizona State. As a college sophomore, Mickelson was defending his U.S. Amateur title.

Earl wasn't afraid to hype the matchup. He told Jaime Diaz of the *New York Times* that "Tiger would like to become the first man ever to win the U.S. Junior, Amateur, Open and Senior championships, something even Nicklaus hasn't done . . . I know Phil wants to repeat, but he might just run into a Tiger."

Mickelson never did run into Tiger at the Honors. Burned out from the Canon Cup, and an eight-hour trip that took him from Colorado Springs to Dallas and Atlanta, Woods didn't have enough time to get in a practice round and shot 78–74 to miss qualifying. Playing on adrenaline, he three-putted his first two holes and could never get it going.

"He didn't even think about this tournament until he got on the plane," Earl said. "I wanted him to have total fun at the Canon Cup, which was really about playing as a team with friends, and he was so excited that his team won. As many individual tournaments as Tiger plays, golf can get a little cold and impersonal. Playing in the Amateur is a great experience for him, but it's really just the other tournament at the end of this trip."

The 91st U.S. Amateur was just another stop on Tiger Woods's road to fame and fortune. At an age when most boys have their heads in video games and *Playboy* magazines, Tiger was thinking about his financial future. At 15, Tiger told Earl he wanted to learn to manage the people who managed his finances. He said he wanted to open the books, understand them and hold people accountable. That's why, when he wrote Wally Goodwin, he made a point of asking about Stanford's accounting program and mentioning that he wanted to obtain a quality business education. "I want to keep track of my money so they won't steal from me like Kareem Abdul-Jabbar," he said.

10

CALLING MR. WOODS

Greg McLaughlin got the telephone number from directory assistance in Orange County. He was amazed to find it there, because Tiger Woods was already pretty big in Southern California. In the summer of 1990, McLaughlin considered giving Woods a spot in the 1991 Nissan Los Angeles Open. As tournament director, it wasn't his call, and he was voted down by a committee.

But the next year, after Tiger won the Junior Amateur, he had little problem selling it. He called Earl Woods in August, making a preliminary inquiry.

"Hello, Mr. Woods? This is Greg McLaughlin with the Nissan Los Angeles Open. I'd like to know if your son would consider taking an exemption into our tournament?"

Earl Woods measured his response.

"Sir," he said. "My son would be honored to receive an exemption into the L.A. Open."

On the other end of the line, Greg McLaughlin was beaming. A golf game was arranged at Riviera in September with Rich Davis, an L.A. attorney who coordinated the volunteer force at the Nissan Open. Davis is a one handicap at L.A. North, but Woods beat him and the official invitation was extended. They played again in November, and Tiger came out for media day, stealing the show from defending champion Ted Schulz.

Greg McLaughlin had bagged the Tiger.

"What I remember about it is that Earl let Tiger make the decision," McLaughlin says. "It wasn't like he was micromanaging the situation, overburdening his son."

11

SHARK ENCOUNTER

In late December 1991, right after he won the Orange Bowl Junior Classic in Miami, Tiger Woods drove up I-95 and met Greg Norman on the back end of the range at Old Marsh Golf Club in Palm Beach Gardens, Fla. He was on his way to Orlando, to play matches against Mark O'Meara and Ian Baker-Finch. This was a recruiting trip and a way for Tiger to see how his game stacked up against three of the best players in the world.

Old Marsh was Norman's home club and the meeting had been arranged through IMG, which at the time represented golf's Great White Shark. By putting Woods together with Norman, O'Meara and Baker-Finch, Hughes Norton was continuing to lay the groundwork for the day when Tiger would make a choice about career management. Earl Woods was already on the IMG payroll as a "junior golf scout" for what sources said was a six-figure salary. IMG claimed that Earl's wages were minimal. It was all perfectly legal, although the other agents who wished to represent Tiger were claiming that IMG had crossed the line of professional fairness. Norton would always dismiss it as professional jealousy, which would make the other agents hate him even more.

It was New Year's Eve, the day after Tiger's 16th birthday. After loosening up on the range at Old Marsh, Norman and Woods headed over to the second tee in a golf cart. They were going to play a quick eight holes around the Pete Dye–designed layout before Tiger hit the road. The second hole is a reachable par-five, with a generous landing area, so Norman could let out the shaft and give the kid something to shoot at. That previous year, the Shark had finished second on the PGA Tour in driving distance, averaging 282.3 yards. It was as if he was saying, "OK, kid, top that." Woods certainly tried. His drive came off the clubface like a tracer, and from the tee, it was hard to tell whose ball went farther, Norman's or Woods's. It was a macho thing, an immediate test of manhood, the 180-pound Shark and the 140-pound Tiger checking each other out for the first time. As they drove up to their balls, making small talk, Norman was a little shocked to see that . . . damn! He had been outdriven by the U.S. Junior champion. It wasn't the last time that Norman hit first into a green. "He was 4–5 yards past me," Norman said. "That little shit was driving it by me all day."

Norman was definitely impressed by the kid's maturity, not only with the way he struck a golf ball, but by the way he handled himself both on and off the golf course. For Woods, it was an opportunity to pick Norman's brain, not only about the game, but about being a superstar, handling the media and balancing his life. Maybe this was part of IMG's luring of Tiger Woods, but Norman came away from that day at Old Marsh feeling he had made a friend for life.

"We just had a quiet game of golf," he said at the time. "But I was really impressed with the kid. He asked the most intelligent golfing questions I've heard from any player and not only was his game solid, but just his all-around presence with questions and ambience is fabulous. I'm just impressed by the guy. I like young talent like that . . . the flair, the cool, calm and collectiveness that he shows.''

O'Meara and Baker-Finch, who were also IMG clients, felt the same way. Baker-Finch, who would win the British Open that summer at Royal Birkdale, only beat the kid by two shots.

Tiger Woods came to realize that Rudy Duran was right. If he had a good day, he could hang with the best players in the world.

12

BIG TIME

Three months later, Tiger found himself on the first tee at Riviera Country Club, looking out over that famous cliff 75 feet above the fairway, about to take the bungee jump into the Brave New World of tournament golf on the PGA Tour. Inside, his stomach was doing an earthquake.

A series of three anonymous calls came into the office of tournament chairman Mark Kuperstock, threatening Woods's life and cursing Kuperstock for giving Woods a sponsor's exemption. Three security guards joined the television crews, still photographers and golf writers following Woods's every move at Riviera.

The kid was more concerned with how his game would measure up.

"I might hit the ball farther than some of them," he said. "But that doesn't mean anything. These guys have got their swings fine-tuned. I don't. They know exactly how far they hit it. For me, because my body is growing, every day is different. These guys are awesome."

Tiger was given a sponsors exemption from Nissan, and had to get a pass from the principal's office at Western High School to compete in the tournament. He was scheduled to be sitting in the third row of Glenn Taylor's ad-

vanced geometry class at the hour of his tee time. Taylor
sent him home with the lesson plan. "It's sort of like what
he's doing on the golf course," said Taylor. "Except that out
there Tiger's doing it all in his head without a compass."

Woods knew from his experience in the pro-am not to
hit driver off that first tee. His three-wood was plenty of
club, especially when he felt that rigor mortis had set in and
his hands could barely grip the golf club. With the veranda
packed and the fairway lined with spectators, Woods roped
a sweeping hook that stopped 280 yards out, in the first cut
of left rough. He could breathe again. From the fairway, he
hit three-wood on the green and two-putted for birdie. After
one hole on the PGA Tour, he was already up on the elec-
tronic scoreboards:

T. WOODS   − 1.

L.A. was the tournament Woods wanted to be his
debut. It was the one closest to his home in Cypress, the one
with so much history and tradition. Riviera was Hogan's
Alley. It had hosted a U.S. Open and a PGA Championship. It
had a membership that included Hollywood stars like James
Garner and a former USC running back named O.J. Simpson
who lived in a mansion just down Sunset Boulevard on
Rockingham. In the pro-am, he got to play with Peter Falk
and meet Sam Snead.

It was easy for Tiger to get caught up in the moment.
In the practice round, he stood on the ninth tee and fanta-
sized a little bit. "I'm going to be right here on Friday," he
said. "And it's going to be like, 'Ladies and gentleman, already 19 under par for 26 holes—just playing his normal
game . . . the leader . . . Tiger Woods." He simulated a crowd
roar and busted a drive over the fairway bunkers.

On the driving range and in the locker room, he had

the buzz going. "You hear so much about him," said Billy Andrade, who was an All-American at Wake Forest and a two-time winner on the PGA Tour the year before. "Just looking at his swing, the length he hits the ball and the way he carries himself, he's just way ahead of any junior golfer I've ever seen."

In January, Woods had been the youngest golfer ever to win the American Junior Golf Association's Player of the Year Award. But now he was in the major leagues, and to Earl, it was clear that young Tiger was in his element. "He's going to blow a lot of people's minds," he said.

David Ogrin, one of the deep-thinkers on the Tour, played two practice holes with Woods on the Tuesday before the tournament. "The young man has a gift, a very special gift," he said. "If he knows what he has, he is going to be great. He gave me the feeling he loves the joy of competition, which is important, because a lot of really talented kids find out they don't really like competition. He wouldn't surprise me if he made the cut or even crept into contention."

Everybody seemed to have an opinion, even Sandy Lyle, who, when asked what he thought about the phenom, responded with dry British humor.

"Tiger Woods," he said. "Is that a course?"

The American players gave Tiger a little more respect. They knew who Tiger Woods was, and they knew of his talent. They also knew there were pros and cons to being the youngest player to compete in a PGA Tour event. They used the example of Bob May, who played in the 1986 L.A. Open when he was 90 days older than Woods. May never made it on the PGA Tour, and was last seen playing the Asian Tour.

"I think it's great what he's doing," said Lanny Wad-kins, who made the cut at the Greater Greensboro Open as an 18-year-old freshman at Wake Forest. "Playing against the pros really helped me. I had been kind of in awe, but once I posted the same scores as a lot of them, it was a different deal."

O'Meara, who played with Woods in January, was afraid that Tiger was missing out on some of the best experiences in his life. "I told Tiger to appreciate that he's going through the best years of his golf career," O'Meara said. "To have fun and be as normal as he can be and enjoy his golf. I know he hopes to come out here, but once he gets out here, it's mostly business and responsibility."

Willie Wood, a former U.S. Junior champion who had struggled in his first nine years on the Tour, felt that Tiger might fall into the same trap that he and other phenoms had. "You just have to keep your fingers crossed," Wood said. "It's more than just ability. You have to have the right things happen to you at the right times, and try to withstand the bad times."

In four years, Tiger would learn quickly exactly what Wadkins, O'Meara and Wood were trying to tell him. But at Riviera on those two days in February 1992, he was too busy just trying to keep the ball in play. His goal was to shoot 69, which is two under at Riviera. He shot 72, with a birdie, two bogeys and all pars on the back nine. That put him eight strokes off the lead held by Wayne Levi, and needing 68 or better in the second round to make the cut. "I wanted to walk out there and hand him a course map," said Brunza.

The spectators didn't seem to care what score he shot. They yelled "Youda kid!" and held up a GO GET 'UM TIGER sign. They called him the next Nicklaus and the future of American golf. They stampeded to the point where it was a distraction. "I wasn't used to it," Woods said.

That day at lunch in the card room at Riviera, Tiger sat with his father, Brunza and McLaughlin. He ate a cheeseburger and digested his performance. "He wasn't awed by the whole thing," McLaughlin said. "He fit right in."

The realization was clear in the middle of Friday's round that he would not be around for the weekend. Tiger simply did not drive it well enough, hitting just 10 of 28 fairways, to make the 36-hole cut. He shot 75 on Friday to finish at five over 147. Not bad for a 16-year-old high school sophomore who was in the midst of a growing spurt, who had outgrown his driver and had to visit the Centinella Fitness Trailer because of back pain.

There were literally hundreds of media people waiting behind the 18th green as Tiger came up the fairway. McLaughlin got on his walkie-talkie and called the press tent.

"What are we going to do with Tiger Woods?" he said.

"Nothing," was the response.

McLaughlin was hot. The tent is right near the green. It would create a disturbance for the next group trying to finish, but the PGA Tour had the attitude that this event was for *their* golfers, not some local high school kid from Orange County who shot 147. So that's where Tiger did his news conference, and the only one who didn't lose his composure was Tiger. "There were tons of media," McLaughlin said. "It was a big, big story."

The up side to those two rounds at Riviera was that it showcased Tiger's short game. Earl used the old cliché and called it military golf. Left. Right. Left. Right. At the second, the long par-four that runs back to the clubhouse, Tiger yank-hooked his drive up against the fence near the driving range, behind a row of oleanders. He tried to chip back to the fairway, but the ball hit the curb of a cart path and came back at him. No problem for Tiger. He took out an eight-iron and busted it 170 yards onto the green, four feet from the hole. "He was getting up and down like a thief," Earl said. "He recovered and made pars from positions that Riviera hasn't seen in a long time."

Tiger's playing partners were duly impressed.

"He's remarkably mature," said Bobby Friend, a 28-year-old rookie. "It was kind of a zoo out there, but Tiger got the ball up and down from some unbelievable spots. I'd say his game is on the level of a good college player, possibly, and All-America."

Ron Matthews, an experienced Tour caddy who worked for Tiger, thought Woods was mentally as sound as an eight-year veteran. "You'd think the kid was 30 years old," Matthews said.

Tiger and Earl took the week for what it was worth: On Monday, he was back in Mr. Taylor's advanced geometry class and Western opened its high school golf season with a match against Gahr High in Anaheim. It was a rainy day at Dad Miller Golf Course and he was out there with Bryon Bell and the rest of the Pioneers, carrying his golf bag, ducking under his own umbrella, while the television crews followed along in the back of a flatbed truck. The match was never completed, but it was just as well. He was still harking back to Riviera, critiquing what went wrong. "It was a learning lesson," he said, "and I learned I'm not that good."

It was still the two best days of his life, and despite the death threat, Tiger Woods was quite comfortable playing to the big crowds. Even when he hit a bad shot, the people clapped. He realized how good he could get in that environment, playing golf fulltime.

In his debriefing, Earl thought his son should have used

a one-iron more, but realized it was just a building block to Tiger's foundation. Earl Woods knew it would take a little time. "Our goal is long-term excellence at the highest echelon," he said. "Not instant short-term gratification."

13

REPEAT

It already seemed like an endless summer, and it was only July. By the time Tiger Woods arrived at Wollaston (Mass.) Golf Club for the U.S. Junior Championship, he had taken his road show to Chicago for the Western Juniors, Roswell, Ga., for the Rolex Tournament of Champions and San Diego for the Optimist Junior World Championship, with the AJGA Boys Championship in Dallas next up on the schedule. He had no time for a Red Sox game at Fenway Park, or a tour of Boston Garden or a trip to historic Faneuil Hall. This was not a sightseeing visit to Boston—this was strictly business.

No player in the 45-year history of the U.S. Juniors had successfully defended his title, and Tiger was once again intent on rewriting history. His only diversion was a junior clinic he put on early in the week at an inner-city public park. Boston mayor Raymond Flynn presented Woods with a proclamation of thanks, which seemed to perk the kid up—"Wow, from the mayor," he said. But otherwise, Woods spent his time away from the course conserving energy and mentally preparing himself for the grind of another match-play pressure cooker.

"Competitive golf is so tiring," he told the writers in

New England. "You are so focused, it is so mentally draining, that when school begins I don't touch a golf club for
two months. Pros have it relatively easy because their
schedule is spread out over nine months. (He would soon
learn differently.) But competitive junior schedules run
from the end of school in June through August. With only
three months of tournament golf, you try to play as many
events as you can. But all the travel, changing time zones,
packing, unpacking, and eating on the road gets old. By the
time September rolls around, I'm glad to get back in school
and be with my friends."

The L.A. Open was an awakening for Woods. It showed
he had the game to play on the big-time level, and he coveted more opportunities to prove it. Part of him was already
ready to take on Greg Norman, Freddie Couples and Nick
Faldo: "One thing I can say is that I'm not intimidated.
That's something my folks instilled in me." On the other
hand, part of him knew he wasn't ready: "I try to live by
the belief that you should always be yourself and always do
the things that are right for you. That means being realistic
about your goals."

His goals were to be the best golfer of all time. Not
black. Not white. Not Asian. *The* best, regardless of race,
color or creed—period. But he was finally confident enough
to realize that nobody can win all the time. Not even Tiger
Woods on the AJGA circuit.

At 16, Tiger had assessed his strengths—and his weaknesses. He had trouble controlling the distances of his
shots—one six-iron would travel 170 yards and the next
would go 185. And he wasn't yet where he wanted to be in
the mental process. There were too many inconsistencies in
his game to compete against the big boys on a regular basis.

"I'm not mature enough," he admitted. "My body

hasn't finished growing and my swing's not good enough yet. It's not fine-tuned. The guys on the pro tour don't make dumb decisions. Their thinking is very clear. With me, 16-year-old problems sneak in there every once in a while. I still take too many chances, get too emotional and try things that aren't very smart."

On the junior level, he could get away with his mistakes, and at Wollaston, he did. In qualifying, he shot 68–75—143, cruising through the second round and still winning medalist honors. He liked the course and thought it reminded him of Lake Merced Golf Club in San Francisco, where he was knocked out in the semis of the 1990 Junior Amateur by Dennis Hillman. Wollaston had taller trees and cleaner air. "This is a patient man's golf course," he said.

In his opening round match, Tiger took Brian Bombard of Rochester, N.Y., to the woodshed, winning eight and seven. He won his next two matches four and three, then dusted Ryan Armour in the Round of 16, eight and six. Jonathan Bartlett of Ocala, Fla., gave him a little game in the semis, but Tiger won three and two to set up a final against Mark Wilson of Menomonee Falls, Wis., who was runner-up in qualifying at 147.

The gallery on Sunday was unprecedented. Tom Meeks, who runs the U.S. Junior Amateur for the USGA, described it as being bigger than anything he had seen on any day of a U.S. Amateur. "I talked with people who drove 150 miles to see him," Meeks said. "The gallery got so big people were leapfrogging to the next hole to wait for him."

The Woods-Wilson match provided great theater. Woods started slow, bogeyed the first two holes and was quickly two down. It was the first time all week he trailed in a match, and it looked like three down when his drive at the par-three third hole landed in the right rough. An eight-foot putt saved par and halved the hole. "That got my juices flowing," he said.

Wilson went two up again, winning the 11th and 12th holes, but he was always looking in his rearview mirror at Woods and Brunza. "I knew he'd come back," Wilson said: "I knew about his reputation and I knew about his caddy."

It was as if Wilson talked himself into it. Woods won the 14th, 16th and 18th holes to win one up. Only four players—Mason Rudolph, Eddie Pearce, Mike Brannan and Tim Straub—were able to reach the finals twice in the under-18 championship. It hit the Woodses, Earl and Tiger, as they hugged for more than a minute behind the 18th green. As they cried in embrace, the gallery of more than 1,000 at Wallaston continued their applause in a tribute to the father and son team.

"Just like Faldo," Woods said, referring to Nick Faldo's emotional British Open victory the previous week at Muirfield, Scotland. "I'm not one who usually does that. It just all came out. You just can not believe how much tension I was feeling. It's over, finally."

14

AIR TIGER

After the Junior Amateur in Massachusetts, the Tiger Road Show played the American Junior Golf Association Boys' Championship at the Four Seasons–TPC at Los Colinas in Irving, Texas. There, on the sixth tee of a practice round, the legendary Byron Nelson pulled up in a golf cart.

It wasn't their first meeting. Nelson was at Bel Air for the Friends of Golf Tournament in 1991. They didn't get a chance to spend much quality time in L.A., but Nelson wanted to lay the groundwork for a longterm friendship. Tiger noticed him driving up to the tee, and greeted Lord Byron with a smile and an extended hand.

"Tiger, I'm glad to watch you play," Nelson said. "I enjoyed watching you at Bel Air."

He delighted in watching him that day in Irving even more, as Woods shot 67 from the back tees on the same TPC course that hosts the GTE Byron Nelson Classic. After eight holes, Nelson returned to the clubhouse and reported to Jeff Rude of the *Dallas Morning News* that he didn't see any weaknesses in Tiger's game, that it was as sound fundamentally as any professional. Five months later, he would handwrite a personal letter to Tiger, inviting him to play in the 1993 GTE Byron Nelson Classic. "You look at his swing and it doesn't look like he hits it long, but he does," Nelson said. "His rhythm is so good. I think he's the best 16-year-old I ever saw . . . unless there's somebody hiding in the woods."

Tiger was getting a little burned out on junior golf. He was having a hard time with the media attention—answering the same questions—and he missed being home in Cypress where he could hang out and rest. Friends like Bell would call wanting to know if he wanted to check out a movie, or maybe the girls down at the mall, but Tiger would beg off. The golf and the traveling and the growing spurts left him exhausted—he shot up 6½ inches in two years and now stood at 6'1". But no matter how many trips to McDonald's he made, no matter how many pizzas he ate and milk shakes he drank, he couldn't gain any weight. It was his metabolism, but it was also the stress. "The summer I have is very challenging and I focus very hard, so I need all the rest I can get," he would say. "I go home and I usually don't even leave my room."

All this running around didn't seem to affect Tiger's game. He won the AJGA Junior Championship at the Four Seasons and the Independent Insurance Agent Junior Classic at Pinehurst for his seventh and eighth victories of the year, then led the West team to a victory in the Canon Cup at Bloody Point Golf Club on Daufuskie Island, S.C. It was costing Earl about $20,000 a summer to finance his son's career, and all that hopping back and forth from California made Tiger realize that Florida would be his eventual home. "When you fly (from the) west you always lose time," he said. "That's tough on your body, especially on a 16-year-old body, and I'm sick of that."

15

TAKING HIS LUMPS

The summer of '92 was not over for Tiger until he made the trip to Dublin, Ohio, for the U.S. Amateur Championship. By winning the Junior Am, Woods could skip local qualifying and move into stroke play at Muirfield Village. Without making any bold predictions, Tiger pointed toward the National Amateur when he left Massachusetts in July. In 1991 at the Honors course, he failed to advance through to match play. But at Muirfield Village, he overcame an erratic opening-round 78 with a 66. At 144, he was eight strokes behind David Duval, who shot 69–67 for a total of 136 and medalist honors. Some of the other names to advance were Jay Sigel, Justin Leonard, Allen Doyle, David Berganio and Manny Zerman, but the media and the gallery were predominantly there for one person—Tiger.

"It made me concentrate knowing I had to shoot low to get in, and I did it," he said. After the first day, Woods was 172nd out of 319 qualifiers. He made quadruple bogey eight on the par-four 12th, but dug himself out of the hole with a par-birdie-birdie-eagle start. After that, he turned off his birdie switch and conserved himself for match play.

"The pressure I deal with to win that second junior amateur is something that is going to help me," he said. "If I can play like I did today, I can win."

Woods was in the bottom half of the draw, and would face Ted Gleason, a 22-year-old senior at UCLA. This was a different game now, where the competitors wouldn't be intimidated. Still, he had more game than any 16-year-old golfer in the world. Zerman, a 22-year-old All-American from the University of Arizona, who lost in the Amateur finals in 1990 and 1991, said that "Tiger's game is definitely that of a top contender." Zerman added that Tiger's lack of experience may get him, "but in match play," he said, "you never know."

Woods started out slow against Gleason. He was three down after three holes, but rallied and was two up through 13 when the rains came. After a 5½-hour delay, any momentum Woods had going shifted. Gleason birdied the 14th and won the 15th and 16th holes when Woods three-putted. With two holes to go, Gleason was one up.

That's when Tiger found his late passing gear. At 17, Gleason drove out of bounds. At 18, Woods saved par from a deep-faced greenside bunker and Gleason missed an eight-footer for birdie. On the first playoff hole, the 440-yard first, Woods hit three-wood and then a 205-yard six-iron to 15 feet. Gleason never had a chance to attempt his seven-foot par putt. Woods rolled in the birdie and advanced to the Round of 32.

"It was gut-check time," Woods said. "I'm proud I had the guts to do it at this level. It's going to help me in the next match . . . but it's different on this level. These guys don't fold. You have to hit better shots to make them fold."

Gleason thought that if Tiger could keep his composure, he could advance well beyond the first round of match play. The player Woods drew in the second round was Tim Herron, a University of New Mexico All-American that his friends back home in Wayzata, Minn., nicknamed

"Lumpy." If there was a match in his young career that Woods could relate it to, it would be the final round of the PGA Juniors against Couch. Lumpy Herron came out hot and stayed that way. He birdied Nos. four, five and six to build a four-up lead, then closed out Tiger at the 14th hole with his fifth birdie of the match. Woods complained of back spasms, but made no excuses. He could just never get it going.

"I was playing well coming in here," Woods said. "But if I had to run into a buzzsaw like today, I probably would still have lost even if I'd played my 'A' game. It might have been a little early. My game's not fine-tuned enough for this yet. The swing's not there yet. And these guys, they're gooood."

Although he had an easy time of it, Herron saw the potential in Tiger's tired game. "He's aggressive," Herron said. "He hits the ball a long way. And he has a good attitude. My advice to him is to just keep playing."

That was John Merchant's advice too. As the only African-American member of the USGA's executive committee, Merchant, a Connecticut lawyer, was working on ways to give minorities greater access to golf. His meal ticket was obviously Tiger. "You'll see him in the finals one of these years," Merchant said.

And we would also see Merchant one day working for Tiger, as his attorney.

After the Amateur, Woods headed to Seattle with his father, where he participated in a halfday golf clinic before returning home to Cypress and his junior year at Western High School. He would put the clubs away for a while, run the 400-meter event for the track team (his best time was 52 seconds) and get ready for the spring golf season. The only time he talked about his sport was when a classmate brought it up.

"Our team's not very good," he said. "But that's all right."

As a freshman, Woods was medalist in 27 of his team's 29 matches, and led the Pioneers to a share of the Orange League Championship. But high school golf was clearly down on his list of priorities. "When he plays some of the tournaments against some of the best kids from all over the country, that's the big time," said his high school coach, Don Crosby. "Not to downplay our events, but that's the way it is."

16

BIRTHDAY SPANKING

The 1992 Orange Bowl International Junior Invitational was a real turning point in Tiger Woods's career. The final round fell on his 17th birthday, and on the first tee, tournament officials and spectators in the gallery at Biltmore Golf Course in Coral Gables, Fla., serenaded Tiger with song and merriment. Earl sensed this was not a good idea.

Tiger was tied with Lewis Chitengwa of Zimbabwe and was the favorite to close out the year with his eighth title. But early in the match he wasn't playing well, and Chitengwa took a one-stroke lead with a birdie at the sixth. At the next hole, Tiger missed a six-footer for bogey, and from there on in, he pouted like a baby who hadn't gotten his rattle. Chitengwa shot 71 to win by three strokes. Woods shot 74 and had to win a playoff for second place. In the bus back to the hotel, his father blistered him.

In junior golf, parents are not allowed to talk with their children during competition, so Earl was forced to watch his son's petulance and insufferable behavior. But when they were alone, he gave Tiger the type of chewing-out his son had never heard before, a dressing down that Earl hadn't given someone since his military days.

"Who do you think you are?" he said. "Golf owes you

nothing. The nerve of you quitting out there on the golf course. You never quit! You never quit! Do you understand me?"

Tiger was so afraid of his father that he did not say a word all the way back to the hotel, or on the trip to the airport. He would never forget that day at the Biltmore. No matter how many holes he was down, he would never quit.

17

THE WHOLE PACKAGE

The invitations went out early. From the Bob Hope Chrysler Classic. From the L.A. Open. From the Honda Classic. And from Byron Nelson. Players on the bottom half of the PGA Tour food chain were getting jealous. During a player meeting at the AT&T Pro-Am, Ed Dougherty stood up and half jokingly said, "The kid's got a better schedule than I do."

He turned down the Hope, but went to Riviera for the L.A. Open, figuring he had a good chance to make the cut. He knew what to expect, both from the crowd and the course, and wasn't going through the same growth pains. He had a driver's license, his father's 1988 Toyota Supra and his first girlfriend—Dina was her name, according to Earl. Tiger Woods, age 17, was growing up.

"To be honest," he said, "my chances this year have doubled."

But the 1993 L.A. Open was another humbling experience. He shot 74–78 and was five strokes higher than the previous year. Four days later, he was playing for Western High in a match against Lakewood. Six days after that, he was at Weston Hills Country Club in Fort Lauderdale, Fla.

McLaughlin was now the tournament director for the

Honda Classic, but selling Tiger wasn't a slam dunk because of Tiger's connections with the Nissan tournament. (Nissan is Honda's big rival.) Eventually McLaughlin prevailed, and Tiger was set up with a courtesy car (which Earl drove) and a two-bedroom suite at the Bonaventure Resort and Spa (which Earl paid for). McLaughlin had done his homework. On Monday he arranged a game for Woods with Dan Marino, John Elway, Bernie Kosar, Phil Simms and Mark Rypien. On Tuesday, he had him in a practice round with Brad Faxon, Billy Andrade and Dudley Hart. On Wednesday, he convinced a pro-am patron to give up his spot, and paired Woods with John Daly.

It was as if Woods and Daly were the only two golfers on the course at Weston Hills. They stood on the 17th tee at Weston Hills that day, separated for a moment from the big crowd following them, surveying the yardage, with Woods trying to decide whether to hit the hard seven-iron or feather-cut a six-iron to a pin that was 203 yards away. They had a little bet going, nothing that would hurt the kid, just a little action to make it interesting.

"Aren't you giving me two shots a side?" Woods said.

Daly grunted.

"Shoot," he said. "You ought to be giving *me* shots."

Daly remembered Woods as the 107-pound kid from that junior tournament in Arkansas they played in 1989, when he had to birdie three of the last four to beat him. He saw a bigger Tiger Woods now, a young man who had grown mentally and physically from Texarkana Country Club.

"He's very, very mature for his age," Daly said. "He's got all the shots, too. He's a good ball striker and he's got a good short game. He's gonna be good—shoot, he already is good."

Daly was asked if he had any advice for Tiger.

"I'm just kind of leaving him alone," he said. "He's played in a few of these PGA Tour events, so he knows what it's going to be like when he gets out of college. I never had that opportunity. When he gets out of college, he knows what he's going to be going up against. It's a great experience for him."

In a way, Daly could relate to the type of pressure that Tiger was under. They were both incredibly long, which the fans loved, and after Daly won the 1991 PGA Championship, he had become one of the biggest box-office attractions in golf. Everybody wanted a piece of them—no matter which way he turned, there was somebody there wanting an autograph or a picture or a handshake or an interview. They'd come 150 miles to see Daly and Woods hit it off the face of the Earth.

"He's kind of like me," Daly said. "People think they're putting pressure on him making all these expectations. I think Tiger's in control of it. He's like me in that we just expect what we can do. Our expectations are different than everybody else's. I don't think he's going to worry about what people put on him."

Tiger liked hanging out with Daly, Faxon, Andrade, Hart, Marino, Elway and the guys. He was especially excited about hitting balls next to Nick Faldo on the practice tee at Weston Hills. But there were other perks, like the perfect turf on the range and the shiny new Titleist balatas, the private omelette chef in the locker room, the sports trainers in the fitness van, the courtesy car Earl was driving and the suite at the Bonaventure. It was all pretty sweet.

"It's like a trial marriage with all the rights and privileges except one—you don't get paid," said Earl. "But it is truly amazing how he takes to the competition and the way of life. He said to me last night, 'Daddy, I can get used to this very easy.' "

Woods's scores still didn't measure up. He shot 72–78 to miss his third cut in a PGA Tour event. But he showed enough game to have Andrade making bold statements.

"He's got the whole package," said Andrade. "The fact is, he can play on this tour right now."

All the hyperbole and predictions had some people worried about Tiger. Tom Kite, the all-time leading money winner on the PGA Tour, couldn't believe the amount of ink the kid was getting. "Stop to think about it," Kite said. "He isn't out of high school yet, and everybody's talking about how good he is."

The names of the other golfing prodigies were rattled off: Eddie Pearce, Bobby Clampett, Bruce Fleisher. Of the first 45 winners of the U.S. Junior title, only two, Gay Brewer (1967 Masters) and Johnny Miller (1973 U.S. Open and 1976 British Open), subsequently had victories in one of the four major professional championships. The consensus was that Tiger should follow Phil Mickelson's blueprint for success. Go to school, stay for four years, and get not only the degree, but the college experience.

"He's got a fun process ahead of him," Mickelson said. "The next four or five years, he's going to have a lot of fun playing in amateur events and collegiate golf. That would be what I would tell him—have fun."

Pearce seconded that. At 12, he won the National Pee Wee by 12 shots. When he was 16, he lapped a field in the U.S. Juniors that featured Ben Crenshaw, Bruce Lietzke and Gary Koch. But Pearce read too many of his press clippings, partied too much, dropped out of Wake Forest, lost his card and attempted a comeback at age 40. He didn't want to see that happen to Tiger.

"Tiger Woods is a great junior golfer, period. End of story," he told Larry Dorman, then of the *Fort Lauderdale*

Sun-Sentinel. "To put all this on him, it's not right. Nobody can tell how good the kid is going to be. You don't know how tall he'll be, how he'll react to the pressures. The kid hasn't even had a beer yet.

"The advice I would have for the kid is to follow in Phil Mickelson's steps to the letter. Follow that program. Go to college, get a degree. Play college golf and keep learning."

Tiger Woods kept saying he would do just that, but he was not Phil Mickelson or Eddie Pearce. Three years down the road, he would have his own set of circumstances. He was already saying that playing the junior circuit can be a bigger grind than playing the PGA Tour. "Some of our tournaments are Friday through Saturday, others are Tuesday through Friday, then maybe Sunday through Wednesday," he said. "I could be gone four or five weeks and play five or six events." And he had not yet experienced the petty restrictions of the NCAA, or the downside to balancing the dual role of student and athlete at Stanford.

In March 1993, Tiger Woods was a 17-year-old senior at Western High School in Anaheim. He was taking honors courses and had a 3.3 grade-point average out of a possible 4. He would go out on the tour and the turf on the practice ground would be better than some of the greens he putted on in high school matches. And the practice balls? They were brand-new balatas.

"I'm like a kid in a candy store," he said. "This is a job to these guys. It's not my job."

Not yet, but it soon would be. Tiger Woods was smart enough to know advanced algebra wouldn't help him shoot four rounds in the mid-60s. He would go to college until his game was ready, or until there was nothing left to accomplish as an amateur. Then he would turn pro and change the face of the game.

18

THREE-PEAT!

On the road, Tiger had already been taking on the responsibilities of an adult. He made all the travel arrangements, told Earl what time he wanted to wake up, go to the course, practice, eat, sleep. "It is very gratifying to see how this life prepared him for adulthood," Earl said. "It is the development of the individual—golf is just the medium."

He traveled to the Nelson in May and shot 149 to miss the cut. He returned to California and won the Southern Section Individual Golf Championship, but wasn't satisfied with his score, which was 68, and complained of being in a slump. In U.S. Open Qualifying at Valencia Country Club, he shot 77–74 for a total of 151 and missed by seven shots. It was the week after finals. He left two days later to play in the Sunnehanna Amateur in Pennsylvania, where he would finish fifth and match the record set by Jack Nicklaus, who was the only other junior to crack the top 10 in that prestigious event. But all the travel, and all the golf, caught up with him. In mid–June, Tiger was diagnosed with mononucleosis. He could not pick up a club for three weeks.

"I knew how much he played compared to everyone else, and I used to tell him, 'Tiger, if you don't want to do

something, then don't,' " said Crosby. "Everybody said it
was God-given ability, but that's a bunch of baloney. He'd
work four hours a day for four years. He'd wear guys out.
They'd leave and he'd still be there—and he was the same
way in the classroom. I had him for two years in accounting, and he came in the classroom and worked just as hard
as he did at golf. He was a very competitive young man who
wanted to be the best no matter what it was. If he didn't get
the top grade in class, he studied harder the next week. He
was always so goal-oriented and he never got off track.
Deep down he knew what he wanted all along."

A third-straight Junior Amateur was one of those
goals, but by the time he reached Waverley Country Club in
Portland, Tiger was not certain what to expect. He shot 143
in qualifying, which was three strokes back of medalist
honors won by high school rival Ted Oh of Torrance. He
cruised through his first three matches, defeating Ryan La-
voie of Pasco, Wash., six and five; Chad Wright of Ventura,
Calif., four and two; Grady Girard of Newport, Vt., six and
four, and Aaron Wright of Anna, Ill., three and two. This
set up a semifinal against Oh, who at 16 had become the
second-youngest golfer in history to qualify for the U.S.
Open.

Woods made his point by birdieing three holes early on
the second nine, and won easily four and three. In the finals,
he would face Ryan Armour of Silver Lake, Ohio. In the
1992 U.S. Junior at Wollaston, Woods crushed Armour in
the quarterfinals eight and six. It didn't figure to be much of
a match, but Armour refused to be humbled again.

"I didn't want to go out like that," he said. "Last year
I went out without a prayer. This year I wanted to go out
with a fight."

An Amateur record crowd of 4,650 was in attendance

at Waverley. Through 14 holes, neither player had been more than one up. At the 15th, Armour rammed in a 40-footer for birdie and at No. 16, Woods three-putted. Armour was two up with two holes to go and thinking, "Two pars and the national title is yours."

Woods may have been down, but he was not dead. At the 432-yard 17th, a hole that registered nearly as many bogeys as it had pars in the competition, Woods carried a bunker that guarded the dogleg, and drove some 70 yards past Armour. With a nine-iron in his hands, Woods hit it approach shot to eight feet. Armour had a tap-in for par. Woods had to make, or it was over.

"Got to be like Nicklaus," he told Brunza, who was carrying his bag. "Got to will this in the hole."

Bang. Birdie. One down. One to play.

The 18th at Waverley is a 578-yard par-five. Woods nearly reached it in two shots. Armour played it safe, hitting iron off the tee, laying up with his second shot and hitting wedge to 45 feet. Earl noticed Tiger's face had hardened. He realized that by going the conservative route, Armour was daring Woods to make birdie.

For a moment, Armour's strategy looked semi-decent. Woods's three-iron approach from the light rough drifted into a greenside bunker, 40 yards from the green. The long bunker shot is one of the hardest to hit in golf, especially when the pressure is on. Woods hit his third shot to 10 feet. "I'm thinking, he'll be lucky to get it on the green," Armour said. "And he knocks it to 10 feet. How good is that?"

Armour hadn't seen anything yet. Woods was still locked into his Nicklaus mode. He willed the putt in the hole to even the match.

Advantage Tiger.

"I knew I had to birdie 17—no ifs, ands or buts about

it," Woods said. "And at 18 it's either make the putt or go home. I knew I had to play two of the best holes of my life, and I did."

The playoff hole was a formality. Armour three-putted for bogey. Woods tapped in for par and another place in history. "To finish birdie-birdie on this course is awesome," Armour said. "It was mine. I had my hands on it, but he was teasing me. It was like he was following a script. I don't think many people could have done what Tiger did, professional, amateur, junior amateur, whatever. That's why he's the best."

Woods was wiped out. The travel. The mono. Two down with two holes to play, needing two birdies and a miracle, needing those two putts, thinking how Nicklaus would think, then executing. This was better stuff than being three down after six holes in his first Junior Amateur at Bay Hill, or two down with six to play at Wollaston in 1992. It was the most amazing comeback of his career, and he wept in the embrace of his dad on the 18th green.

"I did it, I did it," he said to Earl.

"I'm so proud of you. I'm so proud of you," Earl said, over and over.

Tiger had once again done the impossible.

He made time stop.

19

GETTING PAGED

The 93rd U.S. Amateur at Champions Golf Club was Tiger Woods's last chance to pull off the historic double. He came to Houston as a three-time Junior Amateur champion, and no golfer had won the Junior Am and the U.S. Am in the same year. If anybody had the game to pull it off, it was Tiger.

Long and demanding, Champions figured to be Tiger's kind of golf course, and early in the competition, it was. He shot even-par 142 and advanced through the 36 holes of stroke-play qualifying, then made three birdies and an eagle in 14 holes to dispatch Christopher Sladish of Oswego, N.Y., in the opening round of match play, six and four. Afterward, he told reporters that there should be more match-play events in golf. "Each match is so different," he said. "You have to always think and be aware of what the other guy is doing."

By beating Sladish, Woods had advanced to face Paul Page, who the week before had represented Great Britain/Ireland in the Walker Cup matches. It looked like another easy win, but like Tiger said, there are no certainties in match play.

Page, who was 0–2 in the Walker Cup loss at Inter-

lachen, birdied the eighth and ninth holes to go one up.
Every putt the Engishman needed, he made. Woods hung
tough, but Page went one up again with a birdie at the
par-3 12th. Woods was having trouble with the swing
changes he tried to make at the range, and double bogeyed
the 16th. Page was two up, the same situation Ryan
Armour was in at Waverley.

Lightning was in the skies, but it didn't strike twice.
Woods was in the woods right of the 17th green and Page
was plugged in a greenside bunker when play was sus-
pended. They went to the locker room and waited for five
hours. When they came back out, the bunker by the 17th
green had washed out, and Page's ball was completely covered with sand. Trey Holland, the USGA's rules official, ordered that the bunker be raked, and Page's ball returned to
its place. Every effort was made to re-create the lie, but Page
definitely caught a break. He got up and down to save par
and win the match, two and one.

"It was not the way I envisioned to lose, on a rake drop
like that," Woods said.

Paul Page would join Dennis Hillman and Tim Herron
as the answers to a golf trivia question.

He would be the last player to defeat Tiger Woods in
USGA competition. Tiger would win 18 of his next 18
matches, capture three U.S. Amateur titles and run his
USGA match-play record to 42–3.

20

BUTCH

One of the first calls Earl Woods made after Tiger was eliminated from the Amateur was to Butch Harmon at Lochinvar Golf Club. Butch had been credited with reworking Greg Norman's swing, and helping The Shark win the British Open that summer at Royal St. George's.

Butch's father, Claude, won the 1948 Masters back in the days when touring professionals took club jobs to support their families. Claude was the professional at Winged Foot in the summer and Seminole in the winter, so he had the best of both worlds, plus a wonderful family that included four sons—Claude Jr. (Butch), Craig, Dick and Billy—all of whom grew up to become club professionals. Butch was the oldest, and he learned all the shots and the golf swing while caddying for his father. Besides Norman, he had worked with Davis Love III and Steve Elkington.

Tiger didn't like the way he was driving the ball, and Norman was the best driver of the golf ball in the world. Harmon had been at Champions, watching Tiger's match with Page before the rain delay. He saw a lot of clubhead speed, but also a loose swing with a big hip turn that produced inconsistent results.

At first they just talked. Butch bought them lunch and

they discussed the golf swing, what Tiger was trying to accomplish and what Butch had seen at Champions. Butch eventually asked if Tiger wanted to hit some balls, and it wasn't long before they were on the practice tee, Butch with his video camera, Tiger with his clubs.

"Tiger showed me some of the shots that he could hit, and I made some suggestions to him at the time that would make him more consistent," Harmon said. "It was nothing special but I guessed he liked the results that he saw."

To say he tightened up Woods's swing the way he did Norman's would be an oversimplification. The things Harmon worked on were giving Woods a wider stance for a better foundation, a wider arc at the top of his backswing and less hip turn, which would prevent his club from going past parallel. It was more like what he did with Love, since Davis and Tiger are built similarly.

Harmon kept telling Woods that in order to get to the next level, he had to control the distance on his shots, and work the ball depending on the conditions, or the shape of the hole. Tiger came back the next day, and they worked again. For the next year, they would get together only twice, but a week wouldn't go by without a phone conversation, or a month without Tiger mailing Butch a tape of his swing.

Butch's first question was always: "Where's the ball starting?"

From there, he knew what Tiger was doing correctly, or incorrectly.

Right from the start, Butch Harmon knew that Tiger Woods was the real deal, one of the best young players to come out of the United States in a long time—maybe ever.

That was the good news.

"The bad news," Harmon said, even then, "is that he has to live up to it now."

21

DECISION

It was time for Tiger Woods to pack up and move on. He won the Dial Award as the top high school male athlete in the country, and decided that he was unofficially finished with junior golf. His college decision now was between Stanford, Arizona State and the University of Nevada–Las Vegas. His plans were to visit all three schools by mid-October, and sign early. "I want to get it over with," he said at the Amateur. "I don't want to deal with the hassle anymore."

It came down to Stanford and UNLV, two schools on opposite ends of the spectrum yet close in Woods's confused mind. Stanford was the Harvard of the West Coast. The Cardinals had won the NCAA golf title in the spring, but the school was also known for its academics. UNLV, a college golf power, was known as a party school.

Woods agonized over it to the point where he became physically ill. UNLV had the sunshine and the attractive coeds. Stanford had the academics and his heart.

"School has always come first, and that meant Stanford," Woods said. "I know my golf won't improve as much at Stanford because of the academic requirements, but my main concern was picking the school which will be best for me overall, and I think it's Stanford."

The announcement was made on November 10, 1993, in the gymnasium at Western High. Woods was flanked by his parents, Earl and Tida. In Palo Alto, Wally Goodwin just hit the lottery.

The Stanford golf coach was returning Notah Begay, Steve Burdick, Brad Lanning, Casey Martin and William Yanagisawa from its national championship team. He was flashing the letter that Woods wrote him in the seventh grade. The one so perfectly worded.

"When you're lucky enough to sign the best junior player who's ever lived, you have a star in your midst," Goodwin told Mark Soltau of the *San Francisco Examiner*. "He's not only a great player but a great kid. He seems motivated to help us attain our goal of a national championship. But Tiger won't come in here and be No. 1. They're going to beat him like a drum for a while."

The only downside to Stanford was that the undergraduate business program did not include an accounting major as part of its curriculum. Arrangements were made to accommodate Woods's academic needs. He'd major in a customized economics program.

"The dean, the athletic director and the business director said, 'We'll work with you. We'll create you a major,' " Woods said. "I said, 'OK.' "

It was a decision he never regretted making. He wanted a quality business education. At Stanford, he would get one.

III

MOVE OVER, BOBBY JONES

"Let the legend grow."
—EARL WOODS

22

PRELUDE

The Masters. The U.S. Open. The British Open. These were the Big Three, the majors that Tiger Woods was eligible to play in as an amateur. Earl had made a prediction that Tiger would win a U.S. Amateur and qualify for them while he was in high school. It was too late to fulfill that goal, but Tiger Woods could still qualify for the Masters and the two Opens as a Stanford freshman. On his 18th birthday, December 30, 1993, and over those Christmas holidays, Tiger and Earl plotted a game plan that would prepare Woods for the 94th U.S. Amateur Championship at the Sawgrass–TPC in Florida, and ultimately for the majors.

Behind the scenes, IMG was already working to get Tiger Woods in tournaments that included the best international golfers in the world, fields where Nick Faldo, Greg Norman, Bernhard Langer, Ernie Els, Ian Woosnam and Colin Montgomerie were competing. It was done quietly. It was done discreetly. It was done because IMG saw the immense earning potential of Tiger Woods growing and growing, and 20 percent of that would be a windfall. It all went back to that conversation Hughes Norton had with Earl Woods at that junior tournament when Tiger was thirteen.

"The first black superstar on the tour is going to make

himself and somebody else a whole lot of money," Earl
Woods had said.

And remember what Hughes Norton, the Harvard
MBA, said? "That's why we're here, Mr. Woods."

In the years to come, Tiger Woods would be criticized
for aligning himself for the world's most powerful management firm. The deal would be called shady, and Tiger would
be warned that IMG had a reputation for running its clients
into the ground, that Hughes Norton is the worst guy in the
world to be managing your career, that someday he would
see that and break off to do his thing, just like Nicklaus and
Norman and Price and Floyd did. But there is a huge upside
to IMG, and Woods realized it early. No management firm is
better connected, and at the age of 18, Tiger Woods had a
schedule that included the Johnnie Walker Asian Classic in
Thailand, the Nestle Invitational at Bay Hill in Orlando, the
Buick Classic at Westchester Country Club in New York and
the Motorola Western Open at Cog Hill in Chicago. He also
had a list of high school and amateur tournaments, plus his
final semester and graduation from Western High School.
Tiger Woods would be a very busy young man in 1994.
Later in the summer he would compete for the 94th U.S.
Amateur title at the Sawgrass-TPC, and enroll for his first
freshman semester at Stanford University.

The deal with the Johnnie Walker tournament was
supposedly arranged with the Thai government through
connections Tida had back home. Whatever the case, IMG
ran the event, and it had a reputation in the early '90s for
having one of the best fields in all of golf. While PGA Tour
Commissioner Tim Finchem was struggling to protect his
West Coast swing, Greg Norman and Fred Couples—his two
biggest gate draws—flew halfway across the world to play
IMG's event on the resort island of Phuket, off the southern

coast of Thailand. The reason was obvious. It wasn't the scenery or the hot Thai food. It was the appearance money, numbers that ranged in excess of $200,000 each for Norman, Couples and Faldo, and at least six figures for Els, Langer, Woosnam and Montgomerie.

Tiger wasn't getting paid a cent, but it was a priceless education to play overseas, in the homeland of his mother, against what amounted to the best players off IMG's Sony Rankings. "Tida had contacts in Thailand," Norton explained. "And they made it known that if Tiger was interested, they'd give him an exemption. The initiative came from their government, but we were happy to have him."

Tiger was paired with Langer, the taciturn but highly respected German who in 1993 won his second Masters title and who at the time was ranked No. 3 in the world. Tiger could pick Langer's brain about Augusta, and it made for great TV in Asia and Europe. The first day Bernhard shot 68, the kid a 74. The second day Langer shot 70, the kid a 71 to make his first cut in a professional tournament. Langer, who never overstates anything and who rarely shows his excitement, heaped praise on Tiger, unequivocably touting both his talent and his temperament. "He is a great prospect with great talent," Langer said. "He has a superb short game and although sometimes his mis-hits are way off, he has excellent composure—an old head on young shoulders."

Woods wouldn't let Langer's compliments inflate his ego. He shot 74–73 on the weekend and finished in a tie for 34th at eight over 292, 15 strokes behind Norman, 14 behind Couples, 13 behind Langer, 12 behind Woosnam, 11 behind Montgomerie and five behind Els. (Faldo missed the cut.) "Langer's bad shots are still in play, unlike some of mine, which end up in the next county," Tiger said.

One month later, Woods was back in Orlando for the fourth time in as many years. He had accepted a personal invitation to play Bay Hill from Arnold Palmer, the tournament's host. Unfortunately, the knowledge Tiger gained from playing the course with tournament director Jim Bell in 1990, or winning the Junior Amateur there in 1991, did not help. Tiger shot his worst scores in a PGA Tour event (80–77) and was not happy. A young reporter from the *Orlando Sentinel*, Jeff Babineau, had to write a sidebar and tried to interview Tiger coming out of the scoring trailer. The standard procedure is for players to stop for a few minutes, run down their scorecards, and then head to the locker room. Nicklaus does it. Watson does it. Palmer does it. And they do it whether they shoot 67 or 77. Woods didn't have time for that. He told Babineau that he could do the interview if he walked with him. The kid was 18 years old and he was already big-timing the press. Babineau blew him off. Watson was coming up. He needed that interview more than the one with Woods.

Back in California, Woods finished up his senior year at Western by shooting five under par 66 at LaCumbre Golf and Country Club in Santa Barbara to win the Southern Section Individual Championship. The course was only 6,352 yards long, about 700 yards less than Blue Canyon Country Club in Phuket and Bay Hill in Orlando. He birdied four of the first six holes he played and missed birdie putts on the other two. On the back side, it appeared Woods lost interest. He hit his tee ball out of bounds on the 15th, made double bogey, and indifferently cruised home to a four-stroke victory. That was Woods's last high school tournament. He skipped the CIF-Southern California Golf Association Championships because of a commitment to play in the Buick Classic at Westchester Country Club in New York. He also passed up sectional U.S. Open Qualifying, which was the same day as Western High School's graduation ceremony. In spite of all the golf he was playing, all the travel he was doing, Tiger Woods still had his priorities in order. His education still came first.

That summer was dedicated to getting ready for the U.S. Amateur. Tiger played the Buick Classic, the Motorola Western Open, the California Golf Association State Amateur Championship, the Pacific Northwest Golf Association Amateur, the Southern California Golf Association Amateur, the Porter Cup and the Western Amateur. There were some brilliant moments and some surprising ones.

In the Cal State Amateur, Tiger was two up after 10 holes in his semifinal match against 32-year-old Ed Cuff of Temecula. Cuff got hot on the back nine at Pebble Beach Golf Links and closed out Tiger on the 17th hole, two and one. He missed the cut in both PGA Tour events, shooting 145 at Westchester and 149 at Cog Hill, but finished eighth in the Porter Cup, won the Western Amateur, and won the Pacific Northwest Amateur (while battling a cold brought on by allergies) in front of record crowds at Royal Oaks Golf Club in Vancouver.

"It put a regional tournament on a national level," said Gary Mogg, the director of competition for the PNGA. "Tiger was the biggest name we've had. We obviously had Fred Couples and Rick Fehr, but nobody with as big a name as Tiger at the time. The pro shop was saying they got call after call, especially from kids wanting to know when he was going to be there, when he was going to show up."

The big moment of Tiger's satellite tour came in the second round of the Southern Cal State Am at LaHacienda, when he shot a career low 62 to break the course record and the SCGA Amateur record. It was one of those days where

Tiger could do no wrong; at the third hole, facing a blind shot on an embankment right of the fairway, he hit an approach that landed short of the green, bounced off a concrete curb that lines the cart path, jumped over a bunker and rolled to within a foot of the cup. "You kind of get an idea when something like that happens that you're on a roll," Woods said.

He went on to break the SCGA 72-hole record, shooting 70 on Sunday for a 270 total. Mark Johnson, a 40-year-old truck driver for Anheuser-Busch, thought he played well enough to win and finished second—five shots back. "He plays one of our events," said Johnson, who won the Pacific Amateur, "and he breaks all the records."

To Woods, the important part of the Southern Cal State Am was not the scoring records. It was the fact those lessons he took from Butch Harmon at Lochinvar after the 1993 Amateur were starting to work in competition. Instead of the rope hook, he could hit the left-to-right cut. Instead of one shot, he could dial in two or three. Going to Ponte Vedra for the Amateur, he felt ready to walk on ground that no one else had ever walked on before. Not Jones. Not Nicklaus. Not Mickelson.

Nobody.

23

THE AMATEUR

The 1994 U.S. Amateur Championship would become a benchmark for Tiger Woods. It would define him for the first time before a national television audience, and put him in the starring role of a melodrama that Michael Crichton and George Lucas would have been hard-pressed to script. The suspense started in the semifinal round, when Tiger faced Buddy Alexander, a former U.S. Amateur champion who was coaching the University of Florida golf team. It ended with the most dramatic comeback in U.S. Amateur history.

Tiger had coasted through qualifying, shooting 65 in the first round on the Stadium course and then 72 on the Valley course. In the opening round, 36-year-old PGA Tour rules official Vaughn Moise pushed him to the 17th hole, but Tiger prevailed two up. Moise called Woods a "man-child" and predicted it wouldn't be long before he was working with Woods on the PGA Tour. It wouldn't be that easy against Alexander.

The Gator golf coach was three up playing the 13th and facing a 2½-foot putt for par that would have meant a four up advantage with five holes to go—a trap not even Tiger himself could have clawed his way out of.

But Alexander left the cage door unlocked, lipping out the putt and triggering a comeback that Earl Woods predicted as he sat on his walking stick, looking like Buddha and listening to his jazz tapes. "This isn't over yet," Earl predicted. "Tiger will make another run."

It wasn't so much Tiger making another run as it was his opponent blowing all four tires. Starting with that miss at the 13th, Alexander finished bogey-bogey-bogey-bogey-bogey-double bogey. It was about as ugly as it could get. Afterward, cleaning out his locker, Alexander was exasperated. "I just played lousy, and if you don't make a par from the 13th hole on, you're not going to beat anyone, no matter who he is," Alexander said.

Woods caught a huge break at the par-three 17th, when his nine-iron into the island green caught a gust of right-to-left wind and flirted with the black swamp water. Woods leaned right. His caddy and sports psychologist Jay Brunza leaned right. The ball leaned right, too, stopping eight inches from the edge of danger. Woods exhaled. Brunza exhaled. Alexander three-putted from 22 feet and threw his ball in the moat. "I was about to pass out," Woods said.

The next two matches were breathers for Woods—and he needed it. In the Round of 16 he beat Tim Jackson of Germantown, Tenn., five and four, then took care of Eric Frishette of Carroll, Ohio, in the semifinals, five and three. Against Frishette, an All-American at Kent State, Woods played his best golf since the opening round of qualifying. Starting at No. 6, he ripped off five birdies in eight holes to steamroll into the finals against Trip Kuehne of Oklahoma State. At the 582-yard, par-five ninth hole, he hit a 300-yard drive and a cut three-wood over the branches of a live oak tree to set up a conceded birdie. That green is rarely reached during the Players Championship, but not that many pros can fly a three-wood over 270 yards. "I could have easily reached it if I hit a hook," Woods explained. "But that would have been a dangerous shot on that hole with the woods on the left, so I played a fade, knowing that I couldn't get in any danger."

Danger was the operative word for Woods against Kuehne. He was six down after 13 holes, five down with 12 holes to play . . . and still came storming back. Kuehne, whose sister Kelli had won the U.S. Girls' Junior five weeks earlier, birdied seven of the first 13 holes, none with a putt of more than four feet, and shot 66 for a four-up lead at the lunch break.

Earl wasn't worried. Before Tiger went out for the second 18, he whispered in his son's ear, "Let the legend grow."

Kuehne made birdie at the second to go five up again, but that was his last birdie of the match. Woods won the 4th, 7th, 9th, 10th, 11th, 16th, 17th and 18th holes. After that birdie at the second, Kuehne would win only one other hole, with a par at the sixth. It was the greatest comeback in the 99-year history of the event. And it was punctuated by Woods's fist-pumping birdie at the 17th, that hellish little par-three surrounded by water and haunted by the echoing cries of Pete Dye, who designed it with double bogey in mind.

Tiger stood on that tee, having just made birdie at the 16th to even the match, holding a pitching wedge and taking practice swings as the wind did its dance in the trees. He had saved par from the woods on the 10th and 14th holes, but a miss here and there was no pine straw to catch his ball. A miss here, and Tiger was rinsed and walking to the drop circle.

The wind died and Woods grabbed a pitching wedge

that was loaded with lead tape. He had 139 yards to the hole, the wind slightly at his back, and the heart of a lion thumping in his chest. His target? A stupid question. "The pin," he would say later. "I was going directly at the pin."

This was to be the friction point. The fearless tee shot landed in the Bermuda Triangle of the Sawgrass-TPC, right of the pin at the 17th. At her home in Cypress, Tida Woods rolled off her bed and onto the floor when the ball caught a piece of green, took one hop to the fringe, then spun back, no more than three feet from the water's edge. "That boy almost gave me a heart attack," Tida Woods said. "All I kept saying was, 'God, don't let that ball go into the water.' That boy tried to kill me."

It seemed as if everybody watching was holding his breath—everybody except Woods, who had faith that sand wedge was the right club and that his ball would follow its command and sit on the green. "You don't see too many pros hit it right of that pin," Kuehne said afterward. "It was a great gamble that paid off."

The ensuing putt, which dropped for birdie, was in the 14-foot range, but afterward Woods couldn't remember the distance, the break, or the grain. He couldn't even remember hitting the putt or the celebration that followed. He was too zoned out.

Walking to the 18th tee, Brunza reminded Woods to stay focused. There was big trouble down the left side, and the hole was 440 yards, but Woods was long enough to avoid the water with a two-iron. He flat-out killed it, driving it to a spot that the pros find with their drivers during the TPC. He had only a seven-iron into the green, and two-putted for the win that had the country buzzing. Earl dropped his walking stick and made his way onto the green, embracing his son as applause rained down from the spectators on the stadium mounds. It was getting to be a clichéd scene, but this was the first time it had been broadcast nationally on ESPN.

Kuehne's father (and caddy), Ernie Kuehne, called it "divine intervention." Woods said it was indescribable. Earl put it in historical perspective. "When Tiger won his first U.S. Junior [in 1991]," the old man said, "I said to him, 'Son, you have done something no black person in the United States has ever done, and you will forever be a part of history.' But this is ungodly in its ramifications."

Woods had yet to register for his first semester at Stanford. He hadn't even gone to freshman orientation, and with that stunning and thrilling Amateur victory at the Sawgrass-TPC, there was already speculation about how long he would last in Palo Alto. How could he possibly remain in school for four years, shunning the pro tour to earn his degree as Phil Mickelson did after winning both the Amateur and NCAA titles in 1990 while a sophomore at Arizona State? The millions Mickelson made in endorsement contracts would be pocket change compared to the numbers that Woods could make in golf equipment and clothing contracts.

If he did turn pro early, it wouldn't be because of pressure from Earl and Tida. "We're not parents who are out for the money," Tida said that night from Cypress. "I always tell Tiger that golf is not a priority. Nobody can take an education away from you, especially a degree at Stanford."

Nevertheless, the events at Ponte Vedra would not make it any easier for Tiger, his parents or IMG to ignore the lure of the pro tour. Tiger had stamped himself with the undeniable look of a future megastar.

Not many people knew it, but Woods's 11th-hour heroics in the Amateur actually began three weeks before the tournament. After Tiger won the Western Amateur in Benton Harbour, Mich., he and his father dashed to Chicago for a flight to California, where Tiger had U.S. Amateur qualifying the next morning in Chino Hills. However, traffic on the way to O'Hare turned a 90-minute drive into a three-hour ordeal, and the Woods missed their plane. They had to stand by for the last flight out, knowing that if Tiger didn't get on that plane, he would not make his tee time—and would not be able to compete in the Amateur.

There were two seats on the plane.

"I prayed, and my prayers were answered," Earl Woods said. "Thank God we got on that damn airplane."

24

TIGER GOES TO COLLEGE

On the culturally diverse campus at Stanford University, one of the great bastions for learning in the world, Tiger Woods was allowed to blend into the student body and—to some extent—assume the role of anonymous freshman. On the floor of his dorm was a kid who could split atoms, who got 1,580 out of 1,600 on the SATs. Tiger split fairways and scored over 1,000. It sort of made him feel semi-normal.

Well, almost.

After the Amateur, he received congratulatory phone calls from people ranging from Jesse Jackson to Sinbad. Jackson, of course, was proud to see a young African-American achieve such an honor. Sinbad asked for a resumé so he could work some Tiger material into his act. Cool, Tiger thought. Jesse Jackson and Sinbad. He had no idea what life would be like as a celebrity.

Before leaving for Palo Alto, he was given the key to the city in his hometown of Cypress: "That was unbelievable. I'm 18 years old and getting the key to the city." He went to Knotts Berry Farm and three people asked for autographs: "I've never had that happen before. I've started wearing sunglasses a little more." Producers from *The To-*

night Show with Jay Leno and *Late Night with David Letter-man* called, wanting to book him on their shows. Tiger turned them down: "It's not me. I only do stuff that's me."

Tiger didn't need sunglasses at Stanford. He went to Palo Alto for an education, not a spot on *Entertainment Tonight*. Stanford was a university that schooled Tom Watson and John McEnroe, a place of higher learning that was known for its liberalism and equanimity. Sure, Tiger was a Big Man on Campus—when he returned home after leading the United States team to victory at the World Amateur in France, there was a banner greeting him at the dorm—but for the most part, he was allowed to disappear among the student body. He called it Utopia.

"If it's not the nation's best pianist, or the nation's best swimmer, it's somebody with a brain you can't believe," Woods said. "I'm just lost in a crowd here, which is fine. That's why I came."

His classload was pretty light. He took history, a computer class, a course in Portuguese cultural perspective and a golf unit. He shared a dormitory room with a non-golfer from West Virginia. He missed freshman orientation because of a tournament and found himself photocopying the lecture notes of fellow students to catch up. He had to drop calculus when he fell behind, abstained from television because it was too time-consuming, but indulged in campus parties, where he noticed the kids drank more than they did at Western.

"Nobody sleeps around here," he said. "There's so much work you have to stay up late. But it's easy to blend in here because everyone's so special. You have Olympian swimmers, baseball and football players who are going to be in the pros . . . and I'm not the brightest one, either. There are geniuses here."

Goodwin provided a line of defense against the interview requests. He was the only one with Woods's phone number—not even his teammates were allowed to call. In an interview with Guy Yocom of *Golf Digest*, Goodwin defended his role as gatekeeper for the young Tiger. "I'm not taking it too far," he said. "Tiger is absolutely up to his ass in alligators with schoolwork, adapting to living away from home, handling reporters and trying to play golf. The fact is, nobody can do what he's being asked to do. The whole world is watching Tiger, and he feels that responsibility."

Initially, there was the feeling that Tiger didn't want to be one of the boys, that he was deliberately keeping his distance. In a story that appeared in the *New York Times Magazine*, writer Peter de Jonge quoted Notah Begay saying, "There's Tiger, and then there's the four of us." But de Jonge, who wrote a marvelous piece, might have been guilty of perceiving bad vibes that weren't really there. The problem was that Begay, Casey Martin, Will Yanagisawa and Steve Burdick were all seniors, all All-Americans, all returning from the NCAA championship team, and Tiger was just a freshman who had to prove himself not only on the golf course but just hanging out. When Tiger took off his contact lenses and wore his glasses, Begay nicknamed him "Urkel" after the nerdy little black kid Steve Urkel on *Family Matters*. Tiger hated it. "Tiger told me to stop," Begay said. "But I told him, 'The more you tell me to stop, the more I'll call you that.'"

It was just freshman hazing.

25

THE HALL OF SHAME

In the wooded suburbs of Birmingham, Ala., outside the front gates of a club that was internationally vilified as a capital of Old South racism, three African-American political activists were protesting. It was late October 1994, and Tiger Woods was tied for the lead in the Jerry Pate National Intercollegiate tournament at the site of golf's emancipation, Shoal Creek Country Club. The activists thought that Woods should be out there with them, boycotting the tournament. Woods's half-Pueblo, half-Navajo teammate, Notah Begay, thought it would be much better if Woods went down to Birmingham and kicked some ass. "What a great slap in the face it would be to those who think that minorities are inferior, if he went down and won," Begay said.

In 1990, Hall S. Thompson, founder and president of Shoal Creek, consented to an interview by the *Birmingham Post Herald*. Asked about Shoal Creek's membership practices, Thompson told the reporter that his club "don't discriminate in every other area except the blacks." When asked, "Why not?" Thompson had responded with the damning "that's just not done in Birmingham" line. Until then, the race issue in American golf had been addressed in whispers and swept under the carpet because it created too much discomfort. Hall Thompson and Shoal Creek changed all that.

Golf's black pioneers were Charlie Sifford, Pete Brown, Jim Dent and Lee Elder. They were part of an era when black men and women were still being judged by the color of their skin, and not, as Martin Luther King, Jr., preached, by the content of their character. Until 1961, the PGA of America had membership rules that specifically restricted its members to golfers of the "Caucasian race." The Masters Committee kept changing its invitation rules, preventing Sifford from gaining a spot in their hallowed tournament. Tiger Woods already had carte blanche, and he was only a freshman in college.

"There is no way in hell he will have to deal with the hassles that I had," Sifford said. "Man, the way has already been paved. But the thing is, he will still have opposition. And he will be out there by himself."

Tiger recognized he wasn't a pioneer like Sifford, that he didn't have it as bad as his dad in Kansas, but he knew about opposition and prejudice. Earl taught him about it, and he experienced it first-hand when he was tied to the tree in kindergarten, when he wasn't allowed to play the Navy course, supposedly because he wasn't old enough. Tida would tell him, "Racism is not your problem—it's theirs. Just play your game." But the ugliness and bitterness became a way of life.

In Arkansas, a reporter accused him of entering his first national junior tournament only because he wanted to integrate Texarkana Country Club. Earl told the writer that his 13-year-old son didn't give a damn about that, that he was just there to play the golf tournament. The writer kept pressing. "C'mon," he said. "You know that's not the truth."

The truth? The truth was just what Earl had taught his kid. The truth was that there are two colors in this country: white and not white. The truth was that Earl had African-American, Caucasian, American Indian and Chinese descendants, and that Tida's heritage was Thai, Dutch and Chinese. The truth was that Tiger would get "The Look" when he walked in some country clubs. The truth was that his dad was right. Tiger could feel it. He could sense it. "It makes you uncomfortable, like someone is saying something without saying it," he would say. But instead of slinking away, it motivated Tiger Woods. It made him want to play better and in so doing, speed up the integration process of golf in this country and around the world.

"Golf was originated in Scotland by rich whites," he would say. "When it was brought over here, we made our country clubs exclusively for whites. Minorities, they just served as cooks, porters and caddies. So it's refreshing to see some changes happening."

Shoal Creek, scheduled to host the 1990 PGA Championship, instituted the biggest change. The backlash of Thompson's comments was that the PGA, the USGA, and the Ladies Professional Golf Association had to take a hard look at the clubs that hosted their events. Clubs with discriminatory membership policies—either by race, gender or religion—either had to change, or would lose tournaments. It was that simple. Cypress Point was dropped from the AT&T Pebble Beach rota, Butler National was banned as host of the Western Open and Old Warson lost a Senior Tour event in St. Louis. The PGA lost Aronomink in Philadelphia and Oak Tree in Edmond, Okla., as host sites for PGA Championships and the USGA lost Merion for its Women's Amateur. Shoal Creek eventually complied by admitting one black member, Louis Willie. Even Augusta National fell in line, inviting Ron Townsend to join in 1990 and putting him in the press room at the Masters Tournament, where he would have a high profile among journalists.

Tiger was 14 during the height of the Shoal Creek controversy, and in his words, "a little young to understand what was going on." But as the years passed, he read about it, and gave more thought to it, and realized not only the implications, but his place in the vortex of the storm. "I do understand now," he said. "I thought it was a sad situation. It's not supposed to be like that in the '90s. Then again it woke everybody up that this kind of stuff still happens."

Woods had made it a point to do clinics at municipal golf courses in Boston, Dallas, Seattle, Chicago, Los Angeles and Cleveland. His goal may have been to be the Michael Jordan of golf, and by that he meant the best golfer regardless of skin pigmentation. But in the social environment of this country, he was clearly the Black Hope of Golf, and he took on the responsibilities accordingly. He wasn't Charles Barkley—he didn't mind being a role model.

At Chicago's Jackson Park in August 1993, he told the kids, "Baseball changed. Basketball changed. Golf is sputtering, but it will get there. I would say just give it a chance. Continue playing sports, but give golf a chance. It is a very difficult sport to play. But it's a great sport."

At Manakiki Golf Course in Cleveland in May 1994, at a clinic in conjunction with the National Minority Golf Championships, Woods admitted, "The doors have been shut to African-Americans. It's very easy to see why. There are prejudices out there. Plus it takes money to start a career in golf. The opportunities aren't there. It shouldn't be kept under lock and key. This is the 1990s."

At Hollywood Park Golf and Sports Center in Los Angeles, head pro Bill Wright praised Tiger and the clinic he put on there. "But let's face it," Wright said. "A lot of inner city kids have no idea who he is. To make it out of the inner city and into the golf world, you need money and constant encouragement. Tiger has both, but these kids have neither."

Tiger and Earl were working with grassroots programs like the National Minority Junior Golf Association. Earl knew that golf was the low man on the totem pole in the talent pool, that the good athletes migrated to basketball, baseball and football, that the percentile left over wasn't the strongest or the most coordinated. The important thing, though, was for Tiger to connect with kids whether they were "white, black, brown or green," whether they were preppies from white suburbia or gang members from the ghetto. He had the ability to break down barriers.

"Tiger and I have made a commitment to assist the development of golf," Earl said. "The idea is to generate interest at the lowest level, not only from kids but from corporate sponsors. There are organizations out there trying to do the job but they really aren't getting outstanding financial support. And golf is a game of money. If you don't have money you don't play or practice. What we're trying to do is stir up local interest and local support, to get kids out there and play the game."

At Shoal Creek, Woods was tied for the lead on the 17th tee of the final round. The Stanford team was going to win easily, but Woods was still battling for the individual title. He started the final round three strokes off the lead held by Auburn's Ian Steel. Woods had caught Steel by the turn, but Stanford teammate William Yanagisawa closed with 68 to post a 54-hole total of 208. At the par-five 17th, Woods hit his second shot pin high and two-putted over two humps from 50 feet to take the lead. At No. 18, he rolled in a 25-

footer up and down an incline for a two-stroke victory and his second win in three college tournaments.

Once again, he had been able to concentrate in the midst of all the distractions, the protests, the questions about Shoal Creek. He climbed inside The Zone, put it all aside, shot 67 in the final round and won again.

Waiting for Tiger Woods when he came off the 18th green that day at Shoal Creek, wearing a jacket and tie and floppy hat, was none other than Hall S. Thompson. It was an uncomfortable meeting.

"You're a great player," Thompson said. "I'm proud of you. You're superb."

26

MUGGED

On the night of December 2, 1994, while returning to his dormitory after a charity dinner in San Francisco, Tiger Woods was grabbed from behind in the well-lit parking lot outside his dorm by a man carrying a knife. The assailant demanded Tiger's wallet, which he didn't have, his watch and a gold chain with a Buddha his mother gave him. To punctuate the mugging, he struck Tiger in the jaw with the knife handle, knocking him to the ground.

Tiger didn't want to make a big deal out of it. He reported the incident to campus police, returned to his dorm, took some aspirin and called his father at 2 a.m. "Pops," he said. "You know that overbite I had? It's gone. My teeth are perfectly aligned."

The stars must have been aligned that night, too. Tiger could have been killed, but somebody was looking out for him, that same somebody that carried Earl Woods through Vietnam. Maybe it was that guardian South Vietnamese angel, Nguyen Phong. Maybe it was all those prayers his mother had prayed to Buddha. Maybe it was Jesus Christ, because Earl prayed, too. Maybe it was just plain luck, but Tiger didn't lose his cool, and all the mugger made off with was some jewelry. He didn't stick the knife in Tiger's neck.

Word filtered out through the campus police report. Tiger played down the incident when the media called. He didn't want this to trigger other sick minds. He already lived through one death threat, at the L.A. Open in 1992. "People get mugged every day. I just want to move on from this and put it in the past," he said. "I'm looking forward to the Christmas holidays, and next season."

Brunza did some work with him, just to make sure Tiger wasn't traumatized. He wasn't. Tiger was able to deal with it because Earl always taught him: Prepare for the best, expect the worst. "You grow through experiences like this," Brunza said, "and that's what Tiger will do."

Was this a random act of crime, or was Tiger a target? Nobody seemed to know, but Earl had trained his son how to deal with it, and he walked to the infirmary with nothing more than a headache. "The only thing Tiger can do, from a counterterrorist point of view," Earl told the *L.A. Times*, "is to be alert."

27

ENCOUNTERING AUGUSTA

He arrived on Sunday night at dusk from the Carpet City Classic college tournament in Dalton, Ga., where he lost a head-to-head showdown with Stewart Cink of Georgia Tech. Notah Begay was with him, and his father was waiting with the Pinkerton guards at the front gate. So this was Magnolia Lane. Tiger Woods looked at it curiously, because it had been described as the gates of golf's heaven, the drive to the Cathedral in the Pines.

But Tiger didn't have goosebumps. He felt kind of let down. *Magnolia Lane, is that it?* he thought. Then he arrived at the clubhouse and it appeared to be smaller than it looks on television. The first thing he did, after dropping his bags off in the Crow's Nest, was take a putter and some balls and head to the practice putting green with Notah. At Stanford, he had putted on the hardwood floor of Maples Pavilion, trying to get ready for Augusta. Now, he just had to check out the speed of Augusta's putting surfaces first-hand, to see if they were as fast as they looked on those tapes he watched during Christmas break.

Three men in green jackets approached. Earl froze, expecting Tiger·to be in trouble. The men were part of a welcoming committee. Tiger and Earl would laugh about it later that night at the Green Jacket restaurant across the street on Washington Road. During dinner with Jay Brunza, a British woman asked for his autograph. Her husband explained to Earl that he was a member of the Royal & Ancient, and that he would be welcoming Tiger to the British Open at St. Andrews later in the summer.

Tiger slept for 12 hours and awoke with a full day planned. He stretched out in the Crow's Nest, walked down the creaky stairs from the clubhouse cupola, strolled out on the practice ground, and saw Nick Faldo hitting balls next to his caddy, Fanny Sunesson. His first round at Augusta and he would play with Nick Faldo, the two-time Masters champion. It doesn't get any better.

Jack Nicklaus and Steve Ballesteros played their first Masters tournaments when they were 19 years old. They, too, were heralded, but nothing like this. This was going to be Tiger Woods's coming out party, his first experience with huge galleries and a swarming press corps that would follow him every step of the journey. That Monday, it was relatively quiet. He played with Faldo and British Amateur champion Lee James, but there wasn't much give-and-take. The two-time Masters champion was already zoning.

"A very talented kid," was Faldo's assessment. "He has got the gift of the elasticity of youth because he has an amazing pivot of the shoulders. He turns them so fast he is able to hit the ball as hard as he likes at the moment and it goes such a long way. He kind of makes you feel old."

Faldo and Woods came off the 18th green together, and walked under the oak tree outside the manor clubhouse, not stopping for the mass of journalists desperately hoping for an interview. "That's the rules this week," Woods said, "to make it easier on me." He trailed Faldo into the champions locker room for lunch, then found Trip Kuehne. A $5 match was set up, and Tiger went out for his second 18 of the day.

Kuehne was happy to be at Augusta, but he was still smarting from the Amateur. Tiger wouldn't cut him a break, making par at the last hole to win the bet. They would talk about it that night in the Crow's Nest, which they both said felt like a dormitory. They talked about the history of the clubhouse they were staying in, but it made Tiger uncomfortable to see the plantation caste system at work. Almost all the club's employees were black, and they were dressed in white jackets and called everybody "Sir." Tiger was immensely popular with them. They pointed him in the right direction when he got lost in the maze of the clubhouse.

On Tuesday, a practice round had been scheduled with Raymond Floyd, Fred Couples and Greg Norman. On the second hole, Tiger drove it through the dogleg past everybody and was waiting to hit his second shot. From beside the gallery ropes, he said to the spectators, "What a beautiful day. You know, I could be in the classroom." A marshall was eavesdropping and interjected his thoughts. "You are," he said, "but you would never be getting an education like this."

Woods flashed his toothy smile, and it seemed everyone at Augusta was smiling with him. For some reason Tiger was worried about the way Couples would treat him, but when Freddie let him know that he was accepted, it made Tiger relax. When they got to the 12th hole, the par-three in the heart of Amen Corner, Couples told him to pick a yardage and hit to it. If the ball goes in the water, it goes in the water. If it goes in the back bunker, it goes in the back bunker. If it lands on the green, great. Just make a good, solid swing, and trust it. On Sunday at the 1992 Masters, Couples hit a shot that drifted right of the pin, trickled down the bank toward Rae's Creek, and gripped just inches short of the water. It had been a wet Masters, and the grounds crew couldn't get their mowers down to where Fred's ball had come to rest. Tiger shouldn't expect that sort of luck.

Tiger routinely drove the ball out there with "Fred and Greg"—sometimes even farther. The fifth hole is a 435-yard par-four, one of the toughest on the course. Tiger hit wedge in while Norman needed an eight-iron. At the 13th, the hairpin dogleg that hugs Rae's Creek tributary, Tiger hooked a two-iron through a stand of pine trees and had 20 feet for eagle. Norman had seen enough. "What would be a good tournament for him?" he said. "Probably to win. He's good enough."

Tuesday afternoon was Tiger Woods's first encounter with the media center at Augusta National. The interview was jammed cheek-to-jowl when he came in to face 300 members of the world's golfing press. It was awkward at times, confrontational at others, and occasionally enlightening. The transcript filled up 18 typewritten pages. Tiger started by calling the Masters just another tournament, then qualified, "It just happens to be a major," he said. "You have to treat it that way. At least I do. I don't know what the other guys are doing, but I treat it just like another tournament. I try to go out there and do my best and try to win and see what happens."

A writer asked the correct follow-up.

"Tiger, there are older guys who still get thrilled to be here. Because you played so much golf at such a young age, and accomplished so much at such a young age, do you think you've become jaded at all?"

Tiger obviously did like it.

"In what way?" he said.

"That you don't seem to be thrilled to be here."

"I am thrilled," he said. "But my main focus is on my

game and not the atmosphere here. My main focus is to get my game ready for Thursday.''

Later in the interview, Woods was asked about Arnold Palmer. It was the 40th anniversary of Palmer's first Masters, and there was an obvious hook with it being Tiger's first Masters. A commemorative plaque in Palmer's honor was to be unveiled behind the 16th tee.

''Obviously you know it is way before your time,'' the writer observed. ''But what do you know about him? What have you read about him? What has your dad told you about him?''

Woods didn't want to give up much.

''Basically the only thing I know about Arnold is whatever has been written about him and was shown on TV. That's about it.''

Needing a better quote, the writer persisted.

''Do you have any thoughts about him?''

Tiger barely played along.

''Any thoughts about Arnold?'' he said, indifferently. ''Except that he was one of the greatest players of all time? That is about it. I haven't really got to sit down and talk to him to find out what kind of person he is, for myself, but from what everyone says, he is a fine human being.''

Somebody tried again later.

''Tiger, even though you might not be intimately familiar with Arnold Palmer, it is obvious you know quite a bit about the history of golf. We talk to athletes in other sports. There are baseball players who don't know who Mickey Mantle is and who don't quite care. Why do you think golfers have a pretty good sense of the history of their game?''

''Why?'' Tiger said. ''Hell if I know. I honestly can't answer that because I really don't know. Why do we?''

Tiger was making no effort to "court" the press as Palmer had. His jaw was set. Earl had schooled him. "If you ask Tiger when he was born, he will tell you, 'December 30, 1975,' " Earl said. "He will not tell you he was born in Long Beach Hospital. That's two questions."

The interviewing continued. The golf writers wouldn't let up. Neither would Tiger.

"What has got you going at such a young age?"

"In what way?"

"Well, you mentioned you watched Nicklaus and Watson on television."

"Whoever was leading the tournament. It just happened to be those two at the time."

"And you have taken the time to read about Palmer, you indicated?"

"Somewhat."

Somewhat? Why the attitude? These people were looking for first impressions and they were being slapped around by a 19-year-old kid. This wasn't winning friends. This was bad PR.

"Do you think there is the potential for overloading young athletes?"

"Is there a potential?"

"Yes."

"I think so if you do too many interviews, do too many requests. I think there is a tendency where that might happen, where you might get overloaded. But if you keep a good balance on what you do, what is comfortable with you, I think that should be fine,"

Tiger was questioned about his jacket size (42 long), and about the clubs he hit into the par-fives. Earl was in the room, and was asked to stand and be recognized by Charlie Yates of the Masters Press Committee. It was the first time Tiger and Earl had been able to speak all week.

Question: "Tiger, this is the 20th anniversary of Lee Elder playing here. Have you talked to Lee about what his experience had been in that regard."

Tiger: "In what regard?"

Question: "Just in regard to you being the fourth black to play in this event."

Tiger: "OK, let's see here."

Question: "Have you encountered any problems."

Tiger: "I have not encountered any problem except for the speed of the greens."

Later, Tiger was asked about his ability to handle the media. Couples, the 1992 Masters champion, had a hard time with that aspect of being a personality, and backed off when the spotlight became too bright. "What you have to understand," Woods said. "is that you guys have been following me since I was very young. So it has been a gradual process, something where I could get used to it. Freddie, on the other hand, had a brilliant year and then all of a sudden he was thrust into it. It is a little different story. That is probably the reason why he had such a difficult time with it. I guess I have been brought along with the media and have been interacting with them since the age of three. So I have been around them for a while."

The interview was called to a close by Billy Morris, the owner of the Morris Newspaper Group (which includes the *Augusta Chronicle*), and Tiger did not stick around for any followup questions at the podium the way Nicklaus and Palmer and Watson do at the end of their news conferences. The kid put up the blinders, put on his cold eyes, and bolted out the back door.

Earl explained the tension. "I was talking the other day with someone," he said. "The average golfer that goes there is blown away with Magnolia Lane and the history and tradition of the Masters, and I said that doesn't impress the black golfer. Black golfers have nothing in common with Bobby Jones, no historical ties with Bobby Jones. They prevented blacks from being here for many, many years."

Only three black golfers had competed in the Masters, but it should have been four. Charlie Sifford won twice on the PGA Tour, at Hartford in 1967 and at Los Angeles in 1969. Both times, Cliff Roberts found a way not to invite him. With Tiger, of course, it was a different case. As the Amateur champion, he was welcomed, invited even to stay in the clubhouse as a guest of the club. That still didn't change his opinion of Augusta National. Sifford had become his adopted grandfather, and he had heard all the horror stories.

"Tiger's done something that I never got the chance to do," Sifford said from his home that week in Kingwood, Texas. "I'd like to see him get the chance to do a lot of things I never got the chance to do."

Sifford was so proud of Woods's Amateur victory, he sent Tiger his 1994 PGA Tour money clip, and in Tiger's locker at Augusta was a personal note. Charlie Sifford, age 72, could have attended the 1995 Masters, but he didn't want to be anywhere he wasn't wanted. Sifford said, "It's still tough for a black man. It's still a white man's game. Everything that happens happens for the white men, not for the black men."

These were the undercurrents of racial tension that Tiger Woods felt at his first Masters. These were the thoughts he wouldn't reveal in his news conference on Tuesday at the media center. Later in life he would speak out, but not now. When people asked about trouble, meaning racial trouble, he talked about the speed of the greens. He was trying to focus only on the golf and not become the epicenter of a storm. The next morning, he had a practice round lined up with Greg Norman and Nick Price.

28

THE MASTERS

The Wednesday before his first Masters, Tiger Woods woke up feeling tight. Not mentally tight, just physically a little tight. Thirty-six holes on Monday and all those balls he hit on Tuesday with Butch watching were probably too much, but he didn't want to back out on Norman and Price. The adrenaline would get him through, and he'd loosen up.

Playing the fifth hole, that tough par-four on the back of the Augusta National property, Tiger took a normal swing on his tee shot. Right at impact, he felt a sharp pain in his back, and reached for his left leg. He wasn't scared, but he was concerned, and walked up the fairway to play his second shot, hoping the pain would go away. From the fairway, his second shot hooked hard, left and long of the green. Again, he grabbed for his left leg. "When I saw that," Earl said, "I said, 'Oh no, something's wrong.'" Up at the green, Tiger picked up his ball, and explained the situation to Norman and Price. He better go have it checked out.

It didn't take long for this news to reach the media center and the veranda. Luckily for Tiger, he wasn't at a junior tournament in Southern California when it happened. Dr. Frank Jobe, the noted orthopedic surgeon from Los Angeles, happened to be under the oak tree when Tiger walked by,

118

obviously in pain. The PGA Tour had its fitness van parked on the property.

Jobe performed an examination, and diagnosed that a mild sprain had led to a muscle spasm. Jobe advised Woods to see Ralph Simpson, the Tour's physical therapist. Simpson worked on Woods for about 90 minutes, giving him electro-stimulation therapy, massage and Motrin. This relaxed the muscle, the back spasm subsided, and Woods was cleared to hit balls. Tiger ended up feeling so good that instead of withdrawing from the Par-3 Contest, he and Gary Player hooked up and made an afternoon of it.

The Par-3 is a Masters tradition that began in 1960. Some of the big names skip it, because the crowds are huge and Wednesday afternoon is a good time to either rest or fine-tune on the range. But Player, a three-time Masters champion, wouldn't miss it, and Tiger, in his first Masters, wanted to experience it as well. It was part of the education.

The previous summer, Player had the opportunity to play a practice round with Ernie Els before the British Open at Turnberry. Els had won the U.S. Open at Oakmont in June, and was the hottest young prospect in the world—until Tiger came along. "Certain players, you look at them once, and you see something," Player said. "The first time I saw Jack Nicklaus or Arnold Palmer or Ben Hogan or Sam Snead or Lee Trevino, I saw something special. As soon as I saw Tiger Woods swing today, I thought, 'Man, this young guy has got it!' 'It' is something indescribable. It's the way he puts his hands on the club, the way he stands over the ball. It's agility, it's speed. 'It' is what a great horse has."

Tiger's caddy, Tommy "Burnt Biscuits" Bennett, a 20-year veteran at Augusta, saw the same things. "I don't know if he's unfair or unreal," Bennett said. "Tiger swings so pure, and that ball doesn't want to come down. Sometimes I felt like there just wasn't enough golf course out there for him."

After that scare on the fifth hole, Earl was predicting a good showing. "He's into information overload right now," he said. "He knows too much about the course now. He played Monday with Nick Faldo, he played Tuesday with Greg Norman and Fred Couples, he played Wednesday with Norman and Nick Price. All the time he was askng them a thousand questions about the course. He milked those guys, just milked them of everything they know about Augusta."

Earl also saw that his son was comfortable playing to the big crowds, and that was important to the big picture. If Tiger were to transcend the sport, he had to become a presence. "We have it planned out," Earl said. "We have it planned that Tiger should be a role model. How many athletes are there in the inner cities, in disadvantaged circumstances, who could become top golfers? The problem is the best athletes are pruned out early; basketball takes its share, football, baseball, track and field. Then the kid who's left out—maybe at the age of 12—he decides to become a golfer. But then it may be too late. Our dream is that the next Magic Johnsons or Michael Jordans will want to be golfers, not basketball players."

In a quiet moment that night on the putting green, Tiger told a friend, "Everything here is so perfect. I get to live here, they serve us great food, and all I have to do is walk out the door to use the best practice facility and the best course in the world. How can you not play well?"

That question was answered soon enough. Something happens between Wednesday night and Thursday morning at Augusta. The mower blades get a little lower. The pin settings are put in foolish places by the Masters Competition Committee. And the golf course that seemed so friendly in the practice rounds becomes a devil in a green dress. Just after 1:03 p.m., on a rainy spring Georgia afternoon, wearing his Stanford baseball cap and a Gore-tex pullover, Tiger Woods was introduced on the first tee at Augusta. He took a couple of practice swings and ripped his drive, a high draw over the fairway bunker. He hit it so far that his playing partner, defending champion Jose Maria Olazabal, said he needed binoculars to see how far Tiger's ball had traveled. From the fairway, Tiger took a sand wedge and hit a towering shot that rose above the trees, tore a pitch mark three feet from the hole, and released to 25 feet. The kid was pumped—too pumped.

It was his first Masters' putt and he had a run at birdie, but even with the greens softened by the rain, it was an extremely dangerous putt, one that could get away in a heartbeat. Downhill all the way, the ball had to be hit with just the right speed, or it could stop into definite three-putt land. Tiger had tried that same putt in the practice round, because he knew where the pins were set, but the pace was considerably different on Thursday. Tiger thought he stroked the ball just a little too hard, but it wasn't like the gun went off in his hands. *That's probably three feet by*, he thought. But the ball didn't stop at three feet. It kept rolling and rolling another 18 feet and down the shaved bank, off the green, down toward the ninth tee box. Welcome to the Masters, kid. You just made your first rookie mistake. "I lost my focus on that putt," he would say. "I went brain dead."

Now looking at a double bogey, Woods putted back up the bank, onto the green, 12 feet from the hole. This was not the type of putt to be staring at in your first Masters. Twelve feet for bogey with the world on your shoulders. The only person not worried was Earl. "I've talked to Tiger many times about there coming up in every round an absolute must-make putt," he said. "That putt on the first hole for bogey was his absolute must-make putt. And the way he made that putt, the way he handled adversity and came back from it, was what I was most proud of. But I'm not surprised; he makes most of his must-make putts."

Tiger was both relieved and mad at himself. "I just know it was not the start I wanted," he said.

At the second hole, Tiger pushed his drive over the bunker, through the fairway, and into a stand of white dogwood trees. Taking out a three-iron, and hitting off pine straw, Tiger slashed a 235-yard shot that rolled onto the green, and the spectators roared. One man who was heard above the din was Dave Anderson, the Pulitzer Prize–winning columnist of the *New York Times*. "He believes in the adage," said the spectator, "that trees are 90 percent air." It was the type of daring shot Palmer and Ballesteros pulled off in their assaults on Augusta. Now it was Tiger creating this synergy with the galleries, raising the energy level. Watching her son from the gallery ropes, Tida Woods said, "That's why his name is Woods, because he can hit out of any woods."

From 50 feet, Woods two-putted for his first Masters' birdie, and the roar went up that could be heard back on the clubhouse veranda. They knew; must be that Woods kid down on No. 2 green. Anybody who saw it witnessed a piece of golf history.

The roller coaster ride continued, up and down the Augusta fairways, over its torturous greens. There was a moan at the third when Tiger missed a four-footer for par. Earl was in the gallery wearing a green-and-blue rain suit in a soft drizzle. He was not worried. "Tiger," he said, "hasn't gotten started yet."

He was in the trees again at the fifth hole, punching a four-iron through a narrow gap à la Palmer and Ballesteros, but making bogey from the front of the green. On he went, learning something new with each step, seeing things he didn't see in the practice rounds, soaking it all in. Before the round, he reminded himself that low scores win—that the game hasn't changed, just the arena.

He came to 18 even par. He hit a big tee shot and a solid eight-iron that took one hop and spun back to 10 feet. A roar went up greenside, and as he made that walk up the hill for the first time in competition, hearing the ovation, Tiger Woods felt the goosebumps on his arms. He left the putt right in the jaws, about one inch short of going in. He wanted that birdie. He wanted to shoot under par.

On a day when 55-year-old Jack Nicklaus came in with a 67, 19-year-old Tiger Woods from Cypress, Calif., shot an even-par 72. Following him around that day were the two most prominent symbols of the racial issue in American golf, Lee Elder and Hall Thompson. It had been five years since Shoal Creek, and 20 since Elder was the first black to play in the Masters. Time moves slowly in the South, and so does emancipation.

"I remember the relief of going to that first tee and thinking that [the era when] no blacks had ever qualified was over with," Elder told reporters afterward. "It had really been on my mind and on the minds of the other blacks on the PGA Tour because we had come so close. I had heard so much about Augusta, but we could never get there. It was something I had wanted so much for so long a time."

It wasn't like the red carpet was rolled out for Elder the way it was for Woods. He remembers his meeting with Tournament Chairman Clifford Roberts being cold and brief. "It was a quick handshake, a 'hello' and 'welcome to Augusta,' that sort of thing," Elder said. "He did follow me for a few holes during the Par-3 Contest, and he said a few words to me. But I think he probably would have done that for any first-time golfer at Augusta. But my being black pretty much set me aside from any first-time qualifier."

Behind the 18th green, they were waiting for him, the men and women with the cameras and the microphones, the pads and the tape recorders, pushing and shoving for a spot, jostling like a bunch of horses, just trying to do their jobs. Tiger knew they wanted his thoughts on the social meaning of this round, but this wasn't the time. Let them interject their perceptions. He did the TV stuff and then he did radio and finally print media before escaping to the driving range, which was off limits to the working press and where, if he stayed long enough, they would disperse and leave him alone.

Elder thought Tiger walked too much with his head bowed. "A golfer needs to be in touch with the people who pay to see him," he said. "I would like to see him acknowledge the gallery more. I don't think he's having fun. He looks uptight."

Tiger was just trying to focus. He was driving exceptionally well, and with the exception of that first putt, had stayed out of trouble on the greens. It was his iron play that turned what could have been a sub-par round, maybe something in the 60s into a 72. He was still having trouble controlling the distance of his approach shots, but for the most part, it was a solid start, one that could be measured historically as stellar. Nicklaus shot 76 in his first Masters round. Palmer 73. Player 77. Watson 77. Langer 77. Price 77. Couples and Faldo had 73s. Ballesteros a 74. "I'm having the time of my life," he assured everyone.

Playing with Curtis Strange, Tiger Woods shot another

72 on Friday, and made his first cut in the United States by shooting even-par 144 for 36 holes. He three-putted the 18th after flagging his approach shot, but was in good spirits. Nicklaus, who would win a record six green jackets, the man he was already measured against, shot 150 in his first Masters and missed the cut. Tiger was around for the weekend. The pressure was off.

After Friday's round, Tiger and Earl quietly slipped out of the front gates and took a drive to Forest Hills, a nearby public course where the grass isn't as green as it is at Augusta. Forest Hills is a course where many of the Augusta National caddies play when they're not working, where they'll take your money ($27 weekday, $34 on the weekends) for greens fees, and where they let you play in cutoff jeans just as long as you've got a golf shirt. With men, women and children around, Tiger put on an exhibition off the scruffy turf at Forest Hills. "It's a black thing," Earl said. "We are acknowledging that we know who came before Tiger and that they suffered humiliation and that we realize the debt. It's a way of saying thank you and a promise to carry the baton."

Until 1982, it was a rule at the Masters that touring pros must take Augusta National caddies during tournament week. Jerry Beard, who guided Fuzzy Zoeller to a victory in 1979, saw it as Tiger's way of making a statement. "We have been the forgotten men of the Masters," Beard said. "But maybe Tiger will help us be remembered."

Earl had a microphone and announced to the crowd that Tiger had passed from adolescence to manhood at Augusta, and that he was very proud of him. "Thanks, Pop," said Tiger, who was obviously touched.

Tiger hit some trick shots, big slices and big draws, and boomed his driver out past where anybody had ever hit it at

Forest Hills. He took out a lob wedge, had Earl stand 10 paces in front of him, opened up the clubface and took a full swing. The ball softly floated over Earl, who was as confident as Ziegfield and Roy in a cageful of tigers. "I was in awe," said Doug Coleman, an assistant pro at Forest Hills. "It was his first Masters but he kind of had this swagger about him that you knew he was going to be 'The Man' someday."

Tiger went back to the course with Jay for more practice. He let Brunza hypnotize him and put him in "The Zone." Then he hit balls and was able to assimilate his father's and Butch's instruction. His realistic goal was to finish in the top 24, which would qualify him for the 1996 Masters. At 144, he was nine strokes off the lead held by Jay Haas.

The next day was one of those days that everybody has at Augusta, the type of day when shots roll through greens and into places where not even a Ballesteros could manufacture par. It exposed Tiger's weakness, his inability to master distance control, and it cost him. He started out with birdies at the second and third holes. At two under, he was just another birdie away from a spot on the leaderboard. But at the par-four fourth, a gust of wind knocked his ball into the front bunker, derailing his momentum. He missed a six-footer for par, got on the bogey train and couldn't get off. When they counted them up in the scoring tent behind the 18th green, he had shot 77 and was 15 strokes behind the leaders. "The way I drove it and putted it, I know I could have been in the hunt," he said. "I guess everyone feels that way, but I feel like this place is perfect for me. I guess I need to get to know it better."

Out on the driving range that night, Woods was hitting balls next to Davis Love, trying to put the 77 behind him.

Love, who was in contention, and eventually would finish second to Ben Crenshaw on Sunday, was trying to hit drivers over the 50-foot-high netting at the end of the range. Love, who led the Tour in driving distance in 1994, was 0-for-2 when Woods demurely asked, "Can I try?"

Love nodded. Tiger teed up a ball and sent it sailing over the net and toward Washington Road. A roar went up from the spectators sitting in the grandstands. Players along the range smiled knowingly. On Sunday, Tiger finished birdie-birdie-par-birdie and shot 72 for a 72-hole total of five-over 293. He had averaged 311.1 yards off the tee to lead the field, and had reached the 15th green in all four rounds with nothing more than an eight-iron. The longest club he hit into a par-four all week was seven-iron. This was a place he should tear up, but in his first Masters, Tiger Woods finished tied for 41st. He couldn't wait to get back in 1996, and the only way to do that was by winning another Amateur.

"He has the potential to win over here, and obviously he has to know more about the golf course," Earl said. "He hits the ball very long and very high, which are things very useful on this course. Both he and I know he can do better. He didn't come here to make a cameo appearance; he's here to win. He will not be satisfied with what he did because he's a perfectionist."

With Earl's assistance, Tiger composed a written letter to the officers, tournament staff and members of the Augusta National Golf Club, and presented it to club and tournament chairman Jackson T. Stephens.

It said:

> Please accept my sincere thanks for providing me the opportunity to experience the most

wonderful week of my life. It was fantasy land and Disney World wrapped into one.

I was treated like a gentleman throughout my stay and I trust I responded in kind. The "Crow's Nest" will always remain in my heart and your magnificent golf course will provide a continuing challenge throughout my amateur and professional career.

I've accomplished much here and learned even more. Your tournament will always hold a special spot in my heart as the place where I made my first PGA cut and at a major yet! It is here that I have left my youth behind and became a man. For that I will be eternally in your debt.

With warmest regards and deepest apprecia- tion, I remain,

    Sincerely,

    Tiger Woods.

He read this at his closing news conference. Charles Yates, the former Walker Cup captain and British Amateur champion, was seated next to him. Yates, in his green jacket, extended his hand.

"It has been a privilege and delight," Mr. Yates said. "And as they say in the old country, 'Hasten ye back.' "

As he packed for the trip home, he again noticed the pictures of past Masters champions on the walls of the Crow's Nest. He had a class in history the next morning at Stanford. He had just made golf history as the first black Amateur to compete in the Masters. He looked at the pic- tures of Nicklaus, Palmer, Player, Ballesteros and Watson. He made a promise to himself. "Someday," he said, "I'm going to get my picture up there."

29

OUT CLAUSE

Standing under the great oak tree at the Augusta National Clubhouse, Tida Woods reiterated that her son would stay in college. "These people offer millions," she said. "It means nothing. I love him, but I love him in right way. I would never, never take the money for my son's future. I want that bachelor's degree. I don't want my son to be some kind of dumb athlete. I tell him, 'It's more than a piece of paper. That education in your head, nobody can take it away.' To me, it means that nobody can take advantage of him."

"Quality education, not golf," said Earl, "is the number one priority in our house."

Tiger agreed, or said he agreed. "There's more to life than golf," was the standard line. "I've always had to finish my homework before playing."

But all of this was before the Big Brothers at the National Collegiate Athletic Association started taking a hard look at Tiger Woods's perks. In April, after he returned from Augusta, Stanford had to suspend him from the golf team for a day because of Masters diaries he wrote for *Golf World* and *Golfweek* magazines. Steve Mallonee, director of legislative services for the NCAA, said that Stanford was just playing by the rules. "Because of the inadvertence of the violation, there was no penalty and his eligibility was restored," Mallonee said.

There were also questions raised because Tiger used new irons in the final round that belonged to Harmon, and Maxfli golf balls that Greg Norman suggested he use. Stanford issued the Cardinal golf team with Titleists, and was acting on its responsibility to ensure that one of its athletes was not receiving free equipment from a manufacturer.

Woods was ripping mad. For the first time, Earl intimated that his son might leave school early if the nickle-and-dime stuff continued by the NCAA, and if Stanford's athletic department kept jerking its knee every time Tiger tried a new club or ball. Earl's out clause was that Tiger could leave Stanford if "he achieves a level of performance in which collegiate golf is no longer a viable environment for him."

Tiger even revealed for the first time that his options were open. "If I get to where I can't learn anything more from playing college golf, or if I get burned out like I did playing junior golf, I might turn pro," he said. "I would play the tour during the summer, then go back to school in the fall and winter. In the spring, I'd probably have to take some schoolwork on the road with me. But that's just an option. It's way down the road."

The college golf season droned on. Stanford was the NCAA's defending champion, and with three returning seniors plus Tiger, the Cardinal was heavily favored to repeat. Because of his heavy schedule, Tiger strained a rotator cuff in his left shoulder, and had to withdraw from the second round of the U.S. Intercollegiate at Stanford. He had to skip the Pac-10 Championships in Richland, Wa., on May 1–3, but came back for the NCAA West Regionals in Albuquerque, N.M., and fought his way through gastroenteritis to shoot three 72s. If he had withdrawn that first day, when he was in so much pain, Stanford would have been disqualified as a team because teammate Casey Martin was suffering from the same stomach disorder.

The NCAA Finals were held in Columbus, Ohio, on the Scarlet Course at Ohio State University, the same layout that Jack Nicklaus played during his collegiate days at OSU. On the pro shop wall, a plaque proclaimed "The Ohio State University Courses/Collegiate Home of Jack Nicklaus/ The Greatest Golfer to Play the Game." That same week, Nicklaus was hosting The Memorial Tournament across town at Muirfield Village. Nearly 35 years ago, Nicklaus was three semesters short of graduation when he quit school to continue his insurance practice and play professional golf. In a news conference held while the Memorial Tournament and NCAAs were being held concurrently, Nicklaus addressed a question about Tiger's future.

"Tiger has all the right tools to be a successful and dominant golfer," he said. "He has a college career he wants to finish, but at the same time he'll be receiving invitations to pro events all over the place. It's up to him to determine how much he wants to focus on golf and what his goals are."

Tiger didn't mind being back at college, carrying his own bag, pulling pins and raking his own traps. But the classroom work and the competitive golf were exhausting. College golfers, according to a study conducted by the NCAA in 1990, miss more class time than football or basketball players—and most don't have a schedule that includes the Masters and U.S. Open. "The toughest part of playing college golf is that I'm in school," Tiger said after an opening round 73 on the Scarlet course. "It's hard to handle the workload."

The frustration was not masked by Tiger in the NCAAs. At times he displayed a quiet rage, flipping clubs or slapping the face of an iron against his Stanford bag. When a ball hit a spike mark and darted away from the hole, Tiger pounded it down. When he broke a club on the 12th hole, tournament officials had to give him a warning. Any more outbursts like that, and Stanford would receive a two-stroke penalty. In the post-round interview, Greg Stoda of the *Palm Beach Post* described a "shoulder-shrugging, straight-ahead stare review of his round."

Somebody asked if he was going over to Muirfield Village. He had more important things to do, like three term papers and two final exams awaiting at Stanford. "If the scores are in the paper, I'll look at them," he offered. "Why would I want to be there? I want to be here."

Everybody at Stanford was uptight. Even the usually accommodating Goodwin barked when a reporter wanted two minutes with Notah Begay. "Everybody wants two minutes," he said. "And two minutes times 10 is 20 minutes." The coach claimed he was getting an average of 51 requests a day during the season to his personal office line. All the media attention was too much for the Stanford team to handle. "Being in the spotlight as we are every day has put a lot of pressure on us," Casey Martin said. "It's been a great experience having Tiger, but it's also been tough and has probably hurt our performance somewhat."

Woods brought a 71.35 stroke average in 12 collegiate events to the NCAAs. He had won two tournaments and had six other top 10 finishes, but his performances had been spotty. Once that 73 was behind him, he fought to rounds of 72–70–71 and tied for fifth individually to lead the Stanford team. Overall, though, it was a disappointing week for the defenders from California. Tiger had a 25-foot putt on the final hole that would have given the Cardinal back-to-back titles. This time the putt ran over the dreaded cellophane bridge. Playoff. Oklahoma State, with Trip Kuehne, went on to win the NCAA title and Stanford, with Tiger Woods, returned to Palo Alto for final exams. Tiger Woods ended up with a 3.0 GPA and first-team All America honors his freshman season. He was a perfectionist. He wasn't just making a cameo.

30

WORK IN PROGRESS

There was little or no rest for the weary. After the NCAAs and final exams, Tiger returned home to Cypress to recharge his batteries for a summer schedule that included his first U.S. Open, his first British Open, a return engagement at the Western Open, and a debut in the Scottish Open.

Before he hit the road again, Woods, Bell and some of his high school buddies took a 60-mile bicycle ride up the California coast to Laguna Beach. "Tiger just needed to air himself out," Earl said. He came back, practiced hard for the U.S. Open, and left for Long Island with a renewed spirit. Shinnecock, an open, links-style course, would fit his game. The NCAAs were behind him. So were final exams.

But once they arrived at the Open venue, it was obvious to Earl that his son just wasn't mentally there. It showed right away, too, when Tiger three-putted the second, third and fourth holes. Paired with Ernie Els and Nick Price, the defending U.S. and British Open champions, Tiger shot 74 and was eight strokes off the lead, held by Price. He just wasn't as sharp as he should have been, considering it was his first U.S. Open. "If I had made my putts early, it would have set a different tone," Woods said.

The tone on Friday was one of ambivalence. Standing

on the third tee, he was already one over for the day, and five over for the tournament. Unless he turned it around in a hurry, he was probably going to miss the cut anyway. At 453 yards, the third at Shinnecock is one of the longest par-fours on the course. Tiger took one-iron, and hooked his tee ball into the left rough. Deep in the fescue, he had no shot to the green and decided to bump a wedge back into the fairway. When the club twisted through the heavy grass, Tiger said he felt something "tweak" in his left wrist.

Three holes later, after outdriving Price and Els on the fifth and sixth driving distance holes, Tiger saw Earl behind the gallery ropes and indicated he couldn't go on. It had reached the point, Tiger said, where he could not grip the club without pain. He told Price and Els that he was going to withdraw, accepted handshakes from both, and headed to the clubhouse in a golf cart for treatment. He was seven over at the time.

All it did was reinforce the sentiment that Tiger was either fragile or injury-prone. Since the previous December, Tiger had arthroscopic surgery to remove noncancerous tumors from behind his left knee, almost withdrew from the Masters with back spasms, missed the U.S. Intercollegiate and Pac-10 championships with a strained rotator cuff. Tiger attributed it to his wiry physique, and a product of growing pains. His body had taken a beating.

"I'm kind of bummed out," Woods said. "I felt I was playing well enough to make the cut. But you know, this is what happens when you hit the ball in the long grass. You're supposed to stay away from it."

Earl saw right through it. At the time, he said, "This is just like a teenager who hasn't matured physically, that's all." Indeed, Tiger had lost 10 pounds and was down to 145 after that bout with food poisoning at the NCAA West Regionals. But afterward, Earl admitted that Tiger could have kept playing if he had to, that the injury wasn't that bad. "[The injury] had nothing to do with it," Earl said. "He was absolutely gone because he had just gone through finals. All he could think of was eating and sleeping."

There was a long summer ahead, and maybe it was better for Tiger to preserve himself. He withdrew from the Northeast Amateur, came back out in July and made the cut at the Western, the Scottish and the British Opens. At Cog Hill for the Western, Tiger said the strained wrist was nearly back to 100 percent, and mentally he was ready to go. He shot 69 on Sunday, his low round in a PGA Tour event, to finish tied for 57th, and rushed off to O'Hare for the flight to Scotland. "I just hadn't had time to get my mind clear because of college and all the studying I had to do," he said. "The post-Open break really felt good."

At Carnoustie he recorded his best finish in a professional, finishing tied for 29th, but at St. Andrews the following week, British Amateur champion Gordon Sherry stole the show from him, and clipped him in a five-pound bet. Going into Newport for the 95th U.S. Amateur, it had not been the most productive summer from a results standpoint. But what he did learn, in the gales and hardpan fairways at Carnoustie and St. Andrews, was the little half and three-quarter punch shots that would be vital at Newport. Harmon spent the summer getting Tiger to shallow his swing plane, which would give him a lower, piercing trajectory for shots into the wind. By the time the Amateur rolled around in August, Tiger was rested and ready for his title defense.

31

BACK-TO-BACK

In the merchandise tent at Newport Country Club, Earl Woods raised the Havemeyer Trophy in a toast. "To my son, Tiger," Earl said, raising the trophy with a stiff right arm. "One of the greatest golfers in the history of the United States."

The handful of friends and autograph seekers laughed and cheered. Tiger Woods, age 19, and winner of his second consecutive U.S. Amateur Championship, smiled too—but bashfully. His dad had been drinking champagne from the oldest trophy in American golf. His dad wasn't supposed to be saying those things in public.

But Earl wasn't done.

"I'm going to make a prediction," Earl said. "Before he's through, my son will win 14 major championships."

This one really made Tiger wince, because he saw a writer from *Sports Illustrated* there and he was hoping that quote wouldn't make it in the magazine. They had talked about this goal privately among Team Tiger. With Tiger's ability, and his ambition, 14 majors was certainly doable. But it's not the type of thing that needs to be written in *SI*, where 3.5 million people would read it. Let everybody else do the predicting. Not Pop. Let the legend grow on its own.

Newport, as the headline said the following week in *Golf World*, was "Twice as Nice." Only eight golfers had won the Amateur back-to-back, and none since Jay Sigel in 1982–1983. Tiger was now 36–3 in USGA match play, a perfect 12–0 in the U.S. Amateur. Not since Bobby Jones had anyone put up those kind of numbers, dominated the amateur ranks the way Tiger had. Only Jones (9), Nicklaus (8), JoAnne Carner (8), Anne Sander (7), Hollis Stacy (6) and Glenna Collett Vare (6) had won more USGA titles.

It took six months for the first U.S. Amateur to sink in. This one was easier to comprehend. "It was pretty simple this week," Tiger said. "I knew what I had to do and I kept my focus." Having Brunza on the bag again helped, and he dedicated the victory to his caddy/sports psychologist, who had lost his father a month earlier. Nearly in tears, Brunza said, "Like all the great champions, Tiger has the ability to raise his game when he has to. This tournament was an example of that."

Tiger was not challenged in the early rounds, defeating Western Amateur winner Patrick Lee three and two, Chad Campbell of Andrews, Texas, four and two, and Sean Knapp of Oakmont, Pa., two and one. In the round of 16, he faced Scott Kammann, whose newlywed wife was *looping*. Woods sent them to an early honeymoon by winning five and three. This sent Tiger into the semifinals against Mark Plummer, a former sheriff's deputy turned liquor salesman from Manchester, Maine. Plummer had won the New England Amateur twice, and the Maine Amateur eight times, but he was clearly out of his league against Tiger. He had a corkscrew swing and a grip that Johnny Miller said belonged on a garden hose, not a golf club. "He looks like he was watering a lawn," Miller said.

Plummer pushed Woods to the 18th before succumbing. "I'm probably the happiest loser you'll ever look at," Plummer said. "He has more tournament experience from one summer than I do in my life. He has experience that I only have sitting in my lounge chair watching on television at home."

Emerging from the other bracket was George "Buddy" Marucci, Jr., an entrepreneur from Bernwyn, Pa., whose latest venture was as owner of an import car dealership. Marucci was well-connected in the mid-amateur circles, and had won club championships at Pine Valley and Seminole. At 43, he was 24 years older than Tiger, and from the other side of the tracks from Plummer, who looked like he stepped off a fishing boat. Marucci was always attired in starched khaki pants and a white shirt.

The night before the 36-hole final, when Tiger was sitting down to a helping of his father's special spaghetti, Earl had given him the historical breakdown: "When you have a sense of history, it brings out the best in the best," Earl said. "I talked to him about the last time there were back-to-back winners. I said, " 'Tomorrow, we make history.' "

Sunday brought with it typical Newport weather—a gray, overcast sky and breeze that would come off the ocean, and reverse itself for the afternoon. Buddy went three up on Woods through 12 holes—it was the first time Tiger trailed all week—and had chances on three other birdie putts of less than 15 feet. It may have seemed like a comfortable cushion, but Marucci knew that in a match-play format, three up was nothing. Against Tiger Woods, as was proven in USGA competition, no lead is safe.

Marucci hung on until the 24th hole, where Tiger made four-foot birdie to take the lead. Two holes later, he drew the match back to even with a birdie. In his five previous matches, Woods had only lost 11 holes. Marucci had won eight, and was not backing off. It took birdies to match the 28th and 29th holes. These mid-amateurs like Plummer and Marucci were dangerous. "They may hit it awry occasionally," Tiger said. "But they can get it up and down from everywhere. Great putting can make up for a lot of sins."

Great shotmaking goes a long way, too. Unlike the Masters, where he couldn't control the distance of his approach shots, Tiger found himself able to take a little off a club and land his shots where they would roll to birdie range, not off the back of the green. The work he had put in with Harmon was starting to pay off. Against Marucci, he took back the lead on the 30th hole, and went two up with a fist-pumping 12-footer for birdie two holes later.

Marucci still wouldn't give him. He burned the edge at the 34th hole, and won the 35th when Tiger hit over the green and made bogey. One down with one hole to play, he had honors on the last tee. The 18th at Newport is a 384–yard par-four, doglegging uphill. Marucci had to go after a driver and came off it just enough that his ball drifted into the right rough. Tiger is long enough that he could whistle a two-iron, 265 yards down the middle. Advantage Tiger.

Marucci hit his approach to the upper tier, leaving a tough 23-foot putt for birdie. All Woods had to do was get it inside 20 feet, and his second Amateur was a lock. In the NBC booth, Johnny Miller predicted, "I wouldn't be surprised if he knocks this a foot from the hole." With an eight-iron from 140 yards, Woods sent a lightning bolt toward the green. This was not the type of shot that had been in his arsenal at Augusta, but he and Butch started working on it before the trip to Europe. The ball pitched 14 feet above the flag, and started moonwalking toward the cup, stopping at kick-in distance.

"That's something he couldn't have done at Augusta,"

Harmon said. "Last spring, he would have hit pitching wedge as hard as he could, and it would have sucked back off the green. But, on that last swing, he went down the shaft on an eight-iron and hit it stiff. He was able to flatten the trajectory of the shot, and do it without too much spin. We've worked hard on that, to control the distance and flight of the ball. But under pressure, it's hard to do a lot of things. The fact that he attempted it on the last shot of the tournament is why I'm so proud of him. That was the beauty of all the work we've done."

Walking up to the green, Marucci saw how close Tiger's ball was from the hole. He putted out and conceded Tiger's putt, and the match. He had fulfilled two lifelong dreams, to play in a Masters and make a Walker Cup team. He had lost to a kid who potentially could become the best of all time. He had played college golf at the University of Maryland, and won the Pennsylvania Amateur four times. He had taken this kid to the 36th hole. He would see him at Augusta. "Tiger is the best athlete that this level of golf has seen," Marucci said. "He's lean, he's strong, his swing is marvelous. I couldn't see the ball come off the club for the first 27 holes. It came off the club that fast."

Afterward, Tiger was asked to rank his U.S. Amateur victories, the first with its great comeback, the second at Newport, where Charles Blair McDonald won the first U.S. Amateur in 1895. "This one meant more because it showed how far my game has come," Woods said. "That shot at 18—damn! That's the only shot I could hit close, that half shot. I didn't have it last year. I didn't have it at Augusta."

Marucci concurred. "Tiger wouldn't take a back seat to anyone in my mind," he said. "He's got more game than most people at this level, especially his short game. Some of those wedge shots he hits, those little pitch and run shots

. . . For a guy who hits it 325 yards, he stands there 25 feet from the green and pitches it within a foot of the hole. He's got a tremendous game. There's no question if he stays healthy and well, he's going to be very, very successful. When he stood there in the 18th fairway and knocked that shot next to the hole—that's the sign of a true champion."

At the British Open, Woods had stood on the practice ground at St. Andrews, and had asked Harmon, "Butch, how far away am I? When will I be that good?"

Harmon knew he was already there, but didn't want to tell the kid. "You just have to keep working," he said. "You've got much to learn."

A quick study, this Tiger Woods. If Jack Nicklaus can count his two U.S. Amateurs toward his major championship total of 20, so should Tiger. By Earl's count, his son only had 12 more to go.

Tiger Cub • Flashing that sabre-toothed smile at age fourteen. ALAN LEVENSON/ALLSPORT

Adding 'Em Up • At age seventeen, Tiger shoots 72 in the opening round of his first PGA Tour event, the 1992 Nissan Los Angeles Open at Riviera. GARY NEWKIRK/ALLSPORT

Heavy Metal • After three U.S. Junior Titles, Tiger gets to hold the Havemeyer Trophy after winning the 1994 U.S. Amateur. RUSTY JARRETT/ALLSPORT

Reigning at Augusta • Tiger Woods unleashes his power at his first Masters. MICHAEL O'BRYON

Transcending the Game • Tiger Woods signs autographs at the 1995 Masters. KEIICHI SATO

Local Knowledge • Veteran caddy Tommy Bennett guided Tiger around Augusta National in his first Masters. DAVID CANNON/ALL-SPORT

Father and Son • Earl and Tiger have been
inseparable. Keiichi Sato

Repeat Champion • With the historic clubhouse at
Newport Country Club as a backdrop, Tiger tees off
on Sunday, October 27th in the 1995 U.S. Amateur.
J.D. Cuban/ALLSPORT

Team Tiger • From left-to-right, Butch Harmon,
Jay Brunza, Earl Woods, and Tiger Woods.
J.D. Cuban/ALLSPORT

In the Red • To win his second PGA Tour event in three weeks, Tiger shot twenty-one under to beat Payne Stewart at the Disney Classic, capturing a slot for the Tour Championship. MICHAEL O'BRYON

Hello World • The worst-kept secret in the golf world was that Tiger would turn pro at the Greater Milwaukee Open. J.D. CUBAN/ALLSPORT

Pumped up • Winning the Amateur for an unprecedented third-straight time brought the animal out in
Tiger. J.D. Cuban/ALLSPORT

The Green Jacket • Former Masters champion Nick Faldo presents Tiger with his first green Masters jacket. DAVID TULIS/*Atlanta Journal Constitution*/SYGMA

Fluff • Caddy Mike "Fluff" Cowan guided Tiger to victories in Las Vegas and Walt Disney World. KEIICHI SATO

IV

THE YEAR OF THE TIGER

*"All these people.
They are here
to see my Tiger."*
—TIDA WOODS

32

AUGUSTA REVISITED

Jaded would be a good word to describe Tiger Woods's mood when he arrived at the Masters in April 1996. The NCAA was still hassling him and college golf had become somewhat of a bore. Although his role had changed from freshman gofer to team leader, the tediousness of week-to-week competition was interfering with his schoolwork. He took 21 credits the fall semester of his sophomore year, and he was not the brainiac who pulled down As, like some of his friends. One of the guys he hung out with assembled the parts of a computer from scratch, and the darned thing worked perfectly. Another buddy passed all of Stanford's basic math courses before he enrolled. For Tiger to get good grades, he had to grind harder than he ever did at golf.

"I don't think you work on golf for 20 hours, or stay up all night and drink a pot of coffee," he said. "I have to work hard to get by."

The previous fall, after playing the Walker Cup at Royal Porthcawl in Wales, he made arrangements through IMG to meet with Arnold Palmer during the Transamerica Senior Tour event just north of San Francisco at Silverado Country Club in Napa. Even though Tiger offered to pay, Arnold picked up the check. Tiger came back and told Stan-

ford coach Wally Goodwin about it, and then Goodwin reported it to Susan Burke, the Stanford athletic-affairs
coordinator. Burke then declared Woods ineligible until she
received confirmation from the NCAA that he had broken no
rule. "This was so minor, so incredibly minor, that I knew
it was going to come back fine," Burke said. The problem is
that Woods, who wrote Palmer a $25 check to cover his
portion of the bill, was traveling to El Paso for the Savane
All-America Classic. Burke was unable to reach him with
news of his reinstatement for most of the day, and even
though he won the Savane tournament, Woods was not ap-
preciative of the way Stanford overreacted.

"I was pretty angry," Woods said. "I felt like I didn't
do anything wrong. By having dinner and talking about
things I wanted to talk about, I was declared ineligible. It's
annoying."

Woods had requested the dinner to discuss his future,
and how to better deal with his role as a celebrity. Nobody
is better at it than Palmer, who was glad to offer his advice.
Palmer, of course, thought the whole deal was ridiculous,
and deposited the check for $25 at his bank in Latrobe, Pa.

For the first time, Earl and Tida were acknowledging
that Tiger would have their blessing if he decided to turn
professional. "Could this lead to Tiger turning pro? Hell,
yes," Earl said. "It can lead to a mind-set of, 'I truly don't
need this.' After all, Tiger is human and if pushed hard
enough and consistently enough, he's going to react."

Tida could see the stress of trying to balance the academic workload at Stanford with a full golf schedule. Her
son looked tired, didn't have time for a girlfriend—"It's too
tough. I'm never here"—and complained that his mind is
never clear. "I will support whatever he decides," she said.
"I give him my advice that money is not the issue and to be

careful not to sacrifice his youth. But my boy is a man now, and I trust his judgment."

Earl and Tida were also not happy when Goodwin called, wondering if they would mind donating the canceled check Tiger wrote to Palmer to the university. At a fund-raising dinner in December, a group of Palo Alto business-men had auctioned the check off for $2,500. Earl called the check a piece of golf history that marked the meeting of two great players.

Then, just before the Masters, Tiger was pressured into playing the Far Western Tournament at Pasatiempo Golf Club in Santa Cruz. Because of Tiger, the tournament was scheduled to be televised on ESPN, and he was torn between supporting it and traveling to Augusta. In the end, Tiger played at Pasatiempo because he felt he owed it to college golf.

For the record, he was telling even his closest friends, "I know for sure I will be [at Stanford] next year." Behind the scenes, however, he and Earl were laying the ground-work for Tiger's turning professional. It would depend on how he did in the Masters, U.S. Open and British Open, but his two biggest events in 1996 would be the NCAAs at the Honors Course and the 96th U.S. Amateur at Pumpkin Ridge. If he swept those two events, there would be nothing left to accomplish as a collegian or an amateur, and that would pave the way to a professional career.

"I would know if it's time," Earl said. "It goes back to the AJGA. I knew the moment he had outgrown it. It was at Castle Rock, Colo. He was playing a tournament. He was lethargic and he was playing terrible and he really wasn't concerned about it. He was bored. He had outgrown the AJGA and he never played another event."

The highlight of his second Masters week was the practice rounds, Tuesday with Raymond Floyd, Fred Couples and Greg Norman, Wednesday with Arnold Palmer and Jack Nicklaus. He arrived at Augusta looking broader in the shoulders and thicker in the chest and indeed he was 15 pounds heavier than the previous spring, bulking up in the Stanford weight room and on its training table. Norman could tell the difference right away. Now he was getting outdriven by 50 and 60 yards instead of just 10. And on Wednesday, Nicklaus came in for his annual State of the Bear dissertation, and all but pronounced Tiger as the Second Coming.

"Both Arnold and I agree that you could take my Masters (six) and his Masters (four) and add them together, and this kid should win more than that. This kid is the most fundamentally sound golfer I've ever seen at almost any age. I don't know if he's ready to win yet or not. But he will be your favorite for the next 20 years. If he isn't, there's something wrong."

Nicklaus re-created the scene from the 13th hole. Woods had driven through the dogleg with a three-wood, and was about 45 yards behind Nicklaus, who took driver around the corner. Nicklaus had a two-iron. He and Palmer looked back and saw Woods select an iron of some sort. Palmer figured the kid was going to lay up. Nicklaus, who goes by the nickname Carnac because he always has the right answer, knew better. Woods selected three-iron, and with 215 to the front, hit a high draw past pin high.

"He doesn't use graphite and the other stuff to hit the ball longer," Nicklaus observed. "He's got X100 steel shafts in his clubs. He could hit the ball further if he used something else. I was very, very impressed, to say the least. So was Arnold."

Tiger's Tuesday news conference ran half the length of

the previous year—9 pages instead of 18. He did elaborate on certain questions this time around, depending who asked the question and how it was worded. The race issue did not come up, not once.

Question: "Tiger, with so many college athletes, whether it's golf or basketball, as you well know, all the speculation is, 'When are they going to turn pro?' There was a story in Sports Illustrated, the current issue, that said: All you have to do is turn pro. Do these sort of stories get to your brain a little bit? Do you get tired of reading about them?"

Answer: "I don't read about stuff like that. As soon as I read the article, I move on. I already know what the stuff is all about anyway because I've had to answer those questions. I think the most annoying part is trying to answer the questions over and over and over again. It does tend to get to you after a while if it keeps coming up repeatedly. But the answer's still the same."

Question: "Tiger, it's been said that you feel less pressured this year. Is it because this is the second time or that there is a little less attention to who you are as an individual?"

Answer: "No, I would have to say that it's less, well, internal pressure. Let's put it this way. It's still the same. Externally it's different because I know what to expect now around here. Going through that learning curve was kind of difficult at times because not only did I have to try and play, but I had to get used to all the hysteria that goes around here. Just like trying to find a place to eat is kind of rough. But overall I know what to expect after one year's experience. That has helped. And I'm pleased to say I haven't got lost in the clubhouse like I did last year."

Question: "Tiger, you said you get tired of the questions

about when you're going to turn pro, but most of the guys in this room have difficulty imagining turning down the amount of money you could be making just by signing endorsement contracts. Don't you think about that, just what you could do by signing your signature?"

Answer: "The thing is, you see all the money that's available out there. But where am I going to play? I'm not exempt. I have no security. So if I turn pro and I don't make it out here, where am I going to play? The Nike Tour? The Hooters Tour? Asia? Anywhere but here, I guess."

Tiger played with Ben Crenshaw on Thursday and Tom Watson on Friday. He shot 75 both days, and hurriedly informed reporters that he had to reschedule his flight. "I've got an economics paper due Wednesday and I haven't even started," he said.

Crenshaw, who also missed the cut, had a hard time believing some of the drives Tiger hit. At the 360-yard, par-four third, Tiger's tee shot was 17 paces short of the green. He still only made par. "He's still learning the game, and that takes time," Crenshaw said. "He played the wrong club a few times. He needs to know when to go at it, and when to lay back. With the littlest of help, there's no telling what he could do. The smaller shots from around the green, his short irons and wedges, there's where he has to get razor sharp. But his talent is out of this world."

So were Tiger's total number of putts. He led the field in driving distance and his approach shots were better than in 1995, but he putted like his arms were encased in cement. Sixty-five putts will send you down the road in a hurry, no matter how many greens you hit in regulation. It was just as Nicklaus told him on Wednesday: The key to Augusta National is patience. He missed the cut his first year and had eight three-putts. Five years later he won for the first time. Then, he couldn't be stopped.

"There are only two ways to learn this course," Woods said. "You have to listen to the guys who have played it and you have to go through the diabolical experience of playing it. I'm frustrated that I didn't make the cut, but I'm happy with the way I improved from last year. I know exactly what I have to work on."

There was no silver cup for low amateur to bring home this year, no promises made to himself that his picture would someday hang in the champions locker room. He paid his bill—it costs $10 a night to stay in the Crow's Nest—and flew back to Stanford, to do that economics paper.

33

HONORS STUDENT

ince this was probably going to be his last year of collegiate golf, Tiger Woods adopted the role of guiding hand.
The 1994–1995 Cardinal team was the defending national champion with four seniors returning. The 1995–
1996 team went into the Honors Course for the NCAA Finals
at No. 13 in the *Golfweek*/Taylor Made collegiate rankings.
"This year I'm having more fun than I did last year," he
said. "I think the team this year's a little different because
we have more of a mixture. We have one senior. We have a
couple of sophomores and one freshman. And occasionally
we'll throw in a junior. It depends on who qualifies. So the
mixture is great. Last year it was four seniors and a freshman and I got to sleep on the cot a lot. It was a lot of fun,
but it was also seniority treatment that I had to endure. So
this year's been great in that respect."

Tiger single-handedly carried the Cardinal to the Pac-
10 title by shooting 18-under-par 270 at Big Canyon Country Club in Newport Beach, Calif., opening with rounds of
61-65 on what was called the most spectacular one-day
performance in collegiate golf history. In a 27-hole stretch,
he posted nines of 30-31-31, and was on his way to another
low-60s round when he birdied three of the first five holes.

That put him eight under for the second round, 19 under for the day, but he finally hit the wall, making a bogey and three pars coming in. Arizona State's Scott Johnson, who was 11 under for 36 holes and the closest in pursuit, joked that he was low amateur—and he wasn't far from being right.

The next week, Woods accepted invitations to play the Greater Milwaukee Open and the Quad City Classic, two fall events that fell just after the U.S. Amateur. The Skins Game, which is run by IMG, was also reportedly holding a spot open for Woods. Earl took the credit, or the blame, for adding those two events to Tiger's schedule. "I don't know what he's going to do about turning pro," he said from Cypress. "The decision will rest with him. But I tell you this, I'll be planting arguments against any scenario he might come up with that doesn't call for him staying in school." That was all just a smoke screen, however. Earl had already been in contact with Nike, and according to sources in the golf management and equipment industries, had conducted preliminary negotiations with Phil Knight on the phone and in person. Earl's starting figure was $25 million.

During ABC's telecast of the GTE Byron Nelson, Brent Musburger predicted that Tiger would turn pro. Tiger didn't like the speculation at all. "[Musburger] knows more about my life than I do," Tiger snapped. "Considering the source, it's not hard to understand. He's never asked me anything."

This came out the week of the NCAA West Regional, which Stanford hosted and won. Tiger shot 68–70–67 for medalist honors; it was his fourth win in as many tournaments and his seventh victory in 13 events for the season. Eleven days later, Woods would play in his last college tournament, shooting 69–67–69–80 for a four-stroke victory in the NCAA Championships. The 67 broke the competitive course record last tied by Gary Nicklaus in qualifying for the 1991 U.S. Amateur. That was the year Tiger shot 78-74 and failed to qualify. By those standards, his game had improved 16 strokes over 36 holes in five years.

"To sum it up, I have played smart and intelligent," Woods said at the halfway point. A 69 on Friday gave him a nine-stroke lead going into the final round. He was making it look easy, but warned everyone, "There's still one more day. Anything can happen."

Sure enough, anything did happen on the ninth hole of the final round. With just a pitch shot into the green, Woods ended up dropping three shots to par, then followed that triple bogey with a bogey–bogey–bogey–bogey stretch. He was still the only golfer under par in the tournament, but that bad patch cost Stanford nothing more than third place over East Tennessee State. In the parking lot, Woods had a panic attack about the term paper due Tuesday, and the trip he had to make to Muirfield Village to receive the Jack Nicklaus Trophy as the College Golf Foundation's No. 1 player. "I can't really feel all the emotion of winning," he said.

If it wasn't for Nicklaus, Tiger might have blown it off. But Jack was so nice to him at Augusta, said some things that he took to heart. In Ohio the next day, Woods reiterated that he would not turn pro before his graduation in 1998 "unless something exciting happens." The paper he had due was worth 65 percent of his grade, and he hadn't started it yet. Earl Woods made a point of saying, "The golfer at Stanford gets no slack—absolutely none. Tiger will arrive at the Open like a zombie from studying."

34

BITTEN BY THE MONSTER

Tiger flew back to Stanford, submitted his accounting project on time, made it through his African Literature final exam, and boarded a plane for Detroit. Nobody really understood what this kid was going through, but Earl had prepared him for it back in those days of basic training, when he'd push Tiger to the breaking point, and then back off, push him again, and then back off. The U.S. Open was at Oakland Hills Country Club, a golf course Ben Hogan nicknamed The Monster. It was long and tight with unfair greens and Tiger wasn't exactly prepared for it, but that was the story of his amateur career. He was better prepared for Oakland Hills than he was for Shinnecock, and Tiger appeared somewhat relaxed and in better spirits than during his exits from the Honors Course and Muirfield Village.

At his Tuesday news conference, Woods explained that he planned his class schedule around the NCAAs and the Open, loading up in the fall and winter quarters and taking just two classes in the spring. "The only thing I can say is there's a big difference between this year's Open versus last year's," Woods said. "I remember last year. I had to take three finals on Thursday, pack up on a Friday, leave for the Open Saturday, and then try and somehow play. And during that week [at Shinnecock], I never got any sleep. While I was taking my finals, I stayed up for 46 hours in a row, slept for 3 hours, and stayed up for another 20. Somehow I had to try and get ready for the Open, and I never could."

Woods was also much further along in his development at Oakland Hills than he was at Shinnecock. This was his fifth major championship; he had more shots in his arsenal and had won nine of the 13 college tournaments he played in 1995–1996. He had also shot that 61 in the Pac-10 Championships, and that score wasn't possible before because Tiger's game just wasn't on that level. "My swing just didn't allow it," Woods said. "It didn't lend itself to that. And I have definitely improved my putting, so with all those things combined, I have definitely matured as a player and I think I've matured as a person because of college."

It is a USGA tradition to pair the Amateur champion with the two Open champions, and this put Woods with John Daly and Corey Pavin, the short-hitting Ryder Cup hero. Daly and Woods went back to the 1989 Big I Classic in Texarkana, but Oakland Hills was not the place for a long-drive exhibition. Most of the fairways narrowed out where Woods and Daly hit it. Woods explained that if he had to hit a five-iron off the tee he would. Daly came into the Open equipped with a Wilson Zero iron. If it was driver against driver, Daly could carry the ball farther, which would give him an advantage at Oakland Hills because the fairways were wet. At Augusta, where the fairways are as hard as tabletops, Woods is longer because he can turn the ball over.

Woods went out by himself Monday morning to get a feel for the Oakland Hills greens, and by Thursday's opening round he felt that he had the course wired. He reached the second hole, a par-five of 523 yards, with a six-iron second shot, and made birdie. He one-hopped a 60-degree wedge into the cup at the fifth hole for another birdie. At the sixth, he tore out the back of the hole with an approach shot, but the ball hit the steel cup and ricocheted 50 feet away—payback, Woods thought, for his luck on the hole before. At the 560-yard 12th, he reached the green with a five-iron and two-putted for another birdie.

Going between the 13th green and the 14th tee, Woods looked up and saw his name atop a leader board at a major championship for the first time. If Tiger could get it in the clubhouse at three under par, he would tie for the lead with Payne Stewart and Woody Austin. At the 14th green, he asked for relief from a drain. The USGA rules official denied a free drop, Woods had to chip rather than putt, and he ended up lipping out for par. Tough break, but part of golf.

The 15th at Oakland Hills is a 400-yard par-four with a ridiculously contoured green. Woods drove in the rough and three-putted for double bogey. Back to even par, Woods was still in relatively good shape. The pond in front of the 16th is the only water hazard at Oakland Hills. Woods ringed two shots (six-iron and a wedge) into it, made the dreaded snowman, and finished bogey-bogey for a 76. He did an interview with Johnny Miller on ESPN, had lunch, and came out to review details with the print media. "I hit some bad shots, and it cost me some shots," he said. "The same thing happened in my last competitive round. Unfortunately, it's a common theme."

At the NCAAs, he could get away with it. Not at the Open. Nine dropped shots in five holes, and he went careening from first to 115th. In the parking lot, he slammed the trunk of his courtesy car, hit the gas pedal, and bolted. It was left for Daly to do the explaining. "Those things happen," he said. "It's happened to me a hundred times. He was going along so well. But he's tough. I wish I was that tough at 21."

Woods came back to shoot one-under 69 on Friday, but went 77-72 on the weekend to finish at 294, 14 over par and 16 strokes behind Steve Jones. Like at the Masters, putting was his problem. He three-putted three times during the 69, and concluded the week ranked 68th in putting with 31 attempts per round. Randy Leen, a sophomore from Indiana University, took the silver medal for low Amateur honors. Woods was the third-low am, behind Leen and Trip Kuehne. Thus far the majors in 1996 had been a bust. A missed cut at Augusta and a tie for 82nd at Oakland Hills. There had to be a better way . . .

35

BREAKTHROUGH

ven though he was in England, Tiger Woods felt at home. There were two McDonald's and a Burger King between Royal Lytham & St. Annes and his hotel in Blackpool. Every day, to and from the course, he could stop and get one of his favorite meals. "There's a difference between here and the States, but not much," Woods explained. "The portions aren't as big. I order a super-size fries and get about as many as I get in a large in the States. The food isn't as greasy, either, and I really love the grease. Just about wherever I go, if there's McDonald's there, I'll find it."

Woods also found Royal Lytham to be as good as home cooking. It was bone dry and parched, similar to the conditions he faced at Newport for the Amateur. It took 23 holes to get going, but once he found his rhythm, Tiger played the type of golf that convinced him his game was ready. He played the last 13 holes in seven under to shoot 66 and cruise beneath the cut by two shots. Something just clicked. "I'm finally learning how to play within myself—I'm finally learning what that means," he said. "For the first time in my life, I was able to swing easy at every shot. I'm learning how to control my body speed and my distance, learning not to explode through the ball all the time. At this level, it's all about discipline, how to control yourself, and I'd have to say that after the way things went today, I'm making some progress."

Tiger also showed that he was getting much more comfortable around the crush of major championship media. When asked about his poor record in major championships to that point, he joked that if Jack Nicklaus could count his two U.S. Amateur victories, so could he; in fact, he might as well tack on the three Junior Amateurs as well. "I've got five majors," he said.

The 66 tied the British Open amateur scoring record set by America's Frank Stranahan at Royal Troon in 1950 and guaranteed Woods the coveted Silver Medal for low amateur. But Woods wasn't at Lytham for the Silver Medal. He wanted to capture the Claret Jug, and he was not pleased on Saturday to shoot only 70 on another perfect day. Earl, however, saw the transformation. His son was playing poorly and shooting 70 in a major. "I'm pleased with Tiger's development because that's what it's all about—gaining experience and exposure to the pro game at the highest level," he said. "At age 20, this is his sixth major, and he's made four cuts. All this experience will come back and pay dividends later. I'm not concerned about him going out and winning. I realize he's in over his head but he has the talent and the desire and when you combine those with age, you have a volatile situation—he can catch on fire."

Another 70 on Sunday moved Woods up into a tie for 22nd, his best finish in a major championship and a professional tournament. His 72-hole total of three-under 271 tied the championship record set by Ian Pyman in 1993 at Royal St. George's for the lowest aggregate by an amateur. A bogey at the last hole cost Woods the record, but he was distracted by the noisy fans who had been drinking in the

beer pavilion, and was unable to get comfortable after reset-
ting over his second shot.

"I was looking for the Claret Jug," he said. "But, on
the week, I'd have to say it was a whole lot of fun. It's been
important to me to see my game improve in big tournaments such as this. I'm pleased with how much better I'm
hitting the ball and my decision making.

"Finally, those are starting to show up in my scores."

Michael Bonallack, secretary of the R&A and a past
British Amateur champion, could see the progress Woods
had made since the 1995 Open at St. Andrews. Bonallack
called Woods as good as Nicklaus was at a comparable age,
which was his highest praise.

"I'd have to say he struggled with links golf last year,
especially landing his iron shots softly and on the hard
ground and getting the right feel for pitch-and-run shots,"
Bonallack said. "This year, he has showed a much more
complete game. He's added a new dimension. I think we're
looking at a future champion for many years to come."

Nicklaus, who shot 66 the same day Woods shot 66,
faded on the weekend with scores of 77–72, but was pleased
to see Tiger play so well. "Obviously he has a marvelous
future in front of him," Nicklaus said. "He's getting such
great experience at such an age, competing in important
tournaments like this, and he's making the most of them.
He's going to be around for a long, long time—if his body
holds up. That's always a concern with a lot of players because of how much they play and how many balls they hit.
A lot of guys can't handle it, the physical and mental side.
But from what he's shown me, it looks like he can. I see lots
of brightness in his future."

Tiger knew leaving Royal Lytham that afternoon that
it was probably his last professional tournament as an ama-

teur. On Tuesday, he played a practice round with Davis Love and Brad Faxon, and accompanying them was Titleist President Wally Uhlein. He had met with Uhlein at a hotel in San Francisco to discuss the preliminary terms of an equipment contract, and it was starting to get out that the numbers Nike was talking about would exceed the $25 million Earl had targeted. If he won the Amateur, he would turn pro with the promise to Earl and Tida that he would one day get his diploma.

His canned quote to reporters was still, "I will know when the time is right. As soon as I get there, I will tell you."

36

WALKING THE WALK

olf World came out August 2 with Tiger on the cover, sitting next to a giant Grecian urn outside Versailles. The picture was taken after the World Amateur in 1994. The headline: "Will he or won't he? Tiger Woods faces the decision of a lifetime."

Behind the scenes, the decision had already been made. On *The Tonight Show with Jay Leno*, Tiger said he would turn professional if something viable came along that outweighed Stanford and amateur golf. By "viable" Tiger meant megabucks deals with Nike and Titleist. The contracts hadn't been signed, because that would impinge Woods's amateur status with the USGA. But in Orlando, IMG was already hunting for a townhouse at Isleworth that eventually would be Tiger's tax-free haven. The corporate wheels were in motion.

There was one final sign. Tiger went to the Western Amateur at Benton Harbor, Mich., and was eliminated in the first round by Terry Noe, the 1994 U.S. Junior champion. He was flat, and that told Woods his motivations would be taxed playing amateur golf. It was like that AJGA event in Castle Rock, Colo. "He told me that he was leaning toward turning pro," Earl said. "The reasons he gave were his British Open performance, and his recent collegiate success. Every horizon had been covered. He is mature physically and mentally, and he's ready to move. I told him we would talk again, but it accelerated the preparation I had been doing just in case."

One week later at the PGA Championship, spectators at Valhalla Golf Club in Louisville were puzzled when they couldn't find Tiger Woods's name on the pairing sheet. After all, he played every Masters, U.S. Open and British Open since 1995. Why wasn't he at Valhalla? The answer was that only *professionals* played in the PGA. Tiger would be one soon enough.

Tiger turning pro was now a hot rumor inside golf's inner circles. In the locker room at Valhalla, Joe Moses, the sports marketing manager of Nike's Golf Division, was ducking the other tour reps and agents who had heard it was a done deal, that Earl and Phil Knight had agreed to terms. It was also that week that a handful of writers the Woodses trusted were told that Tiger would turn pro after the Amateur, but they were asked to sit on the information. If they wrote it, they were betraying the trust of the Woods family forever. If they didn't write it, they risked getting beat on the story. The Amateur was still two weeks away. Tiger was home in Cypress, honing his game, still not 100 percent on his decision.

Before he left for the Amateur, Tiger told Wally Goodwin that he'd be back at Stanford for another season. At the Amateur dinner Sunday night at the Portland Marriott, Fred Ridley, chairman of the World Amateur Championship selection committee, approached Tiger and asked, "I'd like to make an announcement that we're going to have you at the Philippines. If there's a problem, I don't need to make the announcement."

"Go right ahead," Woods said.

In the locker room at Firestone Country Club in Akron, Ohio, where they were playing the NEC World Series of Golf, Greg Norman, Fred Couples and Ernie Els already knew that Tiger was turning pro. He had consulted with them, and they all told him that with his talent and market power, he didn't need a college degree. That's what agents and accountants are for. "He made the right choice," Els said at Firestone. "He can't accomplish anything more in amateur golf. He's won everything. He's done everything. If he stays amateur, his level is not going to go up. Out here, he's learning quicker. Give him two years, and he'll be as good as anybody."

Pumpkin Ridge Golf Club in Cornelius, Ore., is located approximately 15 miles from Nike's world headquarters in Beaverton. It was just another piece of convenient fate in the Tiger Woods story that the site of his last U.S. Amateur triumph, and the corporation which would pay him at least $40 million, were located in the same county. Phil Knight, Nike's cofounder and CEO, was in the gallery for five of Woods's six matches. One day he tried going incognito by wearing sunglasses and the shirt issued to tournament volunteers, but Knight's presence was just another harbinger that the Nike-Woods relationship had been verbally consummated. Wally Uhlein, Ely Callaway and Hughes Norton were also among the spectators at Pumpkin Ridge, but it was Knight who had the biggest presence.

"What Michael Jordan did for basketball, [Woods] absolutely can do for golf," Knight said. "The world has not seen anything like what he's going to do for the sport. It's almost art. I wasn't alive to see Monet paint, but I am alive to see Tiger play golf, and that's pretty great."

The hype and speculation swirling at Pumpkin Ridge

was intoxicating. Tiger stayed focused, moving through qualifying and the first five rounds of match play unscathed. He shot 69–67 for medalist honors. The Witch Hollow course at Pumpkin Ridge had five par-fives. Tiger could reach four of them with irons. He wasted J.D. Manning three and two, played the last nine holes against Jerry Courville five under to win four and two, then stiff-armed 17-year-old Charles Howell three and one. Team Tiger was on schedule. Brunza was off the bag, retiring his 36-3 match play record. Replacing him was Bryon Bell, Tiger's best friend from Western High.

There were no hard feelings between Jay and Tiger. After the Manning match, they visited Waverley CC, site of Woods's third Junior Amateur title. Tiger thought Brunza could help better from outside the ropes, and Bell did a better job with club selection. "I trust Tiger's judgment about what he needs to win," Brunza said.

Tiger kept moving through the quarters and semis, dispatching D.A. Points, three and two, and Stanford teammate Joel Kribel, the Pacific Northwest and Western Amateur champion, three and one. At the Western, where he joined Ben Crenshaw, Curtis Strange, Rick Fehr, Scott Verplank and Phil Mickelson among the tournament's two-time champions, Kribel took pride in finally going one up on Woods, who won at Point O'Woods in 1994. "I've got something I can give him grief about," Kribel said. "Before this, it seemed like I was in a total eclipse behind him. Maybe I'm breaking through and people will see me a little bit."

The giant Tiger shadow moved back over Kribel on the back nine at Pumpkin Ridge. Kribel was two up after four holes, shot 32 on the front, but Woods hardened. He got up and down from a bunker, 50 yards out at the 11th, and made two birdies and an eagle coming in. Woods, now 41–3 in USGA competitions, pointed to his head. "All I have to do is stay strong up here," he said.

In the final Woods would face Steve Scott, a University of Florida sophomore-to-be who had lost to Buddy Marucci in the 1995 U.S. Amateur semifinals. Scott barely qualified, shooting 79–66, but moved through his bracket and defeated Florida teammate Robert Floyd for the right to face Woods. "If I should happen to be the one to upset him and keep him from winning three in a row, that would be pretty big," Scott said. Their match would turn into a classic, with 15,000 people overrunning Pumpkin Ridge to witness it. "All these people," Tida Woods said. "They are here to see my Tiger."

Maybe they were, but they ended up seeing a lot of Steve Scott, too. The Gator had his teeth in Tiger for most of the match. Three up after five holes, Scott shot 68 and was five up at the lunch break. He seemed relaxed and poised, spending the intermission in the merchandise tent with his girlfriend/caddy, Kristi Hommel. Woods cursed himself, then sat down with Team Tiger to assess the damages.

"For some reason, I just didn't have it," Woods said. "I can't explain it. I might have been tired. It might have been the situation I was in. I was searching for it. I just couldn't find it."

Harmon spotted a flaw in Woods's posture. Brunza helped him find his focus. He came out in the afternoon a different person and won the 21st, 22nd and 23rd holes to close the gap. At the 27th hole, Woods outdrove Scott by 113 yards, made birdie, and was one down with the back nine to play. "That gave me a big boost going into the back nine," Woods said. But this Scott kid was tenacious. He holed a flop wedge from an impossible lie one hole later, and celebrated by jumping in the air and pumping his fist. Scott shouldn't have done that. That was like tugging on Superman's cape.

Tiger put it right back in Scott's face. He ripped a 357-yard drive at the 553-yard 11th, reaching the green with a five-iron and draining a 45-footer with a 3-foot break for eagle. "I was feeling a little heated," Tiger said. "I took it out on the golf ball and happened to catch it perfectly flush."

Now it was the Gator's turn. He went two up again when Tiger missed a four-footer for birdie at the 32nd hole. This is when Scott sensed he might have delivered the knockout punch. He saw Tiger's head drop. "That's when I thought I'd win the match," he said. "He was looking frustrated. I thought that would rattle him a little bit, but it didn't."

The closest Woods had been to elimination before this was at Waverley, where Ryan Armour was dormie with two to play in the 1993 Junior Amateur. Going back there with Brunza on Thursday night had been an inspiration. He kept telling himself, "I've been here before," and with that to draw on, Tiger Woods did what very few athletes have the ability to do. He became John Elway and Michael Jordan in the fourth quarter.

First, Tiger birdied the 34th hole from five feet. One down with two holes to play. Momentum on his side. A seven-iron into the 35th hole. Another birdie coming up. But Tiger hit a bad shot, blocked in a seven-iron 30 right of the cup. Scott was in good shape. The match could be over right here. He had one option. Waverley. Tiger had to pretend he was Nicklaus, and he had to will the ball in the hole. "It was just one of those putts that I felt no matter what speed I hit it, it was going in," Woods said. His eyes got wide as the ball was tracking to the cup. He had that mask on his face, that wild-eyed look only the great ones get, and he started striding across the green, picking up momentum for that celebration dance of his, where he throws that one big uppercut and then a couple of jabs at the air, as the ball disappears in the hole. Tiger Woods had found that fifth gear once again, leaving Steve Scott standing there with nothing to say but, "Unbelievable."

Woods had hit 28 of the last 29 greens, shot 65 in his closing 18, and sent the match into overtime. Scott's 70 should have been good enough to win, but not against Tiger. In sudden death, he had an 18-footer for birdie on the first hole to putt Woods away. When he missed, short and right, it seemed inevitable. Tiger was already thinking ahead to the cut six-iron he'd hit at the 194-yard 11th, the 38th hole of the match. He smoked it over the flag, 5½ feet away, and Scott was feeling the heat. He missed the green, boldly tried to hole his chip, and lipped out a six-footer coming back for par. Tiger missed his birdie putt, but tapped in from 18 inches for par and the match. Both hands went above his head, almost in disbelief. It was the first time he led all day. It was the sixth time in six USGA finals that he had been taken to the final hole and beyond. "Given the circumstances," he said, "this has to be the best I ever played."

He was too numb to know the significance of winning three straight U.S. Amateurs. Tiger knew that in three days, there would be a news conference in Milwaukee. But when the writers asked that Sunday night at Pumpkin Ridge, he still told them he still wasn't sure of his decision. Then he drove to the house where he was staying near Pumpkin Ridge and told his parents, "Yep, it's time to go."

37

HEY, PRO

avid Fay, the U.S. Golf Association's executive director, had been working with Earl Woods since Tiger won the 1991 U.S. Juniors at Bay Hill, making sure there was never a breach of the amateur guidelines. At the urging of Mark McCormack, they met at Golf House, the USGA's headquarters in Far Hills, N.J., the week of the 1994 Buick Classic at Westchester. Tony Zirpoli, Jr., the USGA's director of regional affairs, amateur status and public golf, also served as a consultant but was not present at that meeting. "When it was clear that Tiger was going to be a prominent player, we made an offer to him and his father, much like we made to Phil Mickelson," Fay said. "The code can be tricky. We told them, 'We're here if you have any questions.' We wanted to make it quite clear that Earl had a grasp on the interpretation of amateur status."

One of the issues that ran through the course of their discussions was a minority golf clinic set up by John Merchant at Brooklawn CC near Bridgeport, Conn., the week of the 1995 U.S. Open. A major corporation was willing to fly Woods from Southampton across the Long Island Sound for the outing, but that would have been a violation of USGA regulations. Tiger could accept auto transportation, but he could not fly in the helicopter.

Merchant, an attorney based in Southport, Conn., the legal advisor to Team Tiger, and the first African American to serve on the USGA's executive committee, practically memorized the rules and decisions pertaining to amateur status. "Under oath, I would say we observed every regulation," he said.

The big question, of course, was Earl being employed by IMG as a consultant. It looked a little shady, but as long as there was no quid pro quo, the Earl Woods–IMG relationship was perfectly within the boundaries of the amateur status code. Just as long as he didn't designate himself as an agent, it was also within the guidelines for Earl to negotiate with Nike and Titleist. The USGA was not, as reported, looking to bust Earl and Tiger Woods.

"If you ask me, Earl always had his son's best interests at heart, and he received good counsel from a number of quarters, including the USGA," Fay said. "We made it clear to him we don't take away amateur status on words. It's actions. Actions by the player himself that would be constituted as legally binding."

It just looked too suspicious when, three days after winning the Amateur at Pumpkin Ridge, Tiger was standing at a podium in Milwaukee, making his announcement, while Hughes Norton worked the room, making sure key people had the right numbers and telling reporters that not in the history of sports has an athlete been as financially secure from day one. Obviously those deals hadn't been done in 72 hours.

Hughes Norton was clearly one of the big winners in this. Up until the last minute, Leader Enterprises of Orlando had been hoping to sign the Woods account and had representatives in the clubhouse at Brown Deer, trying to convince Tida that IMG would have a bad influence on her son's career. Tommy Limbaugh, a former college football coach and recruiter, had been working it hard for Leader. Limbaugh claimed the only reason Leader had a presence in Milwaukee was because Earl promised him at Pumpkin Ridge that IMG did not have Tiger's management contract locked up. Limbaugh interpreted that to mean it was still a ballgame. "They kept trying and trying and trying, but you know what? Ripping IMG worked against them," Norton said. "Tida told me that no one pitched their own plusses. That was all they could sell."

An argument could be made to give Norton golf's comeback of the year award. When Greg Norman and Nick Price left IMG two years ago, Norton had been demoted behind Alistair Johnston as head of Mark McCormack's golf division. By signing, he was once again the golden boy. By signing Tiger, all those hours of working Tiger and Earl had paid off in the most lucrative motherlode in the history of golf.

"I'm a voracious reader, and I had read a lot about Tiger," Norton said. "I'd like to tell you it was brilliance on my part, that I knew he'd win six consecutive USGA championships. The fact is, I was just doing my homework."

So was Wally Uhlein at Titleist, who began laying groundwork with the Woodses and John Merchant by supporting and underwriting the National Minority Golf Foundation long before it was politically correct. It may seem like Uhlein was flying under radar, but, as he states, "We would not be doing our job if we didn't get to know these people, and we don't have to make an apology for knowing them for years." Tiger had been using a Taylor Made driver but at the U.S. Open, he switched to a Cobra model (similar to the one Greg Norman was using) that featured a bore-through shaft. With as much clubhead speed as Norman and Woods generate, the reduced torque creates a more stable feel at impact. Cobra (which is owned by Titleist's parent company, American Brands) gave Woods the option of actually using equipment from two different companies. The other plus with Titleist was that Uhlein would allow Woods to use forged clubs, and not the perimeter-weighted cavity-backed irons that other equipment companies were forcing players to use. Tiger could stay with his Mizuno blades until he was comfortable with a set of irons that Titleist could make for him.

"You do the right things that are in the book," Uhlein said. "At the same time, you're walking the walk."

When Tiger walked to the podium that day in the media tent at Brown Deer Park golf course, and began with the seemingly innocent words, "I guess, hello, world," it began a new era. He was no longer the amateur golfer who hit scruffy two-piece balls out of plastic milk crates at the Stanford golf course range. Eldrick "Tiger" Woods, an African-Asian-American who had been programmed for this day since birth, was now a packaged product, a corporation, and an icon. The Stanford cap and the Lochinvar shirt were gone, replaced by the ever-present swoosh. This was the commercial payoff, a place in Nike's pantheon next to Jordan, Deion Sanders and Andre Agassi. The problem was that "Hello World" happened to be the theme and title for the Nike advertising campaign launched the following day with a $350,000 three-page layout in the *Wall Street Journal*, and in television commercials that aired on ESPN and CBS. The age of Tiger Woods's innocence had ended, but he was still a kid at heart.

Tiger had flown in on the Nike corporate jet, which was part of the deal, and he talked about finally trading in his father's old 1988 Toyota Supra for some new wheels. He was amazed that the Milwaukee tournament had given him a courtesy car, and with all the clothes and bags Nike had delivered to his hotel room. Technically, this was his first week on the job, but he hadn't seen any money yet. The night before at dinner, when the check was passed in his direction, the only thing Tiger could produce were some $25 gift certificates. "I'm still broke," he said. "I guess I'll still be eating at McDonald's for a while longer."

Other than that opening line, Tiger said all the right things. He was articulate, charming, sincere, prepared. He had matured from that opening news conference at Augusta National in 1995. The Stanford experience had served him well.

Tiger on the decision: "My timing is just right because let's go back to the '60s. I don't think I would have been able to play in these tournaments. Or I wouldn't have even been given the opportunity to play a golf course because of the racial segregations at the time. But now the doors are opening. Not all the doors. I'm not saying all the doors. But doors are opening and now we have an opportunity to get more diversity in such a great game. Tennis has come along. Every sport was like that. That's the way it was then. That's not the way it's going to be."

Tiger on the pressure: "One of the beauties is that I'm not even worried about that. It's nice to get a whole lot of money. The great thing is that I get to do something I've always dreamt of doing, ever since I was a little kid watching Nicklaus on TV or watching Watson play well or all those great players play. I'm out here now with them, playing."

Tiger on the value of a Stanford education: "I talked to my parents about that. They told me whether I get my degree tomorrow or 15 years from now, it doesn't matter.

They never gave me a time limit on it. As long as I get my degree. That's all that matters, and I made that promise to them and to myself and I will do that."

Tiger on his strengths and weaknesses: "I think my strongest point is my mind. I think I proved that in the U.S. Amateur, my ability just to hang in there. The weakest attribute is I just don't have the experience out here. I don't know what to say, what restaurants to eat in, so I'm going to have to stick to McDonald's. Something greasy."

Tiger on the money: "It wasn't about money. It was about happiness. Whether the time was right, and how happy am I? And that was the deciding factor. I know my golf game was good enough. Was the time right? Am I ready? And the answers all pointed to yes."

Tiger on his personification of a role model: "I've been very blessed to have the opportunity to become a role model. Not too many people in this world have that opportunity. And if I have the status that hopefully I will obtain, it's amazing how much money I could get to help the youth in the inner city and get them playing if they choose to play golf. But I think the most important thing is to have the opportunity, and hopefully with my status that I'm hopeful to attain that this will happen. God, I sure hope it does."

Sitting on the dais next to Tiger at Brown Deer, decked out in Nike from head to toe, Earl Woods waited for the news conference to end. At one point, Tiger reached around to squeeze his hand, thanking him and Tida for the job they did as parents. "They have raised me well and I truly believe have taught me to accept full responsibility for all aspects of my life," Tiger said.

It was a wonderful moment, not contrived at all, and it would have benefited Tiger if Earl hadn't been in one of his braggadocio moods when the news conference broke up and his father made himself available for interviews. Earl made three declarations at the GMO that did not really reflect well upon him, or Tiger. The first was that Tiger would have a bigger impact on the world than Muhammad Ali and Arthur Ashe. "There is no comprehension by anyone on the impact this kid is going to have, not only on the game of golf, but on the world itself," Earl said. This may turn out to be true, but it's not the type of thing to say before your son has made his first pro check.

The second faux pas came when Earl was asked what his son would do if he wasn't playing golf. "He would probably be a 400-meter runner and he'd be kicking Michael Jackson's ass. If you think his swing is pretty, you ought to see him run." Earl meant Michael Johnson, the 200- and 400-meter Olympic gold medal winner.

Finally there was Earl's Don King quote. "You don't want to tangle with Tiger on a golf course," Earl said. "He's what I visualize in the Old West as a black gunslinger. He'll cut your heart out in a heartbeat and think nothing of it." Again, maybe true, but not the thing you go around saying to reporters. The last thing Tiger needed was his father's hype.

There was already enough jealousy in the locker room. Robert Gamez had popped off. Scott Verplank said, "Those amateur championships aren't going to scare anyone." And Steve Stricker noted, "Here's a guy who hasn't even gotten his Tour card yet, and he's making $60 million." Earl hadn't done his son any favors.

"There will be some guys who will be jealous of him, for sure, the same way they're jealous of Greg Norman and his big airplane and big boat," said Davis Love III. "I've already heard some guys say, 'I hope I get him in the Shark Shootout or the Diners Club Matches,' stuff like that.

They'll be gunning for him, and that's good. That will make him tougher, and he'll prove to them how good he is."

Tiger certainly wasn't intimidated, either. The crowd on the first hole Thursday stretched from tee to green, and was sometimes six deep. He took the worn Tiger headcover off his driver, the one Tida made for him, the one with "Love From Mom" stitched in Thai, and bombed a drive 336 yards down the center of the fairway. People either gasped or laughed. As Larry Dorman wrote in the *New York Times*, ". . . these people were seeing Tiger Woods for the first time and realizing they would be seeing him for a very long time."

There were so many people that it was impossible for Tida to see her son play his first professional round of golf. "I think the only way to watch my Tiger now is on TV," she said. Walking with a media armband inside the gallery ropes, Jeff Rude of *Golfweek* counted 16 Nike logos on Tiger's body. "He wears swooshes like Deion Sanders wears jewelry," Rude wrote. GMO Executive Director Tom Strong estimated the first-day crowd at 20,000. "It's kind of hard to tell, though," he says, "because everybody is following one guy."

Tiger birdied three of the first five holes he played, shot 67, and still trailed by five strokes behind Nolan Henke. What he learned that day is that no matter who it is, somebody is going to shoot a low number on the PGA Tour. On that Thursday at Brown Deer, it was Henke. On Friday, it was Steve Lowery (64). One day soon, it would be him.

"I thought I got off to a really good start," Woods said. "It was an ideal start, really. Perfect. Shooting 67, that's a good number and I'm right in the tournament."

Well, not really. He shot 67–69, the same scores that took medalist honors at Pumpkin Ridge, and found himself eight shots off the lead. "It's weird," Woods said. "I'm going along making pars and then look up and it's like, 'Geez.' But then again, you've got to expect it. These guys can go really low." It all caught up with him Saturday, and he shot 73, returned to his hotel room, and crashed.

Bruce Lietzke, the 22-year veteran, played with him that day, and had nothing but high praise for Tiger's decorum and professionalism. "There wasn't a lot to see today, because he was off his game, but he handled himself wonderfully," Lietzke said. "He didn't let his temper get out of control. We need good guys at the top. If he does become the next ambassador of golf, I think it will be in good hands with him."

A closing 68 on Sunday included a hole-in-one, but even with three rounds in the 60s, Tiger Woods had finished tied for 60th. This clearly was not amateur golf anymore. This was the big leagues, and as Love and Harmon both advised, he'd be the hunted, not the hunter.

The future of golf had just entered the present tense. Let the record show that from August 29 to September 1, 1996, Eldrick "Tiger" Woods played his first tournament as a pro, recorded his first birdie as a pro, made his first hole-in-one as a pro, and deposited his first check as a pro. More important than all that, though, was that he acted like the professional he was.

"All the amateur titles Tiger has won won't mean anything, and he'll have to prove himself in a hard environment where there is no mercy," Harmon said. "He's got the intelligence and the tools to succeed very quickly. My only worry is that he's losing two of the best years of his life to do something that is very demanding for a young person. Considering everything, he's made the right decision, but he's going to have to grow up faster than I'd like him to."

38

DEALING THE RACE CARD

I t all caught up with Tiger Woods by the time he reached Toronto on Sunday night. He checked into his hotel room at the Westin Harbor Castle, pulled the shades on Lake Ontario, and slept in. In the last two weeks, he had played the equivalent of 12 rounds of competitive golf, won his third-straight Amateur, made the biggest decision of his life, had flown from Oregon to Wisconsin and now Canada, and had only really just begun. This week it was the Canadian Open at Glen Abbey. Next week it was Quad City. After that it was the B.C. Open, then the Southern Open, Las Vegas, Texas, maybe Disney, and hopefully the Tour Championship in Tulsa. For now, the goal was to make enough cash to finish in the top 125 on the PGA Tour money list. Do that, and he would avoid the crapshoot at PGA Tour Qualifying School. He made $2,544 at Milwaukee, and stood 344th on the money list. He had a long way to go.

The theme at the Canadian Open was Tiger Woods evolving quickly into a spokesman for social injustice in golf. As an amateur, Tiger always downplayed the race issue. But right out of the blocks, he was portrayed in a Nike television advertisement as an embittered and defiant African American who for years had been denied access to country clubs across the United States. These ads, which ran on ESPN during the GMO, on Fox during its Sunday coverage of the NFL, and on ABC during *Monday Night Football*, stirred an immediate reaction and, in some quarters, a backlash.

Set to a New Age symphony soundtrack and run over highlights of Tiger winning his three U.S. Amateurs, the words that seemed so out of character for Tiger were words that Nike obviously knew would raise brand awareness. Tiger had signed off on them, but nobody had ever heard him say:

> There are still courses in the U.S. I am
> not allowed to play
> because of the color of my skin.
> Hello World.
> I've heard I'm not ready for you.
> Are you ready for me?

On Tuesday night, *Nightline* devoted its entire show to the Tiger Woods phenomenon, focusing on the race issue and opening with the Nike commercial. At Milwaukee, Woods told the media that he had approved the copy because it provoked thought and raised a social issue that needed raising. "It's a message that has been long awaited because it's true," he said. "Being a person who is non-white, I've had to experience that. The Nike campaign is just telling the truth."

Maybe it was, but what bothered many was not the message, but the tenor in which it was delivered. Woods not only had never played the race card, but at the 1995 U.S. Open, he sent a statement to reporters, saying that to call him "black" or "African-American" would be incorrect. Handed out in the media center at Shinnecock Hills, it read:

"The purpose of this statement is to explain my heritage for the benefit of members of the media who may be seeing me play for the first time. It is the final and only comment I will make regarding the issue.

"My parents have taught me to always be proud of my ethnic background. Please rest assured that is, and will be, the case, past, present and future. The various media have portrayed me as African-American, sometimes Asian. In fact, I am both . . .

"On my father's side, I am African-American; on my mother's side, I am Thai. Truthfully, I feel very fortunate, and equally proud, to be both.

"The critical and fundamental point is that ethnic background and/or composition should not make a difference. It does not make a difference to me. The bottom line is that I am an American . . . and proud of it!"

During a news conference at Glen Abbey, Woods explained that he issued that statement out of respect to his mother. "By saying I'm black only it is an insult to my mom," Woods said. "If you understand the Asian cultures in general, denying that is a big insult. I love my mom to death, and I don't want to see her hurt in that way." Woods also confirmed that he received criticism from the African-American community for clarifying his heritage.

The weighty questions raised in the Nike ad were obviously playing off the fact that Woods was black, not a young man of mixed culture. Larry Dorman pointed out the hypocrisies in columns he wrote for the *New York Times* and *Golf World*. "The ads make you think, all right," Dorman wrote. "About exactly how far removed the advertising world is from the real world." Financial affairs expert James K. Glassman followed two weeks later in a column that ran in the *Washington Post*. Glassman called the ad campaign by

Nike "discordant, dishonest and even vile." He wrote: "The ad is telling blacks and other minorities that racism is so virulent in this country that, no matter how good you are, you will be despised and rejected by whites. You have to stand up to them (in Nikes, of course) . . . The only problem is that, in the case of Mr. Woods, it's based on a lie."

Glassman called Nike, requesting a list of the courses that Woods could not play. He got a call back from James Small, the company's public relations director, who admitted that, "Tiger Woods can play on any golf course he wants."

Jim Riswold, creative director for the Wieden & Kennedy advertising agency in Portland and the man who wrote the ad, stuck by his words. The ad was obviously successful, because people were talking about it. "It's created a hailstorm," Riswold said in an interview with Jeff Rude of *Golfweek*. "I can barely sit down, my butt hurts so much. A lot of the criticism comes from the golf community. It's close-knit. They don't like to be surprised. They like to know what's coming. Still, I don't understand why I'm accused of hurting golf."

On the putting green at Glen Abbey, Jim Thorpe said he thought Riswold missed a wonderful opportunity to send a positive message about Tiger Woods and his family. "Nike could have made a beautiful commercial if they had used his photos and used wording like, 'With hard work and education and unity among the family, I made it and you can do it too,' " Thorpe said. "And then Nike comes up with their line . . . I personally don't think Tiger's ever been turned away from a golf course because of the color of his skin. Maybe years ago guys were. But I personally don't think a young man of his status, with the best amateur record since Bobby Jones, and probably as well known as Bobby Jones,

I don't think any club in this country has ever turned him away from playing a round of golf. I personally feel if we let it die, it will all blow over. His job is to just play golf and prove to the world he can compete against the best players in the world, not to make racist statements. The (Charlie) Siffords, the (Lee) Elders, the (Calvin) Peetes, the Thorpes, the (Jim) Dents, we kind of smoothed that over. Just go play golf. I think the only pressure that will be is on his game.''

Until Woods came along, Thorpe was the only African-American playing the PGA Tour. During the Tuesday pro-am at Glen Abbey, he was coming down the 10th fairway, and just saw Tiger coming off the second tee. They had a brief conversation, with Thorpe telling Woods not to worry about some of the jealousy he was hearing in the locker room. He didn't really have the time to get into the Nike ad.

''This isn't anything like Jackie Robinson,'' Thorpe said. ''That road's been paved, plus he doesn't have to worry about making money, where we had to do the Mondays and stuff. Tiger's got it made. Every time Charlie Sifford won a tournament, they changed the rule at the Masters so he couldn't play. With Lee Elder and Charlie, you'd hear the N-word, but I didn't have to go through it. They pretty much paved the way, and every time I see these guys I thank them. I tell them I appreciate it. He told me, 'James, I really appreciate that. Sometimes the efforts we made, people don't give a damn.'

''The PGA Tour has been wonderful, not just for me but a lot of guys. We made a lot of money, met a lot of people, been a lot of places. You know what? My advice to Tiger would be, Just go do it. Forget about the other stuff. We've got political leaders who can take care of the races. It's like coming here. I'd be a damn fool to come to Glen Abbey Golf and Country Club and walk into their membership office and ask if they have any ethnic members. I've got to be stupid. All I have to know is we're playing for that one point two [million]. If they don't have any members, I don't give a damn. As long as we're playing for that money. That's what we have to look at. From the No. 1 player in the world to the guy who finishes rock bottom, if you can play, they're going to pay you. If you're colorful, they're going to pay you more. It's just like I told Calvin Peete one time, 'Peete, you're a wonderful player, you won 12 tournaments in four years. It's not that you're a bad guy. You're just quiet.' When it comes to doing corporate stuff, of course they're going to take the Tom Kites and the Peter Jacobsens over you. It's just that simple. It's not because you're black.

"Tiger should just go out there and be Tiger. He's a household name, a drawing card, one of the biggest drawing cards ever. I'd love to see him work closer with the inner city programs, get involved with a lot of minority programs and see if we can get more Tiger Woodses out there. There's no reason there should be this big a gap between Tiger Woods and me. He's a wonderful young man. God bless him."

Stuck in the middle of this hailstorm was Tiger Woods. At IMG's offices in Cleveland, Hughes Norton and Bev Norwood turned down interview requests from *Good Morning America*, the *Today Show*, *CBS Morning News*, *Later With Tom Snyder*, *ESPN Up Close*, *Outside the Lines*, *Fox's After Breakfast*, *Xtra*, *Nickelodeon*, *Access Hollywood*, *Live with Regis and Kathie Lee*, Roy Firestone, Oprah Winfrey, David Letterman, Jay Leno and Larry King, and guest appearances on *Martin* and *Cosby*. At Glen Abbey, Tiger posed for a *Golf Digest* cover and tried to keep his mind centered. The goal here was a Tour Card. He fought his driver and three-wood early in the week, shot 70-70, rested on Saturday while the remnants of Hurricane Fran wiped out the third round, then came back on Sunday to shoot the day's low round (68) in bad conditions to tie for 11th place.

As was the case in Milwaukee, he attracted a larger gallery during the final round than the last group, which had included tournament winner Dudley Hart. "It's nice to look in the gallery and see so many kids," he said. "They can relate to me. I'm not far from being a teenager myself. When people yell, 'You're the man,' I always say, 'Not legally.'"

The check for $37,500 moved Tiger up to 204th place on the money list, and he headed across the United States border to Quad City after having converted another group of people.

So far, Tiger was two-for-two at the box office.

"He already has a following that is big, or bigger, than J.D. [John Daly]," said David Duval. "He's kind of a cult hero."

39

ONE SWING AWAY

Bev Norwood, IMG's spokesman, told Tiger that he would visit some places during his seven-stop fall swing that he may never visit again. The Quad City Classic was one of those places. It takes a real PGA Tour blue-collar worker to know that the Quad Cities are Davenport and Bettendorf in Iowa, and Rock Island and Moline in Illinois. It is one of those tournaments that makes up in community support what it lacks in big-time atmosphere.

Tiger Woods gave it that big-time atmosphere. A story in the *Quad-City Times* said he was the biggest thing to hit Oakwood Country Club since grilled pork fillets. "We're all grinning so hard our faces hurt," said tournament chairman Todd Nicholson. An extra 15,000 walk-up tickets were printed, but it was not enough. Oakwood never saw crowds like the ones Tiger brought to town. Bob DeGeorge drove 300 miles and brought a three-step stepladder all the way from Brookfield, Mo. "We sold over 31,000 pork chop sandwiches, and that's more than we had people last year when the weather was bad," said tournament director Kym Hougham. "Normally we're at 65,000 people. We had over 100,000 with Tiger. At times we couldn't get tickets out to the gate fast enough, and the volunteers had to use Magic

Markers on the backs of people's hands. As prepared as we were, we weren't prepared enough."

Defending champion D.A. Weibring said he could feel the jolt in electricity that Tiger brought to the Quad Cities. "Tigermania is healthy for golf," Weibring said. "I don't think there's a resentment over Tiger. It's a fascination."

At Milwaukee, Lietzke had said the only resentment toward Tiger was coming from "the typical few bozos who get in trouble on pro-am day." In Canada, however, one player asked Steve Jones if the PGA of America really asked him to sit out the Grand Slam of Golf so Tiger could take his place. And John Cook, after reading Earl's "black gunslinger" quote in the *L.A. Times*, warned that this wasn't going to be quite the same as amateur golf.

"This is not college anymore," Cook said. "There's 150 guys who will look him straight in the eye and say, 'Let's go.' When he learns that and he earns the respect of his peers, he will be fine.

"Tiger's a good kid. He respects the players. I don't think the people around him respect what this is, why he's here and why he just earned all that money.

"That's the only thing that I worry about is people around him think that he can just kind of sidestep everything and go out and win 15 majors. That's not going to happen."

John Feinstein, author of *A Good Walk Spoiled* and a former tennis writer and columnist for the *Washington Post*, made the same point in a story he wrote for *Newsweek*, and in an interview with Forrest Sawyer on *Nightline*. He called Earl Woods a "tennis parent" and drew the comparison to Stefano Capriati, the overbearing father of Jennifer Capriati. "Like Stefano, Earl hasn't had a full-time job since 1988, 'sacrificing' to be at his son's side. Earl Woods says he won't travel fulltime with Tiger. That would be a bonus."

The Woodses took great offense to this characterization of their relationship. Tiger called it "slanderous," but again, Earl didn't do Tiger or himself a great service by being so visible at Quad City, and by telling Tom Johnston, a local columnist, "Before this tourney ends, he will hit one shot that people will be talking about for 30 years." Players read those quotes and started saying, "The kid's all right, but the old man's bad news."

Quad City was held the same week as the Presidents Cup, the international competition between the 12 best players from the United States and the 12 best players from Australasia and Africa, so the field wasn't that strong. Odds on Tiger to be the winner were 20–1 at the Imperial Palace Race & Sports Book in Las Vegas, which looked like a great bet Saturday night after Tiger went 64–67 in the second and third rounds to open a one-stroke lead over Ed Fiori. Leaving Dulles Airport and the Presidents Cup the next morning were Dorman of the *New York Times*, Diaz of *Sports Illustrated*, Ron Sirak of AP, Jeff Babineau of the *Orlando Sentinel* and Phil Rogers of the *Dallas Morning-News*. The press tent on Sunday at Robert Trent Jones Golf Club was deserted as all the top writers flew to Moline Airport for what was anticipated to be Tiger's first professional victory. That 20–1 bet looked like pretty good money.

"He hits wedge to even par four and he reaches even par five in two," Fiori said. "How do you beat a guy like that?"

The answer is: You don't. You let Tiger beat himself. It doesn't happen often, but it did on Sunday at Quad City. Through three holes, Tiger had opened a three-stroke lead. At the fourth hole, a 460-yard par-four, Tiger wanted to hit his patented power cut, a shot where he takes the hands out of his swing and hits it hard, left-to-right. Instead of the power cut, Tiger hit the dreaded "double cross," a left-to-left hook that splashed in a pond. At that point, Tiger probably should have taken his drop, chipped out, and attempted to make an up-and-down bogey from the fairway. Instead, he elected to hit a six-iron 200 yards through an opening in the trees. The heroic shot turned out to be a bad play, as his ball hit an oak limb and took a hard detour into the swamp. From there, it was pretty easy to make a snowman, a quadruple bogey eight. Three holes later, trying to make something happen, Tiger took driver at the 344-yard seventh, hit wedge onto the green eight feet, and proceeded to four-jack for a double bogey. It was like the end of the first round at Oakland Hills, all over again.

But instead of quitting, Tiger sucked it up and finished strong. He played the last six holes in two under to finish tied for fifth, four shots back of Fiori, who won for the first time since the 1992 Bob Hope. "Walking up the 14th fairway, he said to me, 'If I birdie out, can I still win,' " said his caddy, Mike "Fluff" Cowan. "That probably impressed me as much as anything."

Afterward, Tiger admitted he saw progress. "It's hard to say right now what I learned," he said. "I'll know better in a couple of days. I will tell you one thing: I will learn a lot from this."

That night, Woods went out to dinner with Earl, Butch, Norton and Bryon Bell (who was now a premed student at UC San Diego) at their hotel in Moline. They decided that Tiger was mentally fatigued, otherwise he would have punched out on the fourth hole and made no worse than double bogey, and that he never would have four-putted from eight feet at the seventh. By the time dessert came around, they were laughing about how bad Tiger had taken the gas. With the tie for fifth, Tiger earned $42,150 and moved up to 166th in the money standings. He was trending in the right direction. He was one swing away.

"The one thing he's going to learn from this is how hard it is to win a Tour event," Harmon said. "The way things were going, I don't think he thought it was too hard. Even though I wish he had won the tournament, in the long run, this may be better for him. He'll come away from this realizing that it's not easy to win out here, no matter who you are."

40

ALMOST THERE

The B.C. Open is the upstate New York version of the Quad City Classic, with steak and chicken replacing the grilled pork fillets. Going there is like going back in a time warp to the way professional golf used to be in America, before the days of private jets, courtesy cars and $60 million bonus babies like Tiger Woods. Held every September in the Binghamton, N.Y., suburb of Endicott, the tournament is financed by a community that has better things to do with its money than support a $1 million golf event. Yet every year, a good samaritan named Alex Alexander checks the books and decides there's enough in the budget for the B.C. Open to return the following September. There have been 26 B.C. Opens played at En-Joie Golf Club since 1971, but none with as much national and international attention as what Tiger Woods brought to town.

Tiger noticed the deprivation checking into the Best Western Regency Hotel on Monday. This was not the Lodge at Pebble Beach, the Saturnia Spa at Doral, or the Four Seasons Resort and Club in Irving. This was downtown Binghamton, N.Y., after defense contract cutbacks had gutted IBM and General Electric. As Tiger told a friend, "Life looks hard around here." Sixty million bucks would go a long way in Binghamton, N.Y. It was good for Tiger to see this side of the tracks. Hopefully, it made him realize how privileged he was to be 20 years old and never have to worry about money again.

Although he had been denying it in his news conferences, Tiger had reached the point of being golfed-out. This was his fifth straight week of competition, starting with 164 holes in six days at the Amateur. He had no idea what the villa IMG had picked out in Orlando looked like, but he was thinking how nice it would be to put the clubs away for a week and find out. On the phone from his home in Cleveland Friday night, Norton said he hoped Tiger would earn enough to get his card, and skip the trip to Columbus, Ga., for the Buick Challenge.

The B.C. Open was Tiger's first week on the road alone, and he welcomed it. Earl had headed home to California from Moline and Hughes flew out on business Tuesday, leaving Tiger to his hotel suite. This was Earl's way of showing he wasn't the "tennis parent" that Feinstein had characterized him as. "I give him his space to grow, let him make his own mistakes," Earl said from his home in Cypress. "He's out there by himself."

Jerry Chang, Tiger's best friend and teammate at Stanford, also came to Earl's defense. "This idea that his dad manipulates him is totally untrue," Chang said. "All I've seen from his parents is love for Tiger and a lot of respect. If people want to equate that love in the family with manipulation, that's fine."

Tiger's standard line needed no explanation. "My father's my best friend," he said.

En-Joie Golf Club did not set up particularly well for Tiger's game. The greens were spiked up, and he had to hit iron off a bunch of the tees, but once again the crowds were suffocating. His hotel suite looked like an Edwin Watts golf store, with boxes of Nike clothes and stacks of putters and drivers. He stood on the 10th tee at 9:09 Thursday morning with church bells ringing and two anonymous pros named Joe Daley and John Maginnes with them. Daley, an ex–club pro with zero body fat and maybe the worst action on tour, and Maginnes, a swarthy ball beater from North Carolina, were also on the bubble, fighting for a PGA Tour card. It was a clear morning, no wind, and Tiger hit two iron shots to five feet and made the putt for birdie. It was 9:20 a.m., and he was one under. At his 14th hole, a 565-yard par-five, Tiger hit driver-driver to the front fringe, but missed a six-footer for par and scolded himself. He had done the same thing at the Amateur, when he was five down at lunch. He came in the clubhouse, threw his hat around, and started swearing. "I could feel myself getting complacent, probably because I've been on the road so long," Tiger said afterward. "I had to snap out of it. If you do it right, you can channel the anger."

The round ended on the ninth hole, a 425-yard par-four back to the clubhouse. Woods hit a booming, high cut that left him less than 100 yards to the green. Coming off the tee, Maginnes turned and said to him, "It's not fair to hit it like that." Tiger beamed and made birdie to shoot 68, two strokes off the lead. Earlier in the week, he had pumped iron at Gold's Gym in Binghamton, squatting up to 250 pounds and doing chest work with 65-pound dumb bells. At 155 pounds, he was a lot stronger than he looked.

"He played pretty solid today," said Fluff Cowan, his caddy. "But he's picky. He doesn't think he hit it worth a shit, but we'll go to the range and work it out. He practices plenty, but he doesn't need to hit 20 buckets of balls to get the job done. He's pacing himself, because he's trying to do something in seven weeks that everybody's had all year to do. I will say he's got as much savvy as a lot of guys who've been doing it for a long time. He may be 20, but he's way beyond his years."

Down on the driving range, Tiger worked with Fluff and Blaine McCallister to get the speed back in his swing. Harmon wasn't around, but they both knew what Butch wanted out of Tiger: more width to his backswing, stronger flex in his right knee to prevent tilting, and less wrist release through the ball. Tiger gets enough body rotation through the ball—without firing his hands—that McCallister was still raving about a drive Woods hit in the U.S. Open. "Nobody can hit it like him," McCallister said. "I played with him at Oakland Hills, and at 18, he hits it about 10 yards short of the crosswalk. He hit nine-iron, a smooth nine-iron. But look how high his hands get. It just creates more arc. David hit it like that when he first came out of Tour School. I told him to just enjoy it, don't get caught up in it. There's 155 guys out here trying to make a living, but he keeps playing good. I don't anticipate Tiger having too much trouble."

Friday's round ended with an explosive burst of three closing birdies for a 66. He was on every par five in two shots, but still had dropped a shot to the lead. It was Pete Jordan's turn to go off. He shot 64 and was at 131. Tiger was tied for second with Fred Funk and Brian Claar. Even though he teed off at 2:45 p.m., a big crowd awaited at the 18th green. Many of them were there for a Tanya Tucker concert, but Fluff and Tiger didn't know that.

"Don't these people have someplace to go for dinner?" Fluff wondered.

Gary Smith of the Golf Channel asked Woods if he was a Tanya Tucker fan.

"Who?"

"Tanya Tucker! She's a country singer."

"Country? Noooooooooooo. God, no."

He was brought to the press room for an interview. Outside, fans spotted him in the plate glass windows, and they started chanting "Tii-ger . . . Tii-ger . . . Tii-ger." A wave with his Nike cap brought a roar. This would have been his first week back at Stanford. Outside the locker room, there was no security guard. He was ambushed trying to get to his Ford Explorer, which was parked in the Players Lot. He walked up Main Street, signing as he went. Cars slowed down to avoid the wave of people. A white girl, maybe age 12, yelled out, "I love you."

Tiger made eye contact. The girl's girlfriend screamed, "Oh my God! He looked at you!"

On Saturday, Tiger had it two under going to the 13th hole, a 441-yard par-four. He hit nine-iron to 15 feet and made it, then hit four-iron to the 212-yard 14th that floated down to six feet. Denny Shriner, doing play-by-play for The Golf Channel, said, "Tiger's going to have to get some balls with heat shields if he keeps bringing them in from that altitude." He closed out the run by holing a bunker shot for birdie at the 15th and shooting 30 on the back nine again for another 66. It didn't close the gap on the lead, but at least he didn't lose ground. Funk shot 63 to tie Jordan at 197. Tiger was at 200, and still not happy with the way he was hitting the ball.

"My short game gives me the ability to get up and down from a lot of places," he said. "I did that the first two days. I'm still in contention. It's nice when you don't exactly have it, and you're still in contention. Look at the hallmark of all the great players, especially Nicklaus. They've had the ability to turn a 72 or a 73 into a 67 or a 68. I've been doing that a lot on Tour when I haven't had my best ball-striking rounds. I hit it horrible today, just awful."

While there was still daylight, Tiger jumped in a courtesy van for a quick trip to the driving range. He had spoken to Butch on the phone from the locker room, and wanted to work on some things. About 200 children ran two miles at dusk to watch him hit balls. Fluff, who had twice won the caddy tournament, was his eyes. At 6:55 p.m., Tiger ripped the Velcro on his glove and headed to the parking lot. He signed a few autographs when he was through, but didn't stop walking to the van. Would he have any trouble sleeping? "No."

There was no final round. Rain came in and wiped it out. Funk played off with Jordan, and won with a birdie. Tiger was credited with a third-place finish, his best as a pro, and earned $58,000. That moved him up to 128th on the money list, which secured his playing privileges for the 1997 season. A finish in the top 150 made him a Tour member, and guaranteed him unlimited sponsor exemptions. Every sponsor in the world would want him. He was in. He was Tiger Woods.

That night, packing up at the Regency, Tiger assessed the first four weeks of his pro career. Hughes had flown back from Cleveland, and he was going to accompany Tiger on the private jet to Orlando, where he would register for a driver's license to establish Florida citizenship. Tiger Woods had been able to pick up the pieces, put Quad City behind him, and move on. In a month, he had played his way onto the PGA Tour. Now, he wanted more. "I've just got to keep going," he said.

41

ROOKIE MISTAKE

Before he left the B.C. Open, Tiger was asked about the rest of his schedule. If he earned enough money to get his Tour Card, would he take time off, or would he honor his commitments and play out the string? Tiger was diplomatic. He had three tournaments remaining on his schedule, the Buick Challenge, the Las Vegas Invitational and the La-Cantera Texas Open. "They've been nice enough to grant me an exemption and I feel a need to honor them," Woods said. "And if I couldn't do it this year, I would talk to the tournament director about coming back next year."

Woods went back to Orlando and started to have second thoughts. Since August 19, he had played 23 rounds of competitive golf in 35 days. Maybe he was 20 years old, but he wasn't Superman. His tank was empty.

Still, he made the effort. He got back in the private jet and flew to Pine Mountain, Ga., on Tuesday morning, September 24. Bob Berry, tournament director for the Buick Challenge, met him at the airport. Everything, according to Berry, seemed fine. Tiger did a news conference and played a nine-hole practice round with Davis Love and Peter Jacobsen. Tiger talked to Davis about making the Ryder Cup team, but Fluff could see the fatigue. "He looked beat. He was just kind of putting one foot ahead of the other," he said. "But I didn't think it wasn't anything a good night's sleep couldn't cure."

That night, Woods went back to the house he was renting at Callaway Gardens and decided to withdraw. Earlier in the day, he assured Berry that he would be in the pro-am on Wednesday, and at the Fred Haskins Award Dinner Thursday night, where he would be honored as college golf's Player of the Year. Now, he was thinking about withdrawing.

"He looked me straight in the eye and said, 'I'll be there,'" Berry said. But late Tuesday night Berry got a call from Norton, and at 6:15 the following morning in the Buick Challenge tournament office, he and Mark Russell of the PGA Tour staff huddled to come up with a plan. They called Norton and offered to let Tiger skip the pro-am, get some rest, and tee it up Thursday. Norton called back at 6:30. Tiger was already at the airport. The plane was fueled and ready to taxi down the runway.

That day, Norton issued a statement on Tiger's behalf. Claiming he was mentally exhausted, and that it would be a "disservice to myself and those who came to watch me play," Woods elected to skip not only the tournament, but the dinner. "The past five weeks have been the most challenging in my life—and at the same time the most physically and mentally draining," Woods said. "Withdrawing from a tournament at the last minute is not something that I am accustomed to doing. I have expressed my apologies and my regrets to the officials of the Buick Challenge."

First of all, Woods did not personally do that. He let Norton do the dirty work. Secondly, Norton should have stood up to Woods, advised him to rest, maybe skip the tournament, but at least show up for the dinner. His father had committed Tiger to it four months earlier. More than 200 dignitaries had traveled to Callaway Gardens at the tournament's expense. A video was produced. Including flowers, decorations and the special meals, it cost Buick $30,000 to put the event on.

Norton didn't see what the big deal was all about. "It's tough for the tournament here, but [withdrawing] was not something [Tiger wanted] to do," he said. "There wasn't any other choice. He's going to take three days to try and recharge his batteries and relax . . . I'm amazed that it took this long. I thought he might hit the wall before now. I think most people would have withdrawn from B.C."

The reaction was what it should be—pointed and strong against Tiger. He had violated protocol and broken an unwritten rule. It made him appear like he was bigger than the game. "I feel badly for him. But he's stepped off the anonymity sidewalk; he's in the parade now," Jacobsen said. "He's going to be scrutinized, and he'll probably take some heat for this. One thing, you can't compare him to Nicklaus and Palmer anymore because they never did this."

Tom Kite: "I can't ever remember being tired when I was 20."

Davis Love: "Everybody has been telling him how great he is. I guess he's starting to believe it."

Curtis Strange, a former Haskins winner: "This tournament was one of seven to help Tiger when he needed help to get his card, and how quickly he forgot. But I bet the Buick people won't forget."

Tiger was back in Orlando when these quotes ran in *USA Today*. Larry Guest, columnist in the *Orlando Sentinel* and a noted critic of IMG, crafted a "Dear Tiger" column, advising Tiger to be careful in his dealings with Norton. "You'll recover from this deep rough," Guest wrote, "and hopefully learn from this PR gaffe, which doesn't totally surprise me given that your hired advice is International Management Group—an outfit notorious for raising high-handedness to an art form . . .

"The next time a sticky situation arises—and there will be more of them, for sure—address it head-on. *Never, never, never* again leave your IMG rep Hughes Norton and a cold, impersonal, prepared statement to plead your case, as happened this week. The golf world is distrustful of IMG execs, and of Norton in particular. Your own pleasing smile and natural charm will be far more effective in defusing volatile situations and disarming critics.

"Face the music. Be accessible. Openly apologize if the case warrants. This is definitely one of those cases. Say you're sorry. Say you'll try to make it up to Columbus and the Haskins Award sponsors. Cop a plea that you're young and learning. The world will give you the benefit of the doubt and drape an arm around your shoulder."

The problem was that Earl and Butch weren't out on the road with Tiger. They both said that if they had been at Callaway Gardens, Tiger would have been at that dinner. That didn't do the Haskins Commissioner or Bob Berry much good. Berry received a short apology note from Tiger, but it was dictated and not personally written, and it came, unsigned, from IMG's office in Cleveland. There were no promises made to return for the 1997 Buick Challenge, as Tiger said there would be at the B.C. Open. There were no offers to reschedule the dinner.

But Tiger must have read Guest's column, which appeared Friday, September 27. He personally called Berry on Sunday to apologize. "We were right in the middle of the rain delay, and I gave him all the time he wanted, but he didn't have a whole lot to say," Berry said. "He said, 'Maybe

I'll see you next year,' and left it at that. It's history as far
as I'm concerned. I don't have any hard feelings. He's got to
learn, I guess. Maybe when he matures . . .''

Over the weekend, Tiger went fishing with Mark
O'Meara on one of the lakes in the Butler Chain near Isleworth. Sunday they played golf, even though Tiger claimed
that he didn't touch a club during his time off. At one point
in the conversation, Tiger must have thought he had a sym-
pathetic ear.

''The media's been hard on me,'' he said.

O'Meara told it to the kid straight. He told him he
should have gone to the dinner. He also told him, ''The
media made you what you are.''

42

VIVA LAS VEGAS

The call letters on all noncommercial aircraft begin with the letter "N." Greg Norman's Gulfstream IVSP is N1GN. The plane Tiger Woods flew on to Las Vegas, the one parked at McCarran Airport, had the call letters NIKE. Tiger swooshed in from Orlando fresh-faced and ready to go. He was staying at the MGM Grand because Butch is friends with Frank Tutera, and Frank had been a PGA Tour rules official before taking a job as senior vice president at the MGM. Tutera set up Tiger with his own penthouse suite that featured a television in every room, an expansive view of the Vegas Strip, and its own private elevator. It wasn't quite the Best Western in Binghamton, but it would do.

The temptation at the MGM was the blackjack tables Woods walked by every day in the casino. He was still under age, and that fake identification card wasn't working anymore. It was OK for some of the bars at Stanford, where the bartenders and bouncers would let it slide. Now, everybody knew him, and it had gotten him in a little trouble two weeks earlier at Quad Cities.

On September 11, the night before the opening round, Tiger slipped into the Lady Luck Riverboat Casino in Bettendorf. According to an Associated Press report, he played blackjack for 42 minutes before being spotted on surveillance tapes. The story said Woods did not drink alcohol, but did produce a form of I.D. that allowed him to gamble. The legal age in Iowa is 21. Tom Peters, a commissioner's representative for the Iowa Gaming and Racing Commission, told AP that no charges would be filed against the casino or Woods. The Des Moines Register ran the story on the front page of its sports section, on October 13, with the headline: "Underage Tiger Woods gambled on Iowa visit."

Nice. Also in Quad City, Tiger reportedly had tried to enter a popular nightspot called The American Bar. He was stopped at the door by a bouncer, who questioned the I.D. It was pointed out that perhaps celebrity-VIP status should be granted, since this was Tiger Woods.

"I don't care if it's the Lion King," the bouncer said. "You ain't getting in unless you have an I.D."

Harmon claims there is no truth to the Lion King story, because he was with Tiger the whole time. But imagine, for a moment, what it must be like: you're 20 years old, got $60 million in the bank, and you can't spend it. You've done nothing but play golf for a month, and every time you go out, Big Brother is there, watching. He was now more guarded, because he knew the media would write about it, and he could understand that, but still . . . still, couldn't it be the way it used to be?

Now he was in Vegas, Sin City, with the Taj Mahal suite at the MGM. All that money in his pocket. All those blackjack tables at his fingertips. All that temptation tugging at his heart. And he abstained. "To his credit, he didn't try. To his credit and to save my job," Tutera said. "Probably because we stayed in his hip pocket," said Harmon, adding, "I'd hate to have the press covering all my screwups when I was 20 years old. He just happens to be in a fishbowl, and everything he does is news."

Tuesday at the TPC-Summerlin, Tiger conducted his

weekly news conference. By now he knew the questions. He had his programmed answers. The only thing new would be the Buick Challenge and the Fred Haskins Dinner. He'd address it once, and move on.

It hurt Woods that three of the guys who took shots at him—Love, Jacobsen and Strange—were supposedly his friends. Love was a Titleist man. Jacobsen and Strange were both part of the IMG family, and Jacobsen was Mr. Nike. Tiger was prepared for the question, saying he had received messages from the players who criticized him, and turning it around on Steve Hershey, the *USA Today* golf writer who wrote the story. "The guy who wrote it may have had an agenda," Woods said. "Those guys actually had been very nice to me. Davis has been great, Peter's been great, and those guys have told me that that's not exactly what they said, so it's just one of those things."

The tournament started Wednesday, a day earlier than most PGA Tour events, and ran for 90 holes through Sunday. Tiger was paired in the opening round with Nevada governor Bob Miller at the Las Vegas Hilton course. He shot one under 70, and was tied for 83rd. Miller and Woods talked Stanford, since the governor's son was attending the university. The story of the day was Funk, who also played the Hilton course and shot 63, one stroke off the lead. Funk woke Wednesday morning and read quotes in the *Las Vegas Sun* from Tiger's news conference. Asked about the B.C. Open, Woods innocuously said he wished the final round hadn't been rained out, because he thought he had a chance to win. To illustrate just how hypersensitive the middle-class was about Tiger, Funk took it as an insult.

"I think I was walking away with that one and nobody was going to catch me," Funk said. "I sure wasn't going to let him catch me. He failed to mention he was six shots down with about 10 holes to go if we had kept going. I got a little fired up about that, all the articles have been going, 'Tiger, Tiger, Tiger,' kind of forgetting everybody else is playing good golf, too."

Tiger jumped back into the picture on Thursday, shooting 63 at Summerlin in a round that could have been in the 50s. He started with three straight birdies, but went parbogey on the back-nine par-5s that he easily reached in two shots. The upside was his hot putter. On Tuesday night, Harmon spotted Scotty Cameron of Titleist and grabbed one of the limited edition Scottydale models that were earmarked for Japan. Butch just wanted Tiger to have a different look, something to get a little confidence going. He also had Tiger work on putting a little more hinge in his backstroke. Tiger had been getting the blade shut, and pulling a lot of short putts. But all everybody was talking about, still, was the Buick Challenge and the Fred Haskins Dinner, and Tiger.

Paul Azinger shot low (64) that day, and was brought in the press tent at Summerlin. Azinger's always has a good perspective, and he was stopped going out the door by Mark Purdy, the sports columnist for the San Jose Mercury News, and Bob Burns, golf writer for the Sacramento Bee. He stuck around for 15 minutes, which is something Woods has to learn to do. He's got to hang out, develop relationships like the ones Azinger has, and he'll get better treatment in the press.

"The good news," Azinger was saying, "is he doesn't ever have to worry about money as long as he lives. The bad news is there are two potential bad-news scenarios. And one I don't think will ever happen but he could burn out and say, 'Hey, why am I doing this? I don't need the money.' I don't foresee that happening. The other bad news is there's resentment. There's resentment from players and people in general. The unfortunate thing is the numbers came out at all. Nobody knows how much Callaway paid me. Nobody knows how much Titleist pays me. Nobody knows how much Guess

Watch paid me. How much Tropicana paid me. But because of Hughes Norton, *everybody* knows, everybody knows. There are people who resent that. It's just human nature."

"Do you?" Azinger was asked.

"I don't resent it. I think it's great. Now if I play good, it drives my market value up. I love it. Honest to God I don't begrudge anybody anything. It's not for me to determine Tiger Woods's market value. I don't know what Tiger Woods's market value is. Hughes Norton knows what it is. He pulled it off. IMG pulled it off. Those are great numbers. I wished I was gettin' them, but I didn't win three straight U.S. Amateurs and turn pro at the age of 20. I just think that he might have been better served had those numbers not been disclosed."

"Have you talked to him?"

"I haven't talked to him. Everybody really likes Tiger out here. He's an incredibly likeable kid. The withdraw thing [in Georgia], there were a couple of articles I read that suggested, 'Hey man, you've got a tremendous smile and a great personality, and if you have to do it, you do it. Don't let somebody write a withdrawal letter, an excuse for you. I think Larry Guest wrote one of the stories, and the other one was Furman Bisher [in the *Atlanta Journal-Constitution*]."

"Is what he did that big a deal, where his agent says there isn't a player who hasn't done the same thing?"

"Well, at the same time there isn't a pro who can get $40 million from Nike either. He was going to be the main draw, plus there was the dinner. There were a lot of things that opened him up for some criticism. Hey man, I withdrew from the Canadian Open a couple of weeks ago and nobody said a word. No great loss. I withdrew on Monday morning. I was at home. I just never went."

"Is there a difference between withdrawing Monday morning and Tuesday night in protocol?"

"Generally nobody notices. If John Daly would have done it, it would have been a big flap. If Tiger Woods does it, it's a flap. If Fred Couples does it, I don't think there's a flap, maybe I'm wrong. I don't think there's any doubt that Tiger Woods is the No. 1 draw right now on this tour, and the fact that it happened opened him up to criticism, and the way it was handled. Again, I think Hughes should have been a better counselor and advisor to Tiger Woods. He's only 20, man."

"Stuff you had to learn like that at 20?"

"Hey man, I never had to pay income taxes the first four years I tried to turn pro. I lived in a motor home for three years. Nobody knew who I was. I got big gradually, and I wasn't that big. I was never a giant draw . . . nobody has been on this level since John Daly was and still is. He was a giant in this game. He'd walk down the fairway and you could tell it was his group because there would be masses of people following him. Now they're following Tiger Woods. I think what ought to be written is a story about how for so long there were no superstars out here, and where was golf going? Now, Greg Norman's here, Fred Couples is here, John Daly is here, Tiger Woods is here."

Burns read a quote off his notebook from Payne Stewart's news conference, where Stewart said that he wasn't jealous because Tiger Woods had put golf on the front pages of the sports sections during the baseball playoffs and football season.

"That's a great line," Azinger said. "I think for the most part everybody likes Tiger Woods. He's just a nice, likeable guy. The guy's not even legal for crying out loud. He can't even gamble in the casino. He's got to have people around him."

"Do you think if he turned around and went to the dinner last week, this would have a totally different spin?"

"Definitely . . . That's all he had to do. In hindsight I think he probably wished he withdrew from the pro-am and played in the tournament, but obviously he needed to play here, this is the big-money tournament. I think he just realized once he got his card that he just didn't need to play there and it was a perfect place for a week off. Unfortunately he showed up and the dinner was planned and all that happened. It was one of those things where somebody should have said, 'Hey look. If you withdraw Tiger, it's going to be a big deal. Think about it.' It's one of those things where maybe the agent should have said, 'I'm not going to withdraw for you. I'm not going to write the letter to the tournament.' If Tiger handled it himself, maybe it would have gone over better. But the fact it didn't happen that way opened him up to criticism. Eventually people are going to forget about it, but it's a good story right now. He's 20 years old, and he's going to be out here for another 30 years before he goes to the Senior Tour. This is absolutely nothing. The kid withdrew from a tournament. It should have been handled differently, but it's not a big deal. I wouldn't blame Tiger Woods. I would blame his agent. That's what I'd do."

Friday at the Desert Inn, Woods again started hot: Five under through six holes, with an eagle and three birdies. In a 27-hole stretch beginning Thursday at Summerlin, he had gone 15 under par, but instead of taking it deeper, Tiger backed off. At the 15th, a par-five, he hit a long iron approach to the green from an awkward stance, and reinjured the groin pull that had dogged him at the Amateur. From there, Tiger literally limped in, three-putting the 15th for par, missing a little birdie putt at the 16th, making bogey at the 17th, and saving par at the 18th with a gutsy iron shot from a fairway sand trap. He blew off all interviews after the round to get treatment. There was speculation that he might withdraw.

Tiger kept everybody hanging until he came back out Saturday and shot 67. Seeing Woods limp up the 18th fairway, Rude said, "Look at him. Venturi. Congressional. Sixty-four." A closing par and Woods was at 268, four shots off the lead, tied for seventh place. From the gridlock at 83rd on Wednesday, he had climbed 76 places on the leader board. He had six more places to go. A big line formed at the autograph tent. Woods took a glance and turned away. He had to get treatment in the locker room. The MGM stretch limo was waiting outside the clubhouse. Yeah, this beat Quad City and B.C.

Sunday was the stuff that makes for legends. Tiger turned in thirty-two, made birdies at 11, 13, and 14, drove it over the 15th green, 317 yards away, with a three-wood, and made par, then hit driver-six-iron into the 560-yard 16th to shoot 64. It was a high voltage madhouse. Behind the 17th tee, Greg Suttles of Las Vegas screamed out, "LET'S GO, MR. WOODS! SHOW 'EM WHAT YOU GOT! IT'S ALL YUUUUUU." Mr. Suttles was one of the many black men, women and children who traipsed around Summerlin to check this Woods kid out. "Ask Robert Gamez, 'What does he think of my man now?' " Suttles said.

Walking up the 18th, Big Al Ramsey was head of the security force escorting Woods around the course. "He's way cool, man," Ramsey said. "I was at his news conference and the media tried to bait him, get him to react to what some of those old pros were sayin' back east. He told 'em, 'Man, I know those guys. They don't mean it.' "

Standing in the 18th fairway, describing the shot for ESPN, Frank Beard whispered in his hand-held microphone, "The pins back left. The water's left. But nothing seems to bother him. He doesn't know what water and sand are. He certainly doesn't know what fear is."

Tiger Woods hit two-iron, nine-iron into the 18th green on a 444-yard par-four, two-putted for par, and went to the practice tee anticipating a playoff. Love, Mark Calcavecchia and Kelly Gibson were behind him with a chance to tie. Tiger came off the 18th green and Butch was there to tell him, "This isn't over yet," but Woods knew that already. ESPN asked for an interview. He declined. Beard, the on-course commentator, tried again on the practice range. Woods politely said no. "He said he absolutely would not do it," Beard said. "He's a cocky bastard."

Tiger hit balls. He had a three-wood, because he knew it was the club he'd use in the playoff—if there was a playoff. "The Girl from Ipanima" was playing in the Hard Rock tent. The blimp's motors could be heard overhead. The sound of Tiger's shots, one every forty-five seconds, interrupted the background music.

"Can we get a report on what's happening out there?" said Fluff.

"If there's a playoff, do you know what hole it starts on?" said Butch. Michael Carey, operations coordinator, listened to his walkie-talkie.

"Davis just birdied 16 to tie." Frank Cavanaugh of the PGA Tour's field staff drove up in a golf cart. The sudden death playoff would be holes 18, 17 and 18 again, if needed. "All right," he said, "we'll see you on 18."

It was 3:45 p.m.

"Calcavecchia and Gibson had to finish by now," said Fluff.

"I didn't hear any roars," said Butch. Lee Patterson, the tour's media official, came out from the press tent.

"Where's Davis," said Tiger.

"It looks like about eight feet," said Patterson.

"Hell of a shot," said Butch.

"It's a hell of a shot with that water there," said Tiger. Thirty seconds passed.

"Do you know if he made it yet?" Tiger said. Mike Shea's voice can be heard on Patterson's walkie-talkie.

"Rolling . . . rolling . . . rolling . . ." Pause.

"Nooooooo." Pause.

"It looked like it broke right."

Tiger: "It does."

He just had that putt.

"I tell you what," says Fluff, "that's one putt I'll never misread again."

Four p.m.

"The swing feels good," says Tiger. Fluff is cupping a cigarette. "The Girl from Ipanima" is playing. The blimp is circling.

"What shot do you think I should play," Tiger says to Butch.

He hits a cut. He hits a draw.

"Beautiful," says Butch.

"Any updates?" says Fluff.

"Yeah," says Carey. "They went off the air." At seven p.m. Eastern, ESPN cut to its *NFL Primetime Show*. They would come back for live updates. Love hit his drive at 18 left-center of the fairway.

Would this be where Tiger Woods won his first tournament, hitting balls on the range at Summerlin, "The Girl from Ipanima" playing, Fluff puffing and Butchie trying to act cool, calm and collected?

Mike Shea is on the walkie-talkie again, describing Love's second shot into 18:

"Coming in long and right . . . He's got a 30-footer." Tiger pulled a banana out of his bag. Potassium for energy. It was 4:10. He headed to the putting green, and could hear the moan as Love missed.

He is very cool. He is smiling. The P.A. system crackles: "Test. Test. Has everybody had a good time so far?" There's a big roar. He heads to a golf cart, and rides out to the 18th tee.

It is 4:20, and real quiet. Tiger is waiting for Davis.

"Great playing, Tiger."

"You, too, stud."

"I haven't seen you all week. I've seen Butch, but not you."

"I've been here." Love and Woods both use Titleist Professionals, 90 compression. From their short practice round at Callaway Gardens, Love remembered that Tiger used No. 4s. He had No. 3s.

Mike Shea had them draw lots from his hat. Davis won. He had honors.

"Any time you're ready," said Shea.

"Play well," said Love.

"All right," said Woods. "Good luck."

His hand seemed to be shaking, just a little.

Davis had his wooden driver. He roped a low cut. "Good shot," said his brother Mark, who was carrying his bag. "Good one."

It was 4:24. Tiger takes 3-wood, ripped it right next to Davis's ball. Walking down the fairway, somebody outside the gallery ropes yelled, "JUST LIKE THE AMATEURS, TIGER! YOU OWN THIS!"

It was 4:30 in Las Vegas, 7:30 at ESPN's studios in Bristol, Ct. They've cut into the highlights show for Tiger. That's how big this was. Bigger than the NFL. Bigger than Berman.

Tiger did own it. He owned the playoff and he owned Love. It seemed like he owned everything there was to own that day. He was Mr. Woods. The Man. The cheers went up when Love missed his par putt. "TII–GERR . . . TII–GERR."

Inside the mind of that 20-year-old, mixed with the excitement, was the sense that this would happen. He was not surprised. He would wait a couple of weeks, and tell people that he expected to win one of these seven tournaments.

Back in Cypress, he knew Earl was sitting in front of the TV, with Joey and Penny, probably crying. He did the news conference and the trip to the volunteer tent. Outside the clubhouse, Tida was holding court. "I hope this win will tell a lot of people that he is the real one," she said. "Every time the curtain is up, he's right there. Encore every time."

The stretch limo was waiting. He had done enough signing and hand shaking. He compressed his body into the back seat, and rode back into Las Vegas. He rode the private elevator up to the MGM penthouse and looked out over the city. Earl was right again. Something like this had to happen in Las Vegas, the city, Larry Dorman wrote in the *Times*, where there are no sure things, no can't-miss propositions. He had chosen, as Dorman wrote, "the perfect time and place to lay waste to conventional wisdom. He is a sure thing. He is a can't-miss."

Tiger Woods showered and changed clothes, then rode that private elevator down to dinner at a private room Tutera had reserved. Tida was there, and Butch and Jay and Bryon Bell and Jerry Chang. Everybody made a speech and they drank Dom Perignon to toast the winner of the 1996 Las Vegas Invitational, the richest college dropout in America, Tiger Woods. He ordered a big, fat, juicy pepper steak, this kid who earlier in the week had to borrow $20 from his mother so he could go to McDonald's. The waiters brought out the dishes, covered with sterling silver covers, and Tiger was famished. At the count of three, the waiters pulled the covers off the plates.

Sitting in front of Tiger were two McDonald's cheeseburgers.

43

TIGER DOES TEXAS

He was obviously exempt now, but there was another ring to reach for, the Tour Championship. With a $3 million purse and a $540,000 check for first place, the PGA Tour's season-ending event is an exclusive event open only to the top 30 money winners. With the $297,000 for winning at Vegas, Tiger had moved up to 40th on the money list. In the press tent at Summerlin, while he waited for Love to conclude his interview, Tiger sat down next to Tim Dahlberg of the Associated Press. Dahlberg was on deadline, needing to get the story out as quick as possible. Woods read over his shoulder.

"Do you like my lead?" Dahlberg said.

Tiger pointed to the dollar signs on Dahlberg's screen.

"That's what I like," he said.

The Nike and Titleist contracts were paper money. Tiger didn't feel like he earned those zeros. The tournament checks were different, even the C-notes they gave for birdies in the Tuesday Shootouts. One hundred bucks was still a lot of money for a college kid, even if there was an almost unlimited supply of them in some Orlando bank.

Tiger debated whether to play Texas. His groin hurt. He had the perfect out. But he took so much heat for the

WD at Callaway Gardens, and there was so much riding now, that he decided the trip to Texas was in his best interests. In the interview tent, Woods told the press he wasn't sure if he was going. By the time he reached the volunteer party at Summerlin, he was going.

LaCantera Golf Club in San Antonio is a new golf course, designed by Tom Weiskopf and Jay Morrish, and it's not one of their best. Designed on a bad piece of ground, it takes a sherpa to walk it and a lot of local knowledge to play it. The signature hole is a short par-four that plays off a rock cliff to a green that has a roller coaster from the Fiesta, Texas, amusement park to frame it. LaCantera makes the Summerlin-TPC look like Loch Lomond, but it's a golf course and they were playing for $1.2 million, so Tiger put on his best face and showed up.

It's easy to smile when Titleist is willing to throw $20 million at you. That's what the new numbers were, up considerably from the $3 million over five years that had been reported in Milwaukee. Uhlein and the decisionmakers at American Brands obviously felt that Woods was the real deal, and just to keep Ely Callaway from getting too close, decided to wrap up Tiger longterm. Callaway had made overtures to Norton in the weeks after Milwaukee which included a $1 million offer just to try the Great Big Bertha driver, and $3 million to use it in competition. Uhlein got a copy of a letter Callaway wrote to Phil Knight, and took it as an affront. Without taking a deep breath, Uhlein called it "slanderous and vituperative mudslinging by some of our competitors who seem hellbent to cause a disruption and a breakdown in our negotiations . . . which seems to be a byproduct of a condition of envy, jealousy and internal disappointment at not being able to buy what they want." The winner was Tiger. He had been winning a lot lately.

Earl was back on the scene, but was now low-keying it around the media. He did most of his talking while playing golf with friends on some of the local golf courses. One day he played with Roger Clemens at Oak Hills, the Tillinghast layout that used to host the Texas Open before there was a sponsorship problem and LaCantera fronted the purse. On Friday morning, while Tiger was out shooting 68, Earl sat in the press tent next to Pete McDaniel of *Golf World*, chin buried in chest, sleeping and conserving energy for his afternoon golf game.

At night they were hanging out with Tiger's adopted grandfather, Charlie Sifford. The Texas Open tried to make things right with Charlie for some of the injustices of 35 years ago by paying for his transportation from Kingwood and his room and board while in San Antonio. In 1961, Sifford was barred from coming through the gate at Oak Hills. Again, that was another time, another place, but Charlie hadn't forgotten. "Those people are the ones who made the mistake," he said. 'They ran me away. I said, 'OK, but I'll be back. I wanted to play golf and I was going to do whatever it took to play golf."

Charlie has spent plenty of time telling Tiger what it was like to be a black man in that generation. Tiger absorbed it all, and carries it with him. "If it wasn't for him, I wouldn't be able to play the game," Tiger said during his news conference at LaCantera. "If not for guys like [Sifford], Teddy Rhodes, Lee Elder and all the guys who paved the way for minority golf, who knows whether there'd be a Caucasian Clause on the PGA Tour, or how much longer it would have taken for that to fall. Charlie has been great for the game and he hasn't been recognized, which is too bad. I love him dearly for who he is and what he has meant for me and other minorities in golf."

Tiger became a fulltime member of the PGA Tour at the Texas Open. In the scoring tent behind the ninth green on Thursday, Arvin Ginn of the PGA Tour rules staff presented him with his money clip, and outlined the commitment rules. Tiger had until one hour after the completion of play on Friday to enter the Disney Classic. Ginn also offered Tiger a wives' badge.

"What am I going to do with that?" Woods said with a big smile.

Ginn, in his Mississippi drawl, told the kid, "Well, you can give it to your mother, or to your girlfriend."

Tiger Woods didn't have a girlfriend. It was no different out here on Tour than it was at Stanford, in that he didn't have any time for a girlfriend. Word was up that Tyra Banks, the cover model on *Sports Illustrated*'s swimsuit issue, was supposedly interested. But when was Tiger going to put that together? He's out in San Antonio, playing golf, trying to do his job. She's . . . who knows where she is?

Picture it: Here's this good-looking, clean-cut, articulate kid, with $60 million in the bank, about the most eligible young bachelor in the world, and he's got nobody to hug at night. Talk about frustration. The San Antonio Spurs gave him courtside seats at the Alamodome, and who did he take? Pete McDaniel.

Golf, golf, golf. That's all it was. Golf, golf, golf. If there weren't fans asking for autographs, there were golf writers asking questions. It was like he had been sucked up in the movie *Twister*. Tim Herron saw it at LaCantera one afternoon. "He's got a tougher position than most people think," Herron said. "He's 20 years old and he wants to be 20 years old, but in reality he's being treated more like a 35-year-old executive who has to mind his p's and q's. It's tough to kind of be yourself. Everywhere he goes, he's mobbed. He's going to have to work for his money, where most people don't think he is." Even the security guard working the locker room door at LaCantera said he wouldn't trade places with Tiger for all the money in the world. "I wouldn't give a nickel for it," he said.

Tiger was huge after the Amateur. The victory in Vegas made him larger than life. The galleries at LaCantera forced tournament director Tony Piazza to add shuttle buses and open up new parking lots down the street from Fiesta, Texas at Redland Stone. And it seemed like every one of the 125,000 who passed through the Texas Open gates just had to get Tiger Woods's signature. This created a problem. You sign one, you have to sign them all. Or you don't sign any, and you're a jerk. Tiger opted to pick his spots, to sign as he walked, to never stop moving. Nicklaus and Palmer have been known to stand for 90 minutes and sign. Tiger would have to spend four hours every day in the autograph tent to dent the requests. Rather than fight the crowds, one of the tournament's sponsors embarrassingly asked Piazza if he wouldn't mind getting the kid's autograph. When Piazza explained the circumstances, Tiger said, disconsolately, "I wish more people were embarrassed about it."

To Tiger, winning the Amateur meant more than winning at Las Vegas. Winning the Amateur was making history. "That's walking on ground no one else has ever walked before," he said. But to the swarms, it was winning Las Vegas that had Tiger Woods walking on water. "Tiger Woods is not just a golfer," Tony Piazza said. "He's a celebrity."

There were some up sides to being a tournament winner on the PGA Tour, one of which is the pairings. Rather than go off with what the PGA Tour classifies as its "3" players, Tiger jumped into the "1" category. Instead of the dreaded late-early times with no-names and rookies, Tiger teed off at 1:05 and 8:35 with Billy Mayfair and Jim McGovern. Another highlight is that the tee announcer has some material to work with. Friday morning, standing on the first tee, trying to concentrate on his shot, Tiger got to hear some Texan in his best Michael Buffer ring voice bellow, "Ladies and gentlemen . . . Direct from Las Vegas . . . Where he won his first professional event last week . . . The three-time U.S. Amateur champion . . . From Orlando, Florida . . . Tiiiiiii-gerrrrr Woods!"

Don't you think Woods didn't take some teasing for that.

"Direct from Las Vegas?" McGovern said, walking off the tee. "I thought they were going to introduce Elvis."

McGovern, one of the best guys on the Tour, came away totally impressed with Tiger, both as a person and as a golfer. He was hoping that maybe there was something he wouldn't like about Tiger. But after 36 holes, there wasn't. The only thing that bothered McGovern about Woods was that he hit the ball so damn far—it wasn't fair.

Hackensack Mac averages about 265 yards off the tee, which is middle of the pack. Tiger was at 302 yards, about 20 more than John Daly, and that figure was deceptive because on some of the driving distance holes he would use a two-iron to keep the ball in play. Woods, McGovern and Mayfair started on the 10th hole Thursday, a downhill par-five of 541 yards. Tiger hit three-wood and a high, floating three-iron that came down like a soft seven-iron, 15 feet from the hole. McGovern had never seen anything like it, not in seven years on the Tour. Tiger was so long that even on a 7,001-yard course he only had to hit driver three times. When he did, it wasn't even close. On the first hole Friday, Tiger took out driver, put an easy swing on it, and was 70 yards past McGovern's drive. Tiger hit iron to the green. Mayfair and McGovern hit woods to lay up.

"It's hard to believe anybody hits the ball that far," McGovern said. "Plus he's got his head on square. Damn it. He's nice. I bored him with stories about my family. I told him my daughter was watching us on the Golf Channel, and every time we came on TV, my wife would say, "Oh, there's Tiger!" and Melanie kept saying, 'That's not Tigger.' She couldn't find his tail."

Tiger just didn't have it for three days at LaCantera, but again, he was in contention without his 'A' game, turning 72s and 71s into 69–68. He made seven birdies on Thursday. Friday, in the second round, he four-putted the sixth for double bogey, but made six birdies on the back and shot 30. Saturday he shot 73, which was only the second time in 22 rounds since Milwaukee that he failed to break par. That put him seven shots back going into the final round, seemingly out of it, but with Tiger, you never know.

Sunday started out slow. Two birdies on the front. Not much happening. Behind him, David Ogrin and Jay Haas were struggling a little bit, but neither one had a car wreck. Then it happened. At the par-five 10th, Tiger hit four-iron to 18 feet and made the putt for eagle. In a flash, he was two shots back and closing. Ogrin made a surge, but Tiger closed again with birdies at 14 and 15. He was only one stroke back, standing on the 16th tee, a downhill par-four of 380 yards. He did not know that he was only one stroke back, because there were no scoreboards around. He was throwing up grass, trying to judge the wind, and how to play the hole.

Finally he pulled off the Tiger headcover, took out driver, and teed the ball up. The green can't be seen from the tee since it was stuck on a slight dogleg right, behind some scrub trees. Tiger has a reputation for playing slow, any-way, but on this shot, he *really* took his time. The ball came off his clubface so fast that, like Marucci had said at Newport, it was impossible to follow it. It looked high and right, but Tiger had played the draw, out over the trees, and in the distance, in a delayed reaction, a Texas roar went up, the type of sound you'd hear at a Garth Brooks concert or the Houston Livestock Show and Rodeo. There were a lot of "Yahoos!" and "Whoooooooos" coming from the distance. They were getting as excited about Tiger as they do at armadillo races.

"I did it," Tiger said.

"I think you did," said Fluff.

The yardage marker said the green was 380 yards away. Tiger had driven it pin high on the 70th hole of a golf tournament when he had to. Three hundred and eighty yards. OK, so maybe it was downhill. But it wasn't downhill off Mount McKinley, and Hurricane Fran wasn't at his back. Pin high from 380. Palmer did something like that at Cherry Hills in the 1960 U.S. Open. But that was in Rocky Mountain altitude. Tiger did it in San Antonio.

From just off the green, he hit a semi-commercial chip that stopped seven feet from the hole. Fluff looked at his yardage book. The grain went left-to-right. Mark Calcavecchia just had a putt on the same line that went left-to-right. Tiger lined his putt up just inside the left lip and let it go. One foot from the hole it looked perfect. Six inches away and it was jar. Three inches away, and Tiger was ready to pick it out of the hole. But somehow, someway, the putt went left. Left! Tiger slapped his leg and started cursing.

"IT CAN'T GO THAT WAY!" he said. "GAWD! JESUS! IT CAN'T!"

It did.

Tiger tried to put it behind him, said he put it behind him, but went to the 17th tee, a par-three of 183 yards, and pulled the wrong club. He threw up some grass, and it blew back at him. But the wind was swirling. He took six-iron, gripped down to the shaft, and the crowd was yelling "Yes! Yes! Yes!" as the shot flew the pin, the back of the green and landed next to the grandstand, on a trampled lie, under a stand of cedar trees. Ballgame. Tiger made bogey, saved par at 18, and finished with a 67. That put him 11 under for the tournament, and Orgin was on the scoreboards at 14 under. That close to two straight, and in a matter of two swings, it was over.

"The idea was to go out and win the damn thing," Woods said. "You have to believe you have a chance. I did. I just came up short."

In the locker room, Harmon told him, "I know you're upset, but you've got to take away from this how well you played today. You went out a pretty good ways behind, got it in position where you could win, and that's all you want any time you play, is to give yourself a chance."

Tiger Woods went to the airport that night richer by $81,600, ranked 34th on the money list, and in position to make the Tour Championship with another strong finish at Disney. Best of all, he was going home to Orlando. A whole week at Isleworth. The Magic were in town. Maybe it didn't feel like home yet, but it was home.

44

THE TIGER KING

There was a newer, softer Nike commercial that debuted in late October. It was more Tiger and his father, less I, I, I, I. The most memorable passage is an old home movie where Tiger is saying, "I want to win all the big tournaments, the major ones, and I hope to play well when I'm older, and beat all the pros." Cute, poignant stuff. Definitely more appealing, although certainly not as talked about, as the Hello World campaign. "I think they're both great for their own different reasons," Tiger said.

At Nike Headquarters, the company line is the first commercial was not "pulled" because of negative reaction to it. The Hello World commercial was never intended to run more than two weeks. It was just to introduce Tiger Woods. Maybe so, but it didn't help when USGA executive director David Fay called one of Nike's executive vice presidents to point out the logoed shirt Tiger wore to win the Amateur at Pumpkin Ridge was from Lochinvar Golf Club in Houston. Lochinvar is an all-male club.

This didn't come up in Tuesday's news conference at Walt Disney World, but once again the race issue did because every week it was a new tournament, and a new group of writers and a new set of TV people. "Golf has been

such an elitist sport, and—I hate to say it—a white-dominated sport for so long that people have been afraid of
bringing this issue up," Woods said. "They thought the
Shoal Creek incident solved everything. That's wrong. Unfortunately minorities are not allowed to play certain clubs,
or are not allowed to be members. So people of certain religious beliefs are not allowed to join clubs, as well as females.
I'm not usually that blunt, but it's something that needed
to be said."

By now he had it on autopilot, but since this was a
hometown gig, Tiger showed up 20 minutes early and spent
nearly 40 minutes holding court. Then, when it was over, it
was over. There was no hanging around with the writers,
no one-on-ones with radio or TV. That's just the way he
works it. Everybody gets the same quotes. Only a chosen
few get privileged time.

The format, like Vegas, is a pro–am. For some reason,
playing with a bunch of hacks doesn't seem to bother Tiger.
While they're slashing, he does his own thing. They meet on
the green, Tiger maybe reads a putt, and then the amateur
gets out of the way. He knows what to say, how to say it, and
when to concentrate. It's an amazing ability. Butch thinks it's
part of his Buddhist upbringing. Part of a discipline. It also
helped to work with a sports psychologist since age 13.

At Disney, Tiger was without Butch. The coach had to
go home and take care of the members at Lochinvar, but
they communicated on the phone. Earl was with him, but
didn't hang around the golf tournament much. He spent
most of the time back at the Isleworth villa, resting. He
wasn't feeling well.

Tiger kept both of them feeling young, especially
Butch, who's 53 and a former Vietnam vet. He calls his
coach "old man," and teases him constantly about his age
and his putting stroke—"It's so ugly, but you make every-

thing!'' Butch gets his shots in, however. The Monday after Vegas, they went shopping at a mall in San Antonio. Butch wanted Tiger to get some new clothes (''You can't wear Nike 24 hours a day'') and to spend some of the $297,000 he won at Summerlin. When it came time to pay the bill, Tiger handed the salesperson a credit card. It didn't go through the computer. No problem. Tiger whipped out another card. That didn't go through the computer, either.

''Well, you activated them, didn't you?'' Harmon said.

''What's that?'' said Tiger.

Shaking his head, Harmon reached for his wallet.

''That just shows he's a kid,'' he said.

Butch may have developed into Tiger's best friend. But when Tiger's out on the road, playing Tour golf, there's nobody around Tiger's age that he can relate to. His two pals, Bryon from high school and Jerry from Stanford, are both in med school. He likes to listen to Montell Jordan, the new young king of the hip-hop scene. There's not many guys in pro golf who listen to Montell Jordan other than Don Wallace, a former Southwest Louisiana quarterback who works as general manager of the PGA Tour's Scoreboard/Tournament Operations Department. Don and Tiger like to joke about getting mistaken for each other, since they're about the only black faces around other than McDaniel, when he's covering for *Golf World* and the caddies, who are mostly white. At Stanford, there were a lot of people hip to Montell Jordan. You say that name out on the PGA Tour, and most people will probably think you're talking about Montel Williams, the talk-show host.

At least when he was home, he could hang around with his new neighbor, Ken Griffey, Jr., and eventually he would get to know Penny Hardaway, since he lives at Isleworth, too. But early on, there was no denying the cultural and age gap that existed for Tiger Woods.

"What I miss is going to a buddy's house or a dorm at 11 at night and just hanging out," Tiger said. "Those are the good times, when you shoot the bull and you find out a lot about yourself. That part I do miss."

The Disney people were just ecstatic about having Tiger in their field. Tournament director Michael McPhillips had been in communication with Hughes Norton ever since Tiger turned pro. At one point, he sent a set of Tiger head covers to IMG, just in case Tiger needed a spare, and one day, McPhillips called Norton from his car phone, saying he was driving around Orlando with six strawberry milk shakes from McDonald's, and was there a neutral drop point near Tiger's home.

"You're doing your homework," Norton said.

At the Southern Open, Tiger said he wasn't going to play Disney, which triggered the hosts of one Orlando all-sports station to rip him pretty good. The essence of it was: First Shaquille O'Neal leaves and now this kid moves in. We don't need either one of them.

But McPhillips was always hopeful. He had established back-gate security gate clearance for Woods, which would cut 15 minutes off his drive time from Isleworth. He had a newspaper ad prepared, just in case, with a Tiger's head and a Guess Who's Coming headline. When Tiger finally did commit, the Friday of San Antonio, McPhillips was going into a staff meeting outside the Disney Classic office. Trying their best to put on disappointed faces, McPhillips and Disney Golf Director Steve Wilson tried to make it seem like Tiger wasn't playing. "Of course you know Michael made a promise," Wilson said, and with that, McPhillips took off his Foot-Joys and jumped into the swimming pool. "Disney is a place where dreams come true," McPhillips said. "And fortunately mine did."

A whole new operational plan had to be set in motion. Buses were added to the tram transportation. The Port-O-Lets were doubled. Bleachers were put up behind the Magnolia range. More pairing sheets were printed. A detail of four marshalls, two security guards, and two undercover officers were assembled. A welcoming committee met Tiger's plane at Orlando Airport on Sunday night with a courtesy car. And McPhillips had special maps drawn up, showing the courses and also where all the McDonald's were located between Disney and Isleworth.

The Tiger story kept getting bigger, and the press room reflected it. Normally Disney gets a sparse media turnout, but this looked like a Doral press room, with Larry Dorman there from the *New York Times*, Dave Sheinen of the *Miami Herald*, John Feinstein of *Golf Magazine* and Rick Reilly of *Sports Illustrated* joining the usual suspects who normally cover Disney. Reilly flew in from Mark Mulvoy's retirement roast in New York, possibly to write a cover story. Tiger had yet to make an *SI* cover. His three Amateur victories came on the week of the NFL Preview issue. If he won Disney, he'd be on the front of 3.5 million magazines. He did make the covers of *Golf* and *Golf Digest*, the two largest golf publications in the United States. And once again, the big winner on the TV side was the Golf Channel, which had also broadcast Quad City, B.C. and Texas.

Tiger had his usual slow start on Thursday, shooting 69 on the Palm Course. It was a round that started with a bang, as the first fairway was lined four and five people deep from tee to green, a sight Wilson thought he'd never see at Disney. ''Tiger hit that first drive so far, I said, ''He's probably going to have to take a drop in [the] Chip'n Dale [parking lot],' '' Wilson said. ''The ball went forever.'' The round seemed to last that long, too, and Tiger double bogeyed the last hole to shoot three under instead of five under 67. That put him in a tie for 59th place, which was 24 spots better than Vegas but still back in the pack. Friday's round at Lake Buena Vista changed that in a hurry. Tiger lit it up with a 63 that put him two shots off the lead. It can happen in a flash with Tiger, and once again, it did. Tiger said he wasn't that sharp, but he made a couple of snakes and seemed a little disappointed coming off the course. The reason was the bogey he made at the 105-yard seventh hole, his 16th. "I had too much speed at the bottom [of the swing]," he said. "And it was downwind, too. I just hit a bad shot."

There were so many people at LBV that alternate parking had to be opened at Planet Hollywood. Tiger spent five minutes in the autograph tent, headed home, and went to the Magic game that night with Griffey. "It's pretty phenomenal," Fluff Cowan said. "Not many people even realize what a strain playing this many weeks in a row is on a guy, and that's coming off a U.S. Amateur victory. The U.S. Amateur is like playing two golf tournaments in one week. He's been on an incredible stretch, and he's still pretty sharp. His disposition has been pretty good. His disposition is a large part of what allows him to do the things he does."

Woods played that day with Steve Szabo, a psychiatrist from Tampa, who described Tiger as having "an innate goodness about him," and "a young man any family would take pride in."

Szabo's son, Doug, was caddying. "Between nine and 10, at the turn, he said, 'Can you imagine I'm 20 years old. I wake up every day and get to do the thing I like to do most. This is my work now'," Doug Szabo said. "I think it's a very telling thing. He still likes coming out knowing everybody expects a lot of him."

A 69 on Saturday put Woods in a four-way tie for fifth, one shot out of the lead. He three-putted the 18th to lose a piece of the lead, but didn't seem frosted about it. It was a day of almosts, and he was fighting the onset of a flu. One thing that made him feel good was the size and makeup of the gallery. "I think it's great, because look at all the kids out there right now, out there following," he said. "That's our future, and the game's future. They're out there walking with a person they can relate to, me being so young. They can relate to me as a person rather than say a Jack Nicklaus. The age difference is what draws a lot of kids, and I think it's beautiful. It's also nice seeing . . . how can I phrase this nicely? . . . I guess more minorities in the gallery. That's also where the future is heading. That's where the game will go, and where I think it will go."

And no, he did not miss Stanford. It was the 19th of October. Midterms. Tiger is more a guy for finals. As in final rounds.

Sunday he came out wearing red, and red on a golf scoreboard denotes birdies and eagles. He cranked it up by making five straight threes, starting on the third hole, shot 32 outbound, three-putted three times in the final 10 holes, and still won. He did this paired in the final round with Payne Stewart, who has two major championships on his résumé. And he did it with a head that felt like it was going to explode.

"If I felt like this at Stanford, I never would have left that bed," he said. "I got up this morning stuffy, and unfortunately I had to come out here and play. But the good thing is you have to watch out for the sick golfer. For some reason some of the guys play their best rounds when they're sick. Just don't put a needle to my head. It may burst. I can't really hear. I'm so closed. My throat's not doing good. I've got no energy. I'm dizzy. Other than that, I'm great."

Again, Tiger drew a zoo—literally. He had eagled the fourth and birdied the fifth to tie Nolan Henke at five under,

and the crowd was jostling ahead, trying to get better van-
tage points, when it cut through the woods between the
sixth and seventh holes. This intrusion scared a deer, who
attempted an escape through a wetland area. This fired up
an alligator, which started chasing the deer, snapping its
jaws. The deer escaped, but found itself in the seventh fairway, surrounded by, oh, 5,000 people. The poor creature
must not have known what was worse, the gator or Tiger's
faithful. Scared out of its mind, the doe fertilized the grass,
turned and ran—away from the alligator this time, to
safety. Tiger didn't notice the disturbance. He birdied the
seventh and eighth holes to take the lead.

The final postscript to this bizarre day occurred to Taylor Smith, who was told at the turn that his putter grip did
not conform to the rules of golf. He asked to play on, pend-
ing a meeting with the PGA Tour Rules Committee, and
birdied the 72nd hole for what the gallery thought was a
tie. That took a little of the joy out of Tiger, who sat in the
locker room, his feet up on a bench, his head in his hands,
waiting for Smith to finish.

Reilly was in there with him, trying to get a different
quote for his story.

"Oh well. Another win. Some Nyquil. Call it a week,"
he said.

Woods didn't say a word until it was time for the trophy presentation, and the news conference, and then back
in the locker room again, he sat wordlessly as Reilly tried
again.

"So," Rick said. "If you weren't sick, how do you think
you would have done healthy?"

Again, nothing. Reilly had written an *SI* bonus piece on
Woods in 1995, a real positive story. He talked to him on
the phone Saturday night. And Tiger was giving him zero.

He got up, headed out the door, leaving Rick there with his pad.

As sick as he was, as drained as he was, Tiger wanted to spend time in the autograph tent. He had blown everybody off all day, and figured he owed it to the tournament. So McPhillips got a cart and the security force got him to the tent and the line formed back toward the 18th green, as long as a full lob wedge shot. Tiger signed. And he signed. And he smiled. And he made eye contact. And he mixed. Earlier in the day, behind the fourth tee, somebody yelled, "FORGET ABOUT SHAQ, WE GOT TIGER!" Lesley Baker, Jr., said, "What Shaq did for basketball, he's going to do for golf in Orlando. It's a white-dominated sport. That's not disputable. But Tiger's bridging the gap. We're going into the 21st century." Dr. Bob Sims, a close friend of Earl Woods and a man who hosted the Woodses at his home during the 1996 U.S. Open, said, "The whole achievement is not surprising, but it is amazing." Carolyn McCorvey drove over from Merritt Island with her six-year-old son, who is taking up the game. "They used to say golf was boring," she said. "But not with all the money this young man is making."

So Tiger signed and signed and signed. For a good solid 25 minutes he signed. And then, as if a clock went off in his head, he got up, put on the blinders, stopped making eye contact, and walked to his courtesy car in the parking lot. Ten more minutes and he would have signed everything. Arnie would have stayed. Jack would have stayed. Tiger should have stayed. But he's only 20. And he was feeling terrible to begin with. At least he sucked it up and made the effort. Twenty-five minutes is better than nothing. A lot of people went home happy. The other ones are going to learn. They have to get in line earlier next time.

Tiger went back to his villa with the rented furniture, too sick to celebrate.

45

FATHER AND SON

Every player who qualified for the Tour Championship was given the keys to a four-door Mercedes Benz courtesy car, compliments of the PGA.

"Wow!" Woods said. "A Mercedes! I've never been in one!"

"Well, why don't you go buy one?" said Butch Harmon.

"No way!" said Tiger. "Do you know how much this thing costs?"

Here's a kid with all the money in the world at his disposal, and he's worrying about cost. He's like Arnold Palmer in that respect. Arnold carries around a wad of $100 bills, wrapped tightly in a rubber band. Tiger, according to his friends, is just as tight with his fortune.

He could buy four Rolex watches, but he was wearing the one Disney gave him with Mickey Mouse on the dial. He may order pepper steak on special occasions, but he's still fast food over the fast lane.

After practice on Wednesday, for example, Butch asked Tiger if he wanted to grab some lunch. So they jumped in the Mercedes, and Butch was expecting a nice restaurant, an Outback steakhouse at least.

Tiger pulled into a Taco Bell.

Butch was in the passenger seat, and Tiger was blasting Montell on the CD player, signing autographs through the drive-in window. "The hardest part," Harmon says, "is listening to that gawd-awful music he listens to."

They are in Tulsa now. They started this Magical Mystery Tour in Portland on August 20. Tiger had zigzagged to Milwaukee, Toronto, Quad City, Binghamton, Columbus, (Ga.), Las Vegas, San Antonio and Orlando before this final stop. The original goal was to avoid a trip to Tour School. Then it was win. Then, maybe, there was the Tour Championship. Now they were here. Southern Hills. The top 30 money winners on the PGA Tour. Tiger Woods did it in seven tournaments. Seven. His tight man, Woody Austin, was grinding all year, playing so many tournaments straight down the stretch that he was a zombie, trying to qualify for Tulsa. Woody played 36 events. He finished 32nd on the money list. Tiger played seven and was 24th going into the Tour Championship. He'd done in seven tournaments what everybody had all year to do.

It seemed too easy. "Let's not judge Tiger Woods now," Mark O'Meara said Wednesday night on the putting green. "Let's judge him when things aren't going his way, when he's not filled with confidence and enthusiasm. Sooner or later the physical and mental pressure will take its toll, and we'll see that Tiger Woods is indeed human. It may not happen this week, and it may not happen next week. But sooner or later it's going to happen and to me, that's when the true champion is born. Not out of victory. Out of struggling." In Cleveland, IMG had turned down requests from *Newsweek*, *GQ*, *Fortune*, *People*, and *Forbes*. Fan mail was coming in by the sackful, and it wasn't all Dear Tiger stuff. Not from Generation X. One letter began, "What up, fool?" The Boston Pops extended an invitation to read "The Night Before Christmas." Cindy Crawford even wrote, hinting that if Tiger did a deal with Omega watches, she might be available for the commercial shoot. Cindy Crawford! Yow! Things were definitely looking up!

In the media center at Southern Hills, Denise Taylor had her hands full. When Tiger won at Disney, she was deluged with credential requests from *Newsweek*, the *Washington Post*, *L.A. Times*, *Orange County Register* and *Baltimore Sun*. *ABC World News Tonight* and *Dateline NBC* had sent crews. "I mean, it is unbelievable," Taylor said.

Tiger did his usual thing. The Tuesday news conference. The practice rounds. And an even-par 70 in the opening round, which put him four strokes off the lead held by Tom Lehman and Vijay Singh. He was set up for another top 10 finish. He ate lunch with Fred Funk. And then, as O'Meara prophesied, adversity came calling.

At approximately 2:51 Friday morning, October 25, Earl Woods was admitted to the Trauma Emergency Center at St. Francis Hospital in Tulsa, complaining of chest pains. Luckily, St. Francis was across the street from the Doubletree, where Tiger and his family were staying. Tiger was up all night. He had a 12:49 tee time. After three hours sleep, the old Green Beret wished his son luck, and told him he'd be watching on TV. Tiger's body went to Southern Hills, but his head and his heart were back at St. Francis Hospital. He parred the first, double bogeyed the second, then went bogey-bogey-bogey-bogey-par-bogey.

Nobody seemed to know what was wrong. There was a press release issued in the media center, and Brent Musburger reported the story on ESPN, but to the spectators and to playing partner John Cook, it was a mystery.

Going to the 10th hole, Woods mentioned to Cook, "I just want to get done and go see my dad." Cook didn't probe and didn't know what that meant, but Tida showed up and that seemed to change Tiger's spirits. He shot even-par 35 on the back for a 78. It was definitely the gutsiest round of golf Tiger Woods had ever played.

"He showed me a lot today and it wasn't golf," Cook said. "You can lose your mind out here, and he didn't. He didn't have his head down and sulk. He just tried to fight through it. To hold his demeanor like he did was more impressive to me than some of the drives he tried to hit. In a situation like that, you could stomp off and complain, moan and act like a 20-year-old, but he didn't do that. He tried to make the best of a difficult day."

Woods didn't spend much time with reporters. The hard part was not knowing if it was a heart problem or a bronchial problem. Earl still smoked his Merits, and had had bypass surgery 10 years ago. He was 64 now, and slightly overweight. "There are more important things in life than golf," he said. "I love my dad to death, and I'm going to see him right now."

According to *Golf World*, tests revealed some blockage in the coronary arteries and a mild case of pneumonia. Tiger shot 72–68 (with a triple bogey) to finish tied for 21st and break his streak of top-five finishes. He ended the season ranked 24th on the money list with $790,594. His average of $98,824 per event was best on the Tour, better even than Lehman averaged setting the all-time single season earnings record of $1.78 million.

This chapter was over. Ten weeks. Three wins. The Nike and Titleist contracts. All that money. All those memories, and the three sweetest moments were embracing his father's hand, looking in his pop's eyes on the announcement day at Milwaukee, hugging Tida after Las Vegas and hugging Earl after Disney.

Earl Woods was discharged on Tuesday, and said, "I'll take it easy for about a week, and then get back into my regular schedule."

Nguyen Phong would have said the same thing.

46

SECOND SEASON

On November 5, PR man Steve Brener hosted a conference call for the Skins Game. Tiger was seven years old when the first Skins Game was won by Tom Watson at Desert Highlands. He was scheduled to play against Watson, Fred Couples and John Daly on Thanksgiving Weekend at Rancho LaQuinta in Palm Springs. There were 56 people on the call, from coast-to-coast.

Tiger was at his home in Orlando, getting ready to go out and play golf. It was 10 days since the Tour Championship, and he had been "chillin" at Isleworth, playing a little golf, water skiing, fishing, shootin' a little hoop, and going out at night to a Magic game with O'Meara and Junior Griffey, getting his enthusiasm back for golf and a second-season schedule that included the Skins Game, the Australian Open, and the JCPenney Classic, where he was scheduled to play with Trip Kuehne's sister, Kelli, the two-time U.S. Women's Amateur champion.

He had a chance to meet some members of the opposite sex, and admitted, "I think Momma would not accept some of the women I've seen."

And he also had time to reschedule the Fred Haskins Dinner at Callaway Gardens, because, "Admittedly I made a mistake. I know what I did was wrong, and I apologize for any inconveniences I did cause. I'm trying to rectify a wrong."

The previous night, he had been down to the Golf Channel, studying tape of the greatest players from the *Shell's Wonderful World of Golf* series. He watched Watson putt because he made everything back then, and Trevino hit wedges and Nicklaus long irons. He watched how they made decisions on the golf course, how they won all those majors. He called Butch at home in Houston.

"I think we're witnessing something special here," Harmon said. "It could be the birth of something unlike what the sport has ever seen. It's so rewarding to watch his progress. When he first came to me he was this skinny kid with a loose golf swing who hit the ball miles, who had no idea where it was going to go. He's an incredibly hard worker and he's like a sponge. He'll accept advice from everyone, from me, from other players. And he's not cocky. He's not caught up in the hoopla. Every time he wins a check, he says, 'This is my money, I earned this.' I say 'What about your $60 million?' Tiger says, 'I didn't earn that. This I earned.' On the jet coming from Vegas, he had to write the check out to Fluff for $29,000. It was freaking him out. There were too many zeros."

There were five zeros attached to the check written to Tiger by the Australian Open, which was Tiger's first event after the Tour Championship. Tournament officials in Sydney paid him a reported $300,000. It was his first appearance fee, and, although his play wasn't spectacular, there were times when that figure didn't seem like enough. Right off the plane, Tiger played the pro-am and whiffed two flop shots in the deep rough at the Australian Golf Club. Then, walking from the 9th green to the 10th tee in the opening round, Tiger encountered four grinning young men, all of them holding beer cans. At the time he was five-over par for the day, and in no mood to hear the rowdies burst into a chorus of: "Go, Tiger, Go!" followed by a loud "Grrrrr," as he passed by.

A birdie at the last hole avoided an embarrassing 80, which put him 12 shots behind the tournament leader, Greg Norman, who had played his round early, and in relative peace and quiet. "There were some things that were hard to handle out there," Woods said, declining to get too specific, but hinting "the people concerned might have had a few."

Tiger made a strong comeback and finished a·distant fifth, while Norman went on to win the tournament by eight shots over Wayne Grady. Norman, still the No. 1 player in the world, loved the fact that he was suddenly No. 2 with the fans and the media—even in his home country. "Let him have all the attention," the Shark said. "I have been having it for twenty years of my life and sometimes it's nice to stop and see how someone else handles it."

From the Australian Open, Tiger went straight to the Skins Game, where he was again the box office in a field that included Tom Watson, Fred Couples, and John Daly. Over 9,500 attended Saturday's opening round, the largest at a Skins Game since 1986. The real impact, however, was felt by ABC. More than twice as many viewers watched the telecast as the year before, and the overnight ratings for Saturday's program were 8.2, the highest ever for a Skins Game and among the highest-rated golf telecasts in history. It certainly justified Trans World International's decision to hold a spot open for Tiger, even before he turned professional. "There's not a question that Tiger Woods's emergence on tour has created this interest," Watson said. "It's great. The ratings want to see Tiger. It shows the golf world that they want to see him."

Although he won only two Skins, Tiger earned his stripes. Daly told him, "You're going to kick some ass out there. You really are." Skins Game officials had the fairways painted on certain holes with yardage grids to record the long-driving competition between Daly and Woods. Tiger was more concerned with winning every skin, but at the opening hole, Daly pumped one 340 yards, 22 paces past Woods, and the game was on.

"Man, that was a bomb," Tiger said, squeezing Daly's bicep. At the next three driving holes, Tiger averaged 353.3 yards per tee ball. Daly outdrove him two of the three times, including a 380-yarder at the 5th. Finally, at the 17th, a flat, 577-yard par-five, Tiger hit one 322 yards and Daly's blast stopped one yard short of Woods's. "The 17th is the best test, so it's a tie," Tiger said. Daly, who was shut out, nodded.

Tiger clearly loved being in the spotlight. He made only $40,000, but admitted, "I'm having a blast." It was like a high-school match for him, just four guys playing only nine holes a day. Outside the ropes, it was a familiar story: a record media turnout, and everywhere he went, somebody wanted an autograph. Couples and Watson were both worried that the media, and the fan attention, would ultimately wear Tiger out. "Tiger Woods has a lot going on," said Couples. "He does a great job. There's never been anything like this. But you guys should all give this guy a break. If you push him around and drive him crazy, you're going to change him, and he doesn't need to change." Watson noted that it was going to be tough for Tiger to win 80 tournaments like Sam Snead and Jack Nicklaus, unless he learns how to budget his time. "He's a lot like Nicklaus when Nicklaus came on Tour," Watson said. "The different thing is going to be how Tiger deals with the extracurricular things. He's going to have to learn to say no, because he is a great talent."

One commitment Tiger couldn't say no to, not again anyway, was the Fred Haskins Dinner. Before Australia and the Skins Game, he and Earl were back at Callaway Gardens to receive the award given to the 1996 College Player of the Year. Earl stood up at the podium that night, and with a commanding presence, had the room listening to every word. "Please forgive me," he said. "But sometimes I get very emotional when I talk about my son. My heart fills up with so much joy when I realize that this young man is going to be able to help so many people." These words were not scripted, they were from Earl's heart, a heart that needed surgery, and with each thought, Earl Woods became more and more emotional. Soon, everybody had forgotten about the kid's rookie mistake, how he blew out of town in September, claiming burnout. "He will transcend the game," Earl Woods said. "And bring to the world a humanitarianism, which has never been known before. The world will be a better place to live in by virtue of his existence and his presence. I acknowledge only a small part in that. In that I know that I was personally selected by God himself to nurture this young man, and bring him to the point where he can make his contribution to humanity. This is my treasure. Please accept it, and use it wisely."

Again, there were tears in Earl Woods's eyes, and his son was in his arms. All was forgiven. "My actions were wrong," Tiger reiterated. "I've said that all along. I should have attended the dinner. I'm sorry for any inconvenience I have caused anybody. I'll never do it again."

That week, Tiger and Earl were on the cover of *Newsweek*, in what was considered a makeup for that magazine's reference to Earl being golf's equivalent of Stefano Capriati, the overbearing tennis father. The accompanying *Newsweek* article, entitled "Raising a Tiger," was on parenting, and would certainly help promote Earl's book, which was scheduled for a Father's Day release. Word was also filtering out that Tiger would be named as *Sports Illustrated*'s 1996 Sportsman of the Year, the first golfer to win that award solo since Jack Nicklaus in 1978. Gary Smith, *SI*'s premier writer, had been working the story since the Texas Open in October.

This long year, the Year of the Tiger, was grinding to a close. After the Skins Game, Tiger returned to Florida for one more tournament, the JCPenney Mixed Team Classic, Dec. 5–8, at the Innisbrook Hilton and Resort in Tarpon Springs. Early in the week, Tiger clearly wasn't into it. He nearly overslept his pro-am time (Fluff had to roust him from a condo behind the 1st tee), but stepped up, and without a warm-up, busted a hard cut down the left side of the fairway that landed well past the best effort of any pro that day. Once the tournament began Thursday, he was ready to play, and just like any other tournament, he was there to win.

The Mixed Team was added to Tiger's schedule as a favor to his friend Kelli Kuehne, the two-time U.S. Women's Amateur champion, and the sister of Trip Kuehne, who he had beaten at the TPC for his first U.S. Amateur title. With IMG representing her, Kelli had turned pro and signed a $1.5 million, five-year contract with Nike right after the World Amateur. It was an awkward time, because the LPGA Tour's Qualifying Tournament had passed, and Kuehne, a sophomore at the University of Texas, virtually had nowhere to play other than mini-tour events. There was speculation that she did it because her marketability was at its apex, and with Marissa Baena, arriving on the scene and winning the

NCAA Championship as a sophomore at the University of Arizona, Kuehne's stock could be damaged.

That Kuehne got a chance to play in the Mixed Team was an example of the power Tiger wielded with tournament directors and golf's organizations. In October, Hughes Norton had contacted Gerald Goodman, the tournament director of the JCPenney Classic, expressing interest. Goodman could hardly believe it, but soon he learned there was a hook. Woods's choice as a partner was first described as an "unnamed amateur." The problem was that Kuehne was not a member of the LPGA Tour. To get Woods in the JCPenney field, Goodman had to petition Jim Ritts, the LPGA Commissioner. Ritts first declined, then reconsidered and took the matter to the LPGA's Executive Committee. It agreed to give Goodman and the JCPenney one unconditional pick for the good of the game.

The JCPenney issued Kuehne an invitation the day she turned professional. "This is not a question about personality, but about logistics," Ritts said. "What is the fair way to deal with this? This tournament shouldn't be treated differently from anything else. It wasn't a hard decision. Over the years, there have been special circumstances. Let's treat this like other tournaments and simply go to the sponsor exemption pick that we have with every other event. That seemed to satisfy the issue."

It certainly satisfied Goodman, who went into contingency plans designed to handle the galleries Tiger would generate. Route 19, the main artery running north from Clearwater, turned into a parking lot, as more spectators than ever descended upon the Innisbrook. Kelli had a hard time dealing with all the attention; twice she turned down an invitation to visit the ABC booth, referring both requests to her agent, Mark Steinberg of IMG. The irony was that

TWI, IMG's television arm, was actually producing the telecast. On the golf course, Kelli wasn't much help. She made no birdies the first day, and didn't cover Tiger with pars when he made two bogeys. On Tiger's ball alone, they shot 66, and were three strokes off the lead.

Kelli played better Friday, and left Tiger with a 2-footer at the 18th for a 63 and a share of the 36-hole lead. Tiger gunned it through the break ("There are powder burns all over me.") and tapped-in for a 64. Saturday's third round was rained-out, and on Sunday, they both contributed to a second-place finish. At the 14th, Tiger had a six-footer for birdie. "Tiger from six feet. Done. Next hole," and when he missed, she jabbed at the short par putt coming back for a costly bogey. Tiger made that up with a birdie at the 15th, but they both messed up at the 16th. In a modified alternate-shot format, Tiger left Kelli's drive in the front bunker, and Kelli shank-blocked Tiger's drive right-of-right, behind a clump of trees. They made bogey there, but again Tiger made it up with a 5-iron to one foot at the 201-yard 17th.

One shot back going to the 18th, they needed to make birdie. Kelli hit her drive into the right rough. Tiger split the fairway, leaving Kelli just a wedge into the green. Tiger scraped a punch shot onto the putting surface, but it was no birdie putt. Now it was all on Kelli. From just over 100 yards, she pull-hooked a short iron left and short of the green, over a cart path. "As a competitor, you have so much pride within yourself, you don't want to lose," Woods said. "Kelli and I are alike. When we go to a golf tournament, we're trying to win. Granted, we're going to have some fun, but when you get down to crunch time and get in the hunt, your juices take over. It was pretty exciting coming down the stretch."

Tiger immediately went into his chill-out mode, hardly

touching a golf club for the rest of the month. He bought a new house for his parents in Tustin, California, and a Mercedes two-seat convertible for himself. On Dec. 30, he celebrated his 21st birthday with a private party at the MGM Grand in Las Vegas. Frank Tutera and Butch Harmon no longer had to chaperone him. Eldrick Tiger Woods was finally legal. The kid was a man.

The new year was only two days away. A major championship, five victories, and a $2 million season were being predicted. The doubters had quickly become believers. Tiger knew it was on him now. "I've been thinking about this more and more," he said. "People can say all kinds of things about me and Nicklaus and make me into whatever. But it comes down to one thing: I've still got to hit the shot. Me. Alone. That's what I must never forget."

V

RAISING THE BAR

"Tiger's performance has got everyone feeling they have to improve or get left behind."
—TOM LEHMAN

47

CHAMPION OF CHAMPIONS

On the driving range at LaCosta, Tiger prepared for the playoff to determine the winner of the Mercedes Championship. A front had stalled over the Pacific Coast, drenching the San Diego area, and wiping out the final round of the PGA Tour's season-opening event. He had a five-iron, knowing that was the club to hit to the back left pin at the par-3 7th. When Tour officials moved the tees up 5 yards, he switched to the six-iron, and continued to hit draw after draw, knowing that was the shape of the shot he wanted to hit in the playoff.

After 54 holes, Tiger was tied with Tom Lehman, the PGA Tour's Player of the Year, leading money winner, and Vardon Trophy winner in 1996. They had reached this point, at 14-under-par, on Saturday afternoon: Tiger birdied the last four holes, and Lehman, 37, drained a 30-footer at the 18th to regain a share of the lead. After he made the bomb, Lehman came in the press room and declared, "It's like match play. You top what he did and say, 'Take that.' It's like, 'Well, OK, you made your four birdies and took the lead, but watch this one. Swish.'"

Tiger's run to close out the third round was highlighted by the two shots he hit to reach the 569-yard 17th.

In tournament history, only Dewitt Weaver in 1971 had reached that green in two. Around LaCosta, they call this hole The Monster. Tiger whip-cracked his three-wood on the green, and two-putted. Tom Lehman, with his thick chest and forearms, had to lay up. Anticipating an 18-hole showdown on Sunday, Lehman admitted, "If I go out and lose, I'm going to know there's a new kid on the block who's just way better than everybody else. Tom Lehman is player of the year, but Tiger Woods is probably the player of the next two decades. I'm not sure if I feel like the underdog or what, but it's a unique situation. It's almost like trying to hold off the inevitable, like bailing water out of a sinking boat."

Little did Lehman know how appropriate that metaphor would be on Sunday. With the Bob Hope Chrysler Classic scheduled to start on Wednesday in Palm Springs, and with a poor weather forecast for Monday and Tuesday, PGA Tour Commissioner Tim Finchem reluctantly made the call to shorten the Mercedes to a 54-hole event. Only one hole, the seventh, was playable. They would go back and forth on that par three for as long as it took to determine a champion.

Lehman drew the honors. Because the ground was wet, he teed the ball up higher than usual. "Usually the [sudden-death] playoff comes after you've played 18 holes," he said. "You want to have some rhythm and some momentum going. My first thought was, 'I'm hoping it's a good yardage.' You don't want to be in between clubs on something like that. It was a normal six-iron for me, maybe a hard seven."

With the rain coming down, Lehman took the six-iron, and figured the right-to-left wind would help his natural draw. His swing lacked the rhythm he was hoping for, and the ball came off the toe of the club, high on the face, and nose-dived in the pond. Lehman's broad shoulders immediately slumped, and his chin dropped deep into his chest.

Woods was shocked, but he showed no emotion. Instead, he took off his rain jacket, and revealed his bright red Sunday shirt, the color he wore at Vegas and Disney, the color, his mother Tida says, that brings him power. He visualized a high draw that would land right of the pin, away from the water. For most of the week, he had been struggling with his swing, but the extra time on the range allowed him to work it out.

"I was lucky in the fact that I lost the draw," he said. "If it was a clear and sunny day in Southern California, the advantage [in having the honor] would have been Tom's. I had no idea how much the wind was going to blow, but when I saw Tom's ball ride the wind, all I had to do was aim in the middle of the green. I still had to execute the shot."

The shot disappeared in the clouds—Tiger even lost it for a second, because a raindrop hit him in the eye. When it came down and tore a hole next to the pin, the legend of Tiger Woods had once again been injected with steroids. "I overdrew it a little," he would say.

Lehman went to the drop zone, and nearly holed out a wedge for par, but it wouldn't have mattered. Tiger was in pick-it-up range, just six inches from birdie-two and his third win on the PGA Tour. When he tapped in, that made his winning percentage .333. It also converted Lehman, who before the tournament noted that Tiger will eventually become one of the best ever, but he still had some earning to do when it came to respect among his peers.

"You have to take your hat off to the guy who hits it stiff when the other guy is basically in the pocket," Lehman said. "It was one of those deals where you're either totally overjoyed or really bummed out."

48

ACED OUT

Tiger took some heat for skipping the Bob Hope, and the criticism was justifiable. It was Hope who gave him his start, who put him on television at age three, and the tournament director, Mike Milthorpe, took his shots. "The biggest thing for me is, if I don't get him to play, all I'm going to hear is, 'Why isn't he here? He's worth a minimum of 5,000 tickets a day' " Milthorpe said. "I'm watching a promotion on The Golf Channel [in November] for the Australian Open, and it's Norman vs. the Kid. We could have a situation where this is a one-man tour.

"Everywhere I go, all people ask is, 'Is Tiger coming?' I hate it. He's bigger than Norman ever was. I certainly know that if Tiger doesn't come, the media isn't going to be talking about how we've got twenty of the top-thirty players."

The reason he said no to Hope's personal request was that his schedule was basically full starting with the Phoenix Open, the third week of the season. He would play Phoenix and Pebble Beach back-to-back, then fly to Thailand for the Honda Asian Classic, and then on to Australia for the Australian Masters. In other words, he was going to Asia and Australia for two huge appearance fees, and 93-year-old Bob Hope would just have to wait. At least that's the way it came across.

Hope wasn't the only one getting snubbed. Nelson Mandela wrote a personal letter to IMG, appealing to Tiger, and extending an invitation to play in the South African Open. The conflict was the Asian Classic in Thailand, which, to be fair, was his mother's homeland.

On the week of the Bob Hope, Jeff Babineau of the *Orlando Sentinel* contacted Milthorpe. "We wrote Tiger three times, called his father twice, called IMG twice, [and] never got a return call or any kind of correspondence," Milthorpe said. "I don't mind him not playing. He can go play in Thailand for the rest of his life. I just think if Bob Hope . . . calls you up and asks you to play in his tournament, you say yes. Mr. Hope is ninety-three years old and he has done an awful lot for the game of golf. He won't be around forever."

Although appearance fees are forbidden on the PGA Tour, there are certain incentives that tournaments can offer, and the Phoenix Open did, by agreeing to transport 1,500 underprivileged youths to the TPC of Scottsdale for a clinic held on January 20, Martin Luther King Day. Milthorpe hinted that this was unethical, saying, "I guess they've got some creative minds in Phoenix." PGA Tour Commissioner Tim Finchem, doing his best to keep everybody happy, addressed the controversy at the Mercedes Championship.

"Any time you have a player at his level, the tournaments he doesn't play in are disappointed," Finchem said. "There's nothing we can do about that. We're encouraged that Tiger has said he'll make an attempt to spread his schedule around. This is not something that is even close to constituting an appearance fee. A lot of tournaments have already asked us what we can do to make Tiger come."

For almost three days, Tiger was relatively quiet at the TPC of Scottsdale. His opening rounds of 68–68 put him ten shots in back of Steve Jones, the U.S. Open champion, who was on a 62–64 tear. Through 15 holes on Saturday, it was obvious that not even Tiger Woods could pull this tournament out, but that didn't mean he couldn't steal a little of Jones's story.

The 16th at Scottsdale is a par-three of 155 yards that was designed by Tom Weiskopf and Jay Morrish inside a grass ampitheatre that can hold an estimated 25,000 golf fans. On Friday afternoon, and over the weekend, it is a giant outdoor party. In *Sports Illustrated*, Rick Reilly described it as a giant mosh pit of a par-three, a ''Golfapalooza'' and ''Woods-stock.'' The locals call it Sun Devil Hill because of the Arizona State students who make it their weekend frat house. Tiger kind of liked the atmosphere. ''I think it's neat,'' he said. ''It's untraditional. You don't have these people with handcuffs and mittens on.''

Coming off the 15th green, Tiger told Fluff Cowan, ''Maybe I should run up through there like it's a tunnel at a football game and explode onto the tee box and high-five everybody.'' The crowd quieted for only a moment, and Woods nearly backed off in the buzz. All those years of his father's basic training taught him to block it all out and concentrate. He had a nine-iron, and the visualization of a high, soft cut. As soon as the ball came off the clubface, there was an eruption, and when ball hit three feet short of the cup, bounced twice, and disappeared in the hole, the sonic boom could be heard in Tucson. ''Had to be an ace. Had to be Tiger,'' Nick Price said back at the clubhouse. It was called the loudest noise in golf history.

On the tee, Woods high-fived Cowan, and then playing partner Omar Uresti. Beer cups, programs, cans, baseball caps, and cigars rained down, as everybody's arms went up in a touchdown salute. ''Right afterward, I don't really remember anything," Woods said. "It was amazing. People were just going crazy. It was ridiculous how loud it was."

Walking down to the green, Woods gave it his "raise the roof" gesture, and then, after plucking the ball from the hole, threw it in the crowd. It was his second hole-in-one in 10 professional tournaments, and although he finished tied for 18th on Super Bowl Sunday, once again, Tiger Woods had stolen the stage.

49

FIELD OF DREAMS

On Friday night at the Pebble Beach Salon, Tiger Woods was getting a haircut. Word spread quickly around the resort, and outside the window, guests at the Lodge and golf fans peered in at Tiger and Ricki Pilkington. When the phenom was finished, a woman in her 60s came into the shop, and asked Pilkington for a lock of hair. Sorry, the clippings had already been thrown away.

Yes, it was that absurd at Pebble Beach. The convergence of Tigermania with Costnermania made for a rather wild and sometimes rude week on the Monterey Peninsula, where, by the way, there was a golf tournament played and eventually won by Mark O'Meara.

Tiger was originally scheduled to play with his father, but his heart condition prevented that. Replacing Earl was Kevin Costner, star of *Tin Cup*, *Field of Dreams*, *Dances with Wolves*, and a newly addicted golf junkie. The first two days of the tournament, at Poppy Hills and Spyglass, were chaotic. The PGA Tour's "No Camera Rule" is not enforced at the AT&T, and spectators showed no respect for Steve Stricker, who played with Bryant Gumbel in the Woods–Costner pairing. Gumbel picked up on it. "He's a magnet," Gumbel said of Woods. "The only downside—and it's not his fault—is that I know it can be distracting to other golfers." It took them six hours to get around, and Woods was frustrated with the swarming galleries. "They have to realize we're out here trying to earn money," Woods said. "There were a lot of cameras clicking. I think it's great that people come out and it's fine if they take my photo, but not while we're swinging."

When he was playing Poppy Hills, Lehman said he could hear the gallery screaming five miles away at Spyglass. "I said, 'Whoops, Costner must have made another three-foot putt,'" he said. Stricker wasn't nearly as amused. "It was so disappointing," he said. "I might never come back here."

The situation improved slightly at Pebble on Saturday, and Tiger responded by shooting 63 (Stricker shot 72 and missed the cut). He was still seven shots in back of David Duval going into the final round, with Mark O'Meara, his close friend and neighbor, trailing Duval by three. It had reached the point for O'Meara that he no longer attended Orlando Magic games with Tiger because of the accompanying circus. They fish together in O'Meara's bass boat, and play at Isleworth, but he has seen what it's like for Tiger in public, and wants no part of it. "Everybody looks at him and sees his contracts and says he's a great player, a good-looking kid, all that," O'Meara said. "But it's got to be difficult. I don't think I'd want to trade places with Tiger Woods, to be honest."

But O'Meara definitely wasn't going to back off when Tiger started chasing him on Sunday. "I was jacked," he said. "Tiger's the hottest player in the game. We play a lot of golf together. He says to me, 'I just love competition. All I want to do is win. Wouldn't it be great to go head-to-head sometime?' I say, 'You may blow it by me by fifty yards and have a better swing, but I'm going to figure out a way to clip you.' "

O'Meara and Woods didn't go head-to-head in the final pairing at Pebble Beach, but they were the ones slugging it out for the title. Playing one group ahead of O'Meara, Tiger birdied the 16th, 17th, and 18th holes to shoot 64 and conclude a weekend run when he birdied 18 of the closing 36 holes. Tiger hit a seven-iron over the flagstick at seventeen, the par-3 that juts out on a promontory by Stillwater Cove and Carmel Bay. In the 1972 U.S. Open, Jack Nicklaus hit a one-iron at this hole off the flagstick and in the 1987 Nabisco Championships playoff, Curtis Strange used a three-iron to stake the deciding shot. At the 548-yard 18th, Woods left himself 267 to the stick. Into the wind, and in thick ocean air, that shot was considered impossible. "That's a long way, a *long* way," said Jim Furyk, who was playing with O'Meara. "I don't think reaching that green in two even entered anyone else's mind this week."

Tiger had no choice. Behind him, he heard the roars when O'Meara chipped in for birdie at 16, and matched his birdie at 17. To win, he needed eagle.

Since they were playing the lift, clean, and place rule, Tiger teed his ball up in the rough, and unleashed a nuclear three-wood that left him 35 feet from the hole. Never mind that he missed the putt, it was a shot that they'll be talking about for a long time at Pebble Beach. "I made a good run at it," Woods said. "But it was a little too late."

It was still the story of the tournament, and while it made for great drama—many were calling it the best end to a PGA Tour event they had ever seen—it left Tiger mad at himself for making bogey at thirteen. That made the flight to Thailand that night seem even longer. "I think it's great Mark won," he said. "I love him to death. But I'm disappointed. I should've been in a playoff."

50

PRINCE OF THAIS

At 10 P.M. on Tuesday, February 4, 1997, Thai Airways Flight 771 taxied to the terminal at Don Muang Airport in Bangkok, and over 1,000 well-wishers were there to greet the Thai-ger. Inside the first-class cabin, Tiger Woods was startled when the door opened and a TV news crew burst onboard to air his arrival live. Queen Elizabeth and President Clinton had been accorded the same honor.

Around his neck and arms, hostesses draped traditional Thai garlands. He was met by his mother, Tida, who flew over two weeks early, and two dozen relatives and family friends. A banner was raised that read: "Welcome Home, Tiger. We Are Happy To See You Back Again." Riot-gear police and armed militia held back the crowd. A police escort whisked Woods's entourage down a closed freeway to the Shangri-La Hotel on the banks of the Chao Phraya River. The entire 25th floor was reserved for the Woods party, which included Jerry Chang, his former Stanford teammate, Michael Gout, his friend from Cypress, Nike liason Greg Nared, Fluff Cowan, and IMG's Clarke Jones. One newspaper compared it to the arrival of Michael Jackson.

Tiger and Tida had immediate words over a story that first ran in Thailand and was picked up on the wires in

America. In an interview on *Seetoom Square*, a popular TV talk show in Thailand, Tida was asked if Tiger was going to marry a Thai woman. She responded that it was up to Tiger, but the words were twisted and it came out sounding as if she demanded her son marry a Thai woman.

"Mom," Tiger said, "did you say that? It's all over the world."

Tida claimed she was misquoted. "The dad-gum media got it wrong," she said. "All I said was that it would be nice if he did." Tiger brushed it off, but right away he realized how different it would be this time than his two previous trips to Thailand. "I will marry whomever I fall in love with," he said at a news conference.

Tiger visited Thailand when he was 9, and again at 18, but he never before needed a security guard on his hotel room floor, or a police escort everywhere he went. A headline in *The Nation* proclaimed, TIGERMANIA GRIPS THAILAND. When Tiger won the U.S. Amateur at Pumpkin Ridge, it was aired six times in a week on Thai TV. More than 300 media representatives from around the world had descended upon Thai Country Club for the Honda Asian Classic, an IMG-run event on the Omega Tour. Woods was reportedly paid $480,000 to make this trip, although the figure was actually closer to $300,000, which matched the event's purse. Alastair Johnston, the head of IMG's golf division, knew what the skeptics were thinking. "Tiger is here basically for his mother," he said. "Yes, the appearance fee was big, but Tiger doesn't take deals just for money. The fact that this is his mother's country tipped the balance."

The trip was arranged right after Tiger won his third straight Amateur the previous August. Kultida, who was raised seventy miles north of Bangkok, wanted her son to know his Asian roots, but there just wasn't enough time for any of the planned visits to landmarks like the Grand Palace or the Emerald Buddha. His first 24 hours in Bangkok were spent fighting gastroenteritis he contracted on the flight, and he had to withdraw after 13 holes of the pro-am and skip the pro-am dinner that first night. Once the tournament began, he was fine. A helicopter shuttled him 30 miles to the course, and although the heat and humidity were oppressive, Tiger responded by shooting 20-under 268 to win by 10 strokes against a field that included a package of IMG clients Steve Elkington, Frank Nobilo, and Curtis Strange.

The highlight came in Saturday's third round, when Tiger drove the 389-yard 10th hole, but the trip wasn't so much golf as it was about Tiger in the role of dignitary and celebrity. As Strange said, "When you accept the kind of money from a sponsor that Tiger got, for that week they own you." And that part of it was an education for Tiger.

Honda flew in executives from all over Asia. In the aborted pro-am, Tiger was paired with a former Thai deputy prime minister, a Japanese ambassador, and the Asian Honda Motors chairman. On Thursday, after the 70, he conducted a youth clinic for 20 children. "Always keep it fun," he told them. "This game will drive you crazy. You'll love it, hate it, enjoy it. If you don't have fun, you'll never grow as a person or a player."

That evening Tiger wanted to enjoy a quiet dinner with Strange and Nobilo, but Tida had other ideas. She wanted him to attend a function organized in his honor by the government and Thai Airways. Tiger thought he had gotten out of it, until Tida found him in the hotel lounge and convinced him that he had obligations and responsibilities to her and her country.

Accompanied by Chang and Gout, Tiger followed a police car to the Siam City Hotel for a program that included a kick-boxing exhibition and a demonstration of the *rum wong*, a traditional Thai dance. Tiger got up onstage, flashed that megawatt smile, and responded to the good karma the next day by shooting 64, which was the course record. He blew off the post-round news conference and took the helicopter back to the hotel, because that evening a twilight cruise was planned down the Chao Phraya River on the *Oriental Queen*. Tiger spent most of the evening signing autographs. Pradit Phataraprasit, a high-ranking member of Thailand's Democrat Party, and owner of Thai Country Club, presented Tiger with a famous Luang Phor Ngem amulet and gold necklace on behalf of the House Committee on Sports.

"It's important that the boy sees his heritage," Tida said. "It wouldn't have been right for him not to go. I know he did it for me. The boy is a good boy. He got mad because he has no time, but in the end he did the right thing."

Saturday's 66 was followed by an evening at the hotel with his Thai relatives. His 62-year-old uncle, Garvee Punsawad, talked about the honor Tiger brought to his family. Instead of fast food, Tiger ate Thai food, topped off by sticky rice and mangoes for dessert.

His gallery that day numbered only 3,000, and most were carrying umbrellas to block the sun. Thailand has 200 courses, and an estimated one million golfers among its sixty million people, and officials hoped his impact on the game would lead to a rise in tourism and a golf boom for their country. Although small by American and European standards, the galleries that followed Tiger were considered huge for an Asian event. Elkington, Strange, and Nobilo played in relative obscurity.

"A hundred percent of the crowd is following him here," Elkington said. "He's the hometown guy."

"He's the prince this week," said Strange, "and that's fine."

"What Asia has needed is a dominant player," said Nobilo. "And unfairly or fairly, he is considered an honorary Thai this week."

Sunday was nothing more than a victory lap for Tiger. He closed with a 68, and made a quick pass through a reception held at Bangkok's Government House, where Thai prime minister Chavalit Yongchaiyudh presented him with honorary citizenship. Tiger had a plane to catch for Melbourne, where he was getting $300,000 to play the Australian Masters. "Winning, period, is great, but to win here in Thailand is something special," Tiger said before leaving. "It was a hard week with a lot going on, a lot of different forces on me, so I'm proud I overcame that, too."

The trip was more than just a cultural education for Tiger. He realized the demands of international travel, and the tradeoffs made when you accept a big appearance fee. He made friends, but this week had taken a lot out of him. There was no time to relax and have fun, no time to himself. It went against what he told those Thai children at the youth clinic.

"I need to keep golf fun," he said. "I guess I had to learn the hard way."

51

THE RUN-UP TO AUGUSTA

Back in the United States, news of Tiger's victory received better play than O'Meara going back-to-back in California by winning the Buick Invitational right after Pebble Beach. Tiger would've preferred taking the first flight back to Los Angeles, but going halfway around the world just for one tournament didn't make sense at the time, so the Honda Asian Classic was packaged with the Australian Masters at Huntingdale Golf Club.

Tiger was in contention after opening rounds of 68–70, but ran out of gas on the weekend, shot 72–73, and finished tied for eighth, seven shots out of first. There were other more important issues on Tiger's mind. His father was scheduled for triple bypass surgery at the UCLA Medical Center, and he was mentally preparing for that all the way home from Australia.

Earl went in for the operation on February 19, 1997, the week of the Tucson Chrysler Classic, and there were complications that forced doctors to operate again, four days later. He wasn't released until Tiger was playing the Nissan Open in Los Angeles on Saturday, March 1. The travel and the stress of his father's situation were obvious at Riviera, where Tiger snapped at cameramen and was short with the media, many of whom had covered him as a junior.

Early in the week, at his Tuesday news conference, Tiger began to get a sense for what it was like to be a celebrity and a crossover star when an attractive woman from one of the tabloid news shows attempted questioning him on his private life.

"Let me invade your privacy one more time," she said. "When you're relaxing, not playing . . . I mean, I know this is for you and it's your passion, but do you have a girlfriend? Do you go to the movies? Who are you as a person? We know you as a phenomenon."

"Well," Tiger said, trying to be polite, "that's for my friends to know."

Not taking the hint, she pressed on.

"No, tell us," she said. "We want to know. We want to know about you."

Tiger wasn't about to tell her.

"As I said," he said, "that's for my friends to know."

Once the tournament began, Tiger's goal was to play well enough so his father could watch him on television, but with the exception of a few shots, Tiger wasn't a big part of the CBS broadcast. Overall, though, it showed Tiger's maturity. He hung in and shot three-under 281 to finish tied for 20th. "I'm happy with what I did considering everything that is going on," Woods said. "It was hard to get a real deep focus because I was thinking about more important things than a round of golf."

The Doral-Ryder Open was dropped from Tiger's schedule, and Tiger didn't play again until Bay Hill, the third week in March. He offered little at his Tuesday news conference, giving the same stock answers—just as his father taught him—and saying that the surgery was a success and his dad was recovering. Nobody would know until the Masters just how serious the second operation really was.

Tiger had picked up some bad habits playing in the wind overseas, and they weren't totally fixed at Bay Hill. Without his A game, the kid shot 68 in the opening round, and had the other players talking. "I kind of get the impression that we're all chasing Tiger," said Tom Lehman, the 1996 Player of the Year. "I think that he's good for the same. I think that people are aware of the fact that there is a new kid on the block who is extremely talented. And they don't want to step aside."

It was being called the Tiger Factor, and everybody was feeling it: young, old, and middle-aged. "This guy wants to win, and he wants to win badly," said O'Meara. "He's got that burning desire. He brings that element in there, and it's convincing more and more young players—shoot, every player—that when he has an opportunity to win, he'd better try to win. You only have so many chances."

Billy Andrade told a story that occurred after Tiger made the hole-in-one on Saturday at the Phoenix Open. Tiger was 10 shots out of the lead going into the final round when he was approached for an interview by Robert Wrenn, a former Tour player working as an on-course reporter for ESPN. Wrenn asked Tiger if he was going to use the final round to work on certain aspects of his game. Tiger looked him straight in the eye and said, "Next week? If I shoot 55 tomorrow, I might have a shot to win." Realizing that Tiger was dead serious, Wrenn didn't know what to say.

"This kid is twenty-one years old, and he's the best player in the world," Andrade said. "He's not happy finishing eighth or sixth or second. He wants to win. And he's pushing us all to think like that."

Woods ended up finishing tied for ninth at Bay Hill,

which showed his ability to post respectable numbers not only when he was fighting his swing, but putting out fires. On the Friday when he was shooting 71, a fax arrived at the press tent of a story from the April issue of *Gentlemen's Quarterly*. In it, author Charles Pierce arranged to ride in the limousine taking Tiger from his mother's home in Cypress to the *GQ* cover shoot in Long Beach. Naively, Tiger told several racy, off-color jokes in front of Pierce, that he thought were off the record. Pierce, saying sorry, it was too late, used them in the hit-and-run article, and made the point that the language Tiger used—and the jokes he told—was no different than the way most twenty-one-year-olds talk in the dormitory late on a Saturday night. The problem was that Tiger no longer was a twenty-one-year-old at a Stanford University keg party, and on Saturday morning at Bay Hill, IMG went into its damage-control mode, issuing a statement through Los Angeles-based spin doctor Linda Dozeretz. It was the wrong thing to do, because it drew too much attention to the story.

"Thanks to the magazine and the writer for teaching me a lesson," he concluded. "I got the message, even thought the writer completely missed it."

There were many who felt Tiger got what he deserved. After turning down one-on-one interviews with every golf writer except Jaime Diaz of *Sports Illustrated* and Pete McDaniel of *GolfWorld*, he was convinced by agent Hughes Norton that the cover of *GQ*, and an accompanying story, would be great exposure and publicity.

And in some corners, the story actually turned out to be great publicity. Many people felt it humanized Tiger, showed him to be normal after all. Others thought it was hypocritical of him to be telling racist jokes when he was marketed by Nike as the golfer who couldn't play certain courses because of the color of his skin. Either way, it didn't seem to affect his golf. He ended up shooting 71–68 on the weekend to finish tied for ninth with Davis Love III, six strokes back of Phil Mickelson. The next day he drove up to Ponte Vedra Beach for the Players Championship.

Earl was worried about the long-term effects. "That article created a deep hurt," he told Diaz. "It disillusioned him and stayed with him awhile because he realized he misjudged a situation. He thought, 'How could I have been so stupid?' "

Tiger won his first U.S. Amateur at the Tournament Players Club in 1994, and the questions at his Tuesday news conference started with the Golf course, but moved on to such mundane subjects as his golf swing, autograph signing, his play at Bay Hill, his maturity, the upcoming Masters, U.S. Open, British Open, and PGA Championship, his relationships with Butch Harmon, Arnold Palmer, Jack Nicklaus, Jackie Robinson, his father, his fan base, and ultimately, the *GQ* article and his ongoing love affair with the media.

Tiger was asked if his growing irritation had to do with being interviewed by people who don't know golf, and he brought up the scene from the Nissan Open press room.

"I don't know if you guys remember, there was a young lady in the back of the room asking . . ."

"Dumb questions?"

"Yeah, she was from *Inside Edition* or *American Journal*. You are going to get some people like that who—she wanted to talk about my private life."

"Is that what happened in the . . . *GQ* article?"

"I've already answered enough on that *GQ* article."

Early in the new conference, *Golfweek* columnist Jeff Rude tried to break the ice by asking Tiger if he had any good new jokes, but Tiger wasn't amused. He shot Rude a sarcastic smirk and didn't honor the question with a response.

Other than a player meeting, that was his last trip to the press center at the Players Championship. All his interviews were conducted behind the scoring trailer, and with rounds of 71–73–72–73, he finished tied for 31st, his worst finish on the PGA Tour since turning professional at the Greater Milwaukee Open the previous August. On Sunday, he was paired with Faldo and, as always, that was an education. In eleven days, they would be paired for the opening round at Augusta.

Tiger drove home to Orlando that night knowing he had plenty to work on. The distance control on his irons was off, and he wasn't putting very well, but he would take the week of the Freeport-McDermott Classic in New Orleans off to gear up for the Masters. All week he worked at Isleworth, where they shaved the greens down for him. Finally, on the Friday before leaving, he played a practice round with O'Meara.

Mark shot 65. Tiger lipped out two putts, made two eagles, nine birdies, and shot 59.

Fifteen minutes after turning in his card, Tiger was greeted by *Golfweek* publisher Ken Hanson, who is a member at Isleworth.

"That question Rude asked at the Players was bullshit," he told Hanson.

Hanson tried to explain that it was just meant to be a funny one-liner, but Tiger hadn't forgiven him for it."

"That question," he repeated, "was bullshit."

Rude got a call from Hanson at his home in the suburbs south of Chicago.

"How upset would he be with me had he shot 65?" Rude asked his boss. "He should have been dancing with Dom [Perignon]. I guess I should be flattered that he's thinking of me."

52

GETTING IN GEAR

A t 3 P.M. on Tuesday, April 8, 1997, Mr. Danny Yates of the Augusta National Golf Club press committee, sat behind a microphone in the Masters Tournament press room, leaned forward, and said, in a Georgia drawl: "Well, we've got what y'all have been waiting for all day. So, Tiger, say a few words and we'll let them have a go at you."

Tiger seemed guarded, but somewhat amused by Yates's delivery.

"Hi and bye. No, I guess, as always, it's a pleasure to be here at Augusta. I'm definitely looking forward to playing."

"OK. Who's got some questions?"

"Tiger, this being your first pro year on the tour, is it as demanding as you thought it would be?"

"No. A lot more."

"Travel, media, autographs, what?"

"All of it. You hit the nail right on the head. The golf part is actually the easiest part. That part I love to do. Anything else, outside of the golf course, that sometimes can be a little difficult at times, whether it's people wanting a ten-second little stop with you or an interview for ten minutes or whatever. It's just people just want to get a piece of your time."

And so it went, over twenty-two pages of transcribed notes, and it was only Tuesday. For the rest of the week, Tiger kept his head down when he walked under the oak tree outside the clubhouse, tried not to make eye contact with anybody from the news media, and when Jeff Rude called out his name, just to say he was only kidding at the TPC, Tiger kept his stride. He had done his interview.

"I came away from that not only thinking he can't tell a joke, he can't take one either," Rude cracked. "I gave him a chance to endear himself by playfully and jokingly dismissing the *GQ* thing with a laugh, but he took the whole thing wrong. He could have said, 'I'm out of the joke business. I've proved I'm no Richard Pryor.' But he doesn't have that gear right now."

Tiger was simply not in the mood for any bullshit. He was in what his father called the "major mode." It's something he learned playing with Faldo and Nicklaus. "This week of a major, you have to eat, drink, think, dream—just everything—golf," he said. "Obviously, I lack some experience. But being young and having a lot of energy and being psyched to play can also work to my advantage. I can get into that totally obsessed state maybe more easily than an older player, who has done it for years and has more going on in his life . . . But I know how to focus. I've done it before."

Tiger may have been uptight around the media, but his golf game was close to being right where he wanted it to be. In fact, in the news conference, he was confident enough to talk about shooting 59 at the Augusta National, a score that would be four shots lower than the course record. "I'm here to win the golf tournament," he said confidently.

The difference between Tiger at the 1997 Masters and in his two previous trips to Augusta, was that he didn't have to worry about his schoolwork at Stanford. He was dedicating himself entirely to his golf game, so those scores he shot in 1995 (72–72–77–72) and 1996 (75–75) were not true indications of his ability to play the golf course.

It would just be a matter of patience for Tiger. Patience and, as is the case, in any golf tournament, putting. "I just have to go there and play and not try too hard," he said. Cowan, admitting that expectations are never good for a golfer, predicted that if Tiger played well at Augusta—not necessarily super, he could take the place apart.

At the Mercedes Championships in January, he began working with Harmon on the pace of his putts, specifically gearing up for Augusta. When he was at home in Orlando, he would visit the Golf Channel studios and review tapes of past Masters tournaments. He picked up on the way Nicklaus played the course, with safe tap-in pars on the par-threes and par-fours, and a total domination on the reachable par-fives. From Faldo, he gleaned the importance of tee-shot placement in establishing proper angles to those devilish pin placements.

Faldo was asked if he thought it was presumptuous to expect Tiger to tear Augusta up. "Yes, I think there's a learning curve of playing Augusta and the discipline of playing the golf course, when to hit the ball at the pin and when not, when to make that par and walk. You know, as I said, nothing is impossible, but I think that experience does help here."

The key would be getting off to a good start and establishing some confidence early. As he's shown in all his wins—amateur and professional—Tiger does have a passing gear. His usual pattern is to come out of the blocks slow, but never shoot himself out of the tournament, establish a rhythm, then blow by everybody on Sunday. At Augusta, the formula was a little different than the norm.

He was given a 1:44 P.M. tee time on Thursday with Faldo. At Augusta, the tradition is to pair the reigning U.S. Amateur champion with the defending Masters champion, but since Tiger turned pro, there was some question whether the Masters Committee would honor the custom. Normally that late pairing at the Masters is a detriment, because the greens spike up and get harder in the afternoon sun. But this was an unusual circumstance. With the wind-chill, it felt like 34 degrees Thursday morning. By the time Tiger and Faldo stook on the first tee, it had warmed up into the 60s.

Faldo and Woods were at the golf course early, going back and forth from the putting green to the practice tee, concerned more, it seemed, with their feel than their swings. There's always a big difference in the speed of the greens between Wednesday afternoon when the course is close and Thursday morning, and Faldo, especially, was fighting his stroke. With Tiger, it was more a question of distance control with his irons. In 1996, he missed only two of 28 fairways, but was long and left too many times with his approach shots. He needed to be more like Faldo, who had only one putt from the above the hole in his final round of 67.

"It will be a difficult draw for Tiger," predicted Scotland's Colin Montgomerie. "Nick, I'm sure is past the stage of worrying who he's playing with. He's his own man and we know that. He'll get on with his own thing. It will be interesting to see what both of them score, but especially Tiger."

Just before them, former Masters champions Ben Crenshaw, Tom Watson, Jack Nicklaus, Raymond Floyd, Arnold Palmer, Bernhard Langer, and Gary Player had teed off in succession. It was prime time at Augusta, and Tiger was right there in the middle of it with Faldo, the three-time champion.

When he came off the range that final time, and walked through the media under the oak tree, surrounded by security guards, Tiger looked more like a boxer about to climb into the ring, than a golfer going out to play the first round of his first major championship as a professional. He had that mask of intensity and focus on his face, whereas Faldo, paranoid about his putting, was apprehensive.

In truth, Tiger might have been wound a bit too tight. He hit a bad drive down the left side at the first, had to punch out, and made bogey from the front bunker. He missed the fourth green to drop another shot, then bogeyed eight and nine. Four-over at the turn, he steamed to the 10th tee and tried to regroup.

His swing mechanics were off, and then he realized the problem: His backswing had gotten way too long. With Harmon, he had been working on more shoulder turn, which would give him more width, but they had cut down on how far he would take the club back with his arms. Anything too parallel was too long. Seeing his score posted on the giant leaderboards around the course, many wondered: had Augusta and the expectations gotten the best of Tiger Woods? Was he just going to be like the rest of the heirs who never lived up to the predictions?

"I was pretty hot at the way I was playing," Tiger admitted. "I couldn't keep the ball on the fairway. From there, you can't attack the pins, what pins you can attack. I was playing real defensive golf."

The 10th is the longest par-four at Augusta, 485 yards sweeping downhill and to the left. Tiger locked in to his swing thought, hit two-iron and eight-iron to 10 feet, and made the putt for birdie. At the 12th, he flew the green back left with a pitching wedge, but played a beautiful nine-iron chip that he bumped into the bank and released across the green and into the hole. The fortune of that shot carried over to the 13th, where he bombed a high draw around the corner, and reached the green with a six-iron for his third birdie in four holes.

The 15th was Tiger's place to make a statement. He hit a driver and pitching wedge into a hole that is 500 yards long. The pin was cut front left, in a new position designed by Tom Fazio. Tiger didn't even worry about the water, not with a pitching wedge in his hands. His ball stuck to that green, four feet from the hole, and he made the putt for eagle. Five under in six holes, and not through yet.

One more birdie at the 17th gave Tiger nines of 40–30, and at 70, he was only three shots off the lead held by John Huston, with only two other players—Paul Stankowski and Paul Azinger—between himself and Huston. He left a putt hanging on the lip at 18 that would have tied the nine-hole course record, but it was the first time in seven Masters rounds that he was able to break par.

Faldo, on the other hand, three-putted five times on the front nine alone, and shot 75. The kid whipped him by five shots, and looked like he had a good handle not only on his golf game, but the nuances of Augusta. It helps, of course, when you're hitting wedge into most of the par-fours and putting for eagles on the par-fives.

"He obviously played great," Faldo said, keeping it simple, before heading back to the putting green and the range for more work. "Good luck to him."

53

ROUTE 66

The night before Friday's second round, at a restaurant in downtown Augusta, Butch Harmon was having dinner with his wife, Lil, his son, Claude, and Tom Crow, the founder of Coba Golf. There was a sense of excitement and anticipation. That 40–30 comeback Thursday, at least in Harmon's mind, was decisive. Standing up, seeing golf-course designer Tom Fazio and William McKee, the developer of Wade Hampton Golf Club, Harmon made a prediction.

"The kid's going to win this week," Harmon said.

Now, you have to understand where Harmon was coming from, and where he had been: In 1996, as Greg Norman's golf coach, he endured the most devastating final-round collapse in Masters history. He made the mistake a year ago, when Norman had a six-stroke lead after 54 holes, of celebrating too early—and certainly Thursday night at a major championship was not the time to be measuring Tiger Woods for a green jacket.

But there was nobody closer to Tiger Woods and his golf game than Butch Harmon. McKee, who works the range at Augusta as a volunteer, could see the difference in Tiger that night as he hit balls before dark. "What I saw was focused and charged-up and positive and confident," McKee said.

No Masters champion had ever started out with a 40, but Woods had a different look on his face Friday. He was visibly much more at ease, because he knew now that he could play Augusta. He had a score to prove it. The key was not getting in his own way. He had to let it happen.

Harmon escorted him off the range, through the clubhouse, under the tree, and onto the putting green. "I was kidding around when we went through, more to keep him relaxed than anything else, but he didn't need it," the coach said. "Yesterday he was very tight, but he was coming into the biggest tournament in the world and everybody's picking him to win the doggone thing. I'd be nervous too."

Woods's pairing was with Azinger, which was perfect. He made an eagle, five birdies, and his only bogey came at the third, when he drove it pin high on the 340-yard hole, but had the ball roll back down a steep bank. His chip released over the green, and he missed a six-footer for par. At 17, he made his only bad play and swing of the day, going at a pin front right when he should have played to the center of the green. With his short game, he got away with it, and wedged up to tap-in distance.

"He makes the golf course into nothing," said Nicklaus. "That's why this young man is so special. If he's playing well, the golf course becomes nothing. He reduced the golf course to nothing."

Tiger hit wedge into one, five, seven, fourteen, fifteen, seventeen, and eighteen. The most he hit into a par-five was four-iron. He eagled the 13th by hitting three-wood off the tee, and eight-iron into the green. "I'm going to tell you one thing," said Nicklaus. "It's a shame Bob Jones isn't here. He could have saved the words he used for me in '63 for this young man, because he's certainly playing a game we're not familiar with.''

Tiger shot 66 and was at eight-under 136, with a three-stroke lead on Montgomerie. Azinger shot 73, and it felt like 83. "I just got outconcentrated today," he said. "He never had a mental lapse."

That was a tough golf course they were playing. Faldo shot 81 and missed the cut. Norman shot 77–74 and missed the cut. Steve Jones, the Open champion, shot 82–78 and missed the cut. Mark Brooks, the PGA champion, shot 77–82 and missed the cut. Phil Mickelson, winner at Bay Hill and third at Augusta in 1996, shot 76–74 and missed the cut. There was one story at Augusta National now: Tiger Woods.

Waiting by the clubhouse was Phil Knight, and the Nike entourage.

"Great coaching," he said to Harmon, throwing an arm-lock around the teacher's thick neck. "This is what we've been looking for all week. He's making us look smart, isn't he?"

Harmon broke the day down:

"He was a lot looser when he came out to play today," he said. "We had a very good session on the range, more kidding around and going over the basics we go over every time. The club was coming up a little steep, and he had to take back the club a little lower and a little wider. That was about it. On the course, I wanted him to watch his takea-way, and the tempo of it. He tends to pick it up when he gets a little steep. What we're looking for is a bigger shots shoulder turn, and a shorter arm swing. That gives us the tightness that we like to create the speed, and also for him to get the ball a little lower with his trajectory. As you noticed, he's hitting the ball lower now. Other than that, he hit the ball very well. He obviously is unhappy with something he did, because he told me, 'Meet me on the range.' "

It was the second shot at 17. Tiger didn't like it. Neither did Butch, but the mistake was certainly correctable.

"Well, that was the wrong play," Harmon said. "He's got to play that shot left of the flag. That's a false front on that green, and it suckers you into it. But he didn't like it. I saw him make a practice swing after he hit it, but it was a great round. He's eight under par, and at the end of nine holes yesterday, he was four over. That says a lot for him, number one, about his tenacity and how much he wants to win. That just tells you how good he really is. In the middle of a round he knows his faults and knows the keys he works on for those faults. He was able to turn it around on the tenth tee yesterday, and ever since then, he's twelve under. He's in good shape, but we've got to remember, it's only Friday. We've got two more days and we've got to play really good golf to have a chance to win this tournament. That's all we want is a chance."

Tiger fulfilled his obligations with television, but stopped at the range on the way to the press center. It was 7:12 P.M., but working out that shot at 17 was higher on Woods's priority list than pressing newspaper deadlines, so he slow-played the print media. Frank Stone, who works the press room at Augusta as a volunteer, and Carl Reith, a green jacket, hovered nearby, but Tiger wasn't leaving until he was satisfied. Finally, at 7:35, he made his way toward Stone.

Tida was waiting in the parking lot when Fluff arrived to put the Titleist bag in the trunk of a courtesy Cadillac.

"You did a beautiful job," she said to Fluff.

"No," Cowan said, "*He* did a beautiful job."

At 8 P.M., after a quick pass through the locker room, Tiger Woods was asked for another block of his valuable time, this time by Jimmy Roberts of ESPN.

Tiger bent his knees, squatting down to Roberts's height. He was loose now, wanting to stop at a fast-food restaurant on the way home, and then resume his ping-pong tournament with Chang.

Roberts was taping a spot that Mike Tirico would use in the studio.

"It is one thing to spend the majority of your life dreaming about leadng a major, Tiger Woods; it is another thing to come to the weekend of your first professional major as a leader. Tiger Woods, is there anything about this experience thus far that has caught you off guard, that you haven't expected?

Tiger didn't blink.

"Not really," he said. "I've been playing pretty well lately, and playing smart golf."

Roberts, who trained under Howard Cosell, worked to keep the interview going.

"You're playing medal play, not match play against an opponent," he said. "But is there anybody else in the field that you're looking over your shoulder at?"

Again, Tiger did not blink.

"To be honest with you, I don't know who's under par right now," he said. "I haven't had a chance to take a look at the leaderboards or the scores."

Roberts knew he had time for one more question.

"Strategy," he said. "You were on the range for twenty minutes tonight. Is there anything you were working on? What's to work on at this point?"

"Obviously," Tiger said, "I think I can always hit it

better, but overall, I'm striking the ball well, and I'm playing well, but more than anything I'm making good decisions, and that's the key to playing well here.''

Roberts wrapped up the day.

''It's a mind game,'' he said. ''Halfway home, Tiger Woods is your leader. Mike?''

54

42 LONG

It was 4:40 P.M. on Saturday, April 12, and Tiger Woods had just hit a nine-iron from the gallery onto the 11th green, 8 feet below the hole. In the tournament office, Will Nicholson, the Chairman of the Competition Committee, couldn't believe what he'd just seen. "There's no backing off that shot whatsoever," Nicholson said. "It's the wrong angle to go right at the flagstick, but he went right at the flagstick."

When Tiger ran the putt in the hole, and went to 13 under, everybody in Amen Corner, at Augusta National, and watching on television, started to realize that it was no longer a question of Tiger Woods winning the Masters. It was now Tiger vs. the tournament scoring record of 17-under 271 established by Jack Nicklaus in 1965 and tied by Raymond Floyd in 1971.

"I think everybody ought to just go on home," Nicklaus said.

Down in the grandstands at the 12th hole, score reporter Gene Childers wrote a 3 on his clipboard next to the 11th hole, and yelled out above the crowd noise.

"Goodgawdalmighty. Rewrite the record books, boys!"

At 18, he hit sand wedge, and the ball kicked off a bank

and trickled down to within a foot for his seventh birdie of the day. Tiger flashed that megawatt smile and the scoreboard operator behind the 18th green posted that final red number, a 15, which tied Floyd's 54-hole record of 15-under 201, and established a nine-stroke lead over Costantino Rocca of Italy. Tiger had shot 65, and made it look easy.

"It's a done deal," said Jerry Pate, the former U.S. Open champion and CBS analyst. "This one's over with."

Tom Kite, the 47-year-old Ryder Cup captain, still held out hope. "Well, we've got it down to single digits, don't we?" he said. But Colin Montgomerie, who spent the day watching Tiger make birdie after birdie, agreed with Nicklaus: Everybody else *could* go home.

"There is no chance," he said. "We're all human beings here. There's no chance humanly possible that Tiger is going to lose this tournament. No way."

At the Dubai Desert Classic in late February, Monty said he wanted to play Tiger in the Ryder Cup at Valderrama, said the kid only won on resort courses. Friday night, after shooting 67 to earn a spot next to Woods in the final group, Montgomerie hinted that the pressure was on Tiger. On the first tee Saturday, after catching a downslope and skidding a drive past Woods's, he postured to the gallery.

Well, he wanted Tiger, and he got him. "I appreciate that he hit the ball long and straight, and I appreciate his iron shots were very accurate," Montgomerie said. "I do not appreciate how he putted. When you add it all together, he's nine shots clear, and I'm sure that will be higher tomorrow."

When pressed, Montgomerie said there would be no scenario like the events that unfolded in 1996. "This is very different," he said. "Nick Faldo's not lying second. And Greg Norman's not Tiger Woods."

There was a big roar in the media center. Golf writers listening to Montgomerie's interview on headsets typed that quote into their laptops, then moved it up high in their stories. There was time for one more question.

"Colin," a reporter asked, "you said yesterday that you weren't sure with the pressure going into the third round, as the leader, whether he was ready to stand up to it."

Colin Montgomerie, now ready to exit, was losing his patience.

"He is," he said.

Outside the pro-shop door, Fluff Cowan was being interviewed by Bob Verdi of the *Chicago Tribune*, Mark Whicker of the *Orange County Register*, and Rick Reilly of *Sports Illustrated*.

Reilly asked, "Getting any goosebumps?"

"Nope," said Cowan. "This is what I do for a living."

"No thrill by it?" said Reilly, pressing for a better quote.

"Not yet," said Fluff. "We've still got one day left of golf."

The caddy went through the clubs: eight-iron into 12, sand wedge into 14, six-iron into 15, eight-iron into 16, sixty-degree wedge into 17 and sand wedge into 18. Verdi joked that Fluff could lighten his load by taking the three- and four-iron out of the bag.

Seven birdies. Not the hint of a bogey. A perfect round of golf. And the best shot Tiger hit, in Fluff's estimation, was the one nobody talked about: the pitch from the swale left of the 13th green that set up a 10-foot chance for birdie. Woods missed the putt, but Fluff called the setup one of the greatest shots he had ever seen.

"I was seeing the same thing he was seeing, but I didn't

say boo," Cowan said. "That's the first rule. Don't speak unless you're spoken to. But it looks like if he did what he wanted to do, it was going to work, and it did. He executed it perfectly."

Golfers were coming off the range, in awe.

"We knew he was good," said Fred Couples, who trailed by 13. "But we didn't know he was that good."

"I think it's too far," said Rocca. "Maybe if I played nine holes."

"I might have a chance," said Paul Stankowski, who was 10 shots back, "if I make five or six birdies on the first two or three holes."

"Is there any way we can get him to go back to school and get a Ph.D.?" wondered Jeff Sluman, who was 12 back.

"It's what we all kind of visualized coming in here," said Davis Love III, who trailed by 14. "It's not unbelievable, except that no one else is doing it. He's just blowing everybody apart. He's taken the fun out of it for the rest of us."

Underneath the oak tree, on the veranda by the clubhouse, Butch Harmon, Tida Woods, and Phil Knight were holding court.

A copy of *Golf* magazine was out, and Norman was taking shots at Harmon. Now it was Harmon's turn to fire back.

"Tiger Woods is a much smarter player than Greg Norman," he said. "They're both tremendously talented, but Tiger's mental approach to tomorrow is better than Greg's. I don't think you'll see him make mental mistakes. He's so composed. He's made no stupid plays."

Tida Woods wore a silk shirt with a tiger on it. She was asked if she was surprised, and she was only surprised that somebody was actually dumb enough to ask that question. "Does it surprise you guys?" she said, and a few shook their heads. "So why do you ask me those questions?

"This is his ability; you've been seeing it all these years. You've seen him with three straight U.S. Amateurs. This is no different."

Knight, who paid $40 million for Tiger, stroked his red beard and flashed a billion-dollar grin.

"We expected great things from him," he said, "but he's done way beyond what we expected. He's worth what we're paying him. Every penny. When we signed him, one Wall Street analyst, Montgomery Securities, said we overpaid Tiger Woods. I wonder what they think now."

Back at the house they were renting off Wheeler Road in Augusta, Earl Woods watched on TV. Still recovering from open-heart surgery, he was conserving his strength for Sunday. Damned if he was going to miss this one. "Each time I see him I'm amazed at how much his maturity has grown," said his father. "His attitude is, 'I've been there before and I can do it again.' "

At Augusta National, Tiger Woods, soon to be the Masters champion, was riding to the press tent in a golf cart driven by Dan Yates. Walking alongside was Scott Van Pelt of the Golf Channel.

"Tiger, what the hell are you doing?"

"Scott, I have no idea."

"What are you going to wear tomorrow? Something red?"

"Yeah."

"It's going to look a lot like Christmas tomorrow, isn't it?"

"I hope so."

Frank Carpenter, the Augusta National Club steward, had already been informed to get the green jacket ready.

Tiger Woods wore a 42 long.

55

THE RECORD, THE CORONATION

ee Elder couldn't sleep. Finally, at 3 A.M. Sunday morning, at his home in Pompano Beach, Florida, he was able to doze off. Two hours later he was up. At 7:30, he was on a plane at Fort Lauderdale Airport bound for Atlanta. At 11, driving on I–20, he was pulled over by a Georgia Highway Patrol officer for doing 85 miles per hour in a 70 zone. "I've got to get to the Masters to see Tiger Woods win," he told the policeman. The policeman didn't care. He wrote out the ticket.

Butch Harmon couldn't sleep, either. At the home they were renting in Augusta, he rolled over at 4 A.M., and asked his wife, Lil, "You awake?"

"Now I am," she said.

The restlessness of Lee Elder and Butch Harmon was understandable: This was a big day for them, a day that would make the suffering and the waiting and the anticipation seem worth it. For Tiger Woods, it was another step toward destiny, and he was calm and relaxed in its grip. "I slept great, like a log," Tiger Woods would say. "I have no problem sleeping, trust me."

At 3:08 P.M., Harmon and Elder were both near the first tee at Augusta National for the coronation. Harmon gave final instructions, but Tiger Woods's golf game was already on autopilot. Elder gave him a hug, which was an inspiration. It reinforced in Tiger what he had to go out there and do, what his father said when he walked out of the house that morning: "Son, this will be the longest day you've ever spent on the golf course. Go out there and kick some butt."

This was the day, April 13, 1997, that would be a benchmark in golf history, a day when a black man would finally win a major championship in the white man's sport, right in the heart of the Deep South. At the Masters, where they once kept changing the rules to keep Charlie Sifford out, where it wasn't until 1975 that a black man named Lee Elder was let in. At Augusta National, where, until six years ago, there were no black members and where now, there are only two, Ron Townsend and Bill Simms. Yes, this was more than just about golf. This was the emancipation of a sport, the fall, as Elder would say, of the game's last racial barrier.

The kid had been preparing for this since he was in diapers, watching his father hit golf shots into a net in the garage of their home, in Cypress, California. Remember, he made the poster of Jack Nicklaus's major championship victories, and had it on the wall in his room. This would be the first for Tiger Woods: One down, seventeen more to catch Nicklaus on the professional side of the poster; he already had one more U.S. Amateur victory, three to two.

He had 18 holes to make it official, but these 18 holes, the final 18 holes of the 61st Masters Tournament, would be 6,925 yards of victory lap, and when it was over, there would be the first of what Nicklaus predicted would be 10 green jacket ceremonies. When he put on that jacket at dusk, it would represent a unification, the day when blacks and whites and Asians could come together and join in the same celebration. They've always called Augusta National the Cathedral in the Pines. This was the first Sunday when golf really did feel like a religious experience. Nondemoninational, of course. A Black-Thai Affair.

"This is so significantly sociologically. It's more significant to me, even, than Jackie Robinson breaking the [baseball] color line," Elder said. "It's such a great day for golf. It's such a great day for all people. I'm a part of history in the past and now I'm a part of history in the present. After today, we will have a situation where no one will even turn their head to notice when a black person walks to the first tee."

All heads were turned when Tiger Woods walked to the first tee at Augusta. He had on his red shirt and his black pants, and soon a green jacket would complete the outfit. He birdied the second, bogeyed the fifth, bogeyed the seventh, and birdied the eighth. On the back, he birdied 11, 13, and 14 to hit the number, 18 under par, and then he fought to keep it there.

On the 18th tee, a cameraman got him, firing his motordrive at the top of Tiger's backswing, and then twice coming down. His tee shot hooked over the bunker and into the old practice fairway. Tiger whirled on the camera tower, cursing. "That was a noise that's unnatural," Woods said. "Rustling the trees, you don't hear that. But anything mechanical, you hear that; and when they do that on the golf course when it's quiet, it's going to stand out."

The click of that camera was a blessing; it sent Tiger into the maw of his gallery, allowed him to make that walk up the 18th through a tunnel. He thought of many things after he hit that second shot on the 72nd hole. He thought of his father up there at the 18th green waiting for him; his father who just had a triple bypass, his father who put him through basic training, who dedicated his life to his son's career. He thought of his mother, and the talks she used to give him about sportsmanship and Buddhism. He thought of Jackie Robinson and Charlie Sifford and Lee Elder, and the swath they cut through racism. He thought about the dream he had as a kid, the dream where he won the Masters tournament, and now, almost fifty years to the day after Robinson played his first major-league game for the Brooklyn Dodgers, here Tiger Woods was, doing just that.

Then, he saw the putt that was left, and he realized, it wasn't over. "I've got a tough one," he said. "My focus never left me. Even with all the ovations I got and everybody cheering me on, it was a special moment. I knew I had to take care of business first. I was at 18 under par, which is the scoring record."

He had not three-putted all week, and he wanted to walk off this golf course knowing that could be done. He wanted to walk off with the record and he left himself 5 feet for 270.

This story was too perfect for it to end any other way. He made the putt, did the traditional Tiger Woods uppercut, embraced Fluff, hugged his parents, and then shook the hand of Tom Kite, the U.S. Ryder Cup captain who finished second, 12 shots back. And then he headed to the Butler Cabin for the green jacket ceremony on CBS, where Nick Faldo put that 42 long on his back.

Next was the presentation on the putting green, a tradition that began long before television. Surrounded by a phalanx of policemen, he walked out of the Butler Cabin, and toward the green where earlier in the week he had spent hours getting the speed of the greens. And there, out of the corner of his eye, Tiger Woods spotted Lee Elder and he said, "Wait!" and everybody braked.

"Lee, come here," he said, and the two men embraced,

these two generations of black golfers, the first to play the Masters tournament and the first to win the Master tournament. Tiger whispered in his ear, "Thanks for making this possible," he said. There was another tear in Lee Elder's eyes, and Tiger surged forward to the green, where he was presented the jacket by Nicholson, Chairman of the Competition Committee. "I've always dreamed of coming up 18 and winning," Tiger said. "But I never throught this far through the ceremony."

The news conference followed, and outside the interview room, Earl spoke for the first time about his heart operations, and about how close he had come to missing this day. "They almost lost me," he said. "Death was not far away and I was there and I said, 'No.' When I came back, and I came out of it, my surgeon told me, 'You are a true warrior.' And I said, 'Yes, I have been where the ultimate competition exists. I was competing for my life and I won.' "

This happened during the second operation, in the middle of the Nissan Open, but the old Green Beret, now 64, had fought tougher fights. This one he fought without Nguyen Phong.

"I didn't need any motivation," he said. "It's just an inherent will and drive to survive. I have a lot more work to do and many more things to accomplish with Tiger."

There was a dinner that night at the clubhouse, where he sat under a picture of President Eisenhower at the head table. At the back, near the service entrance, the club's black employees, the waiters and the busboys and the cooks, joined the club members and their wives in the applause.

That night, back at the house they were renting, there was a party for the close friends and family of Tiger Woods, the inner circle. Pete McDaniel showed up from *GolfWorld* and when he asked, "Where's Tiger?" Tida and Jerry Chang showed him. They took him to a bedroom, and there was Tiger Woods, fast asleep.

In his arms, he was hugging the green jacket.

EPILOGUE

On the plane ride to Augusta, the Monday before the tournament, Tiger Woods turned to Mark O'Meara and asked, "Do you think it's possible to win a Grand Slam?" After he won the Masters by the largest margin of victory in a golf tournament this century, after breaking the tournament record established by Jack Nicklaus in 1965, Tiger Woods had answered his own question.

"It can be done," he said.

Golf's "Impregnable Quadrilateral," was won in 1930 by Bob Jones, but the rotation then consisted of the U.S. and British Amateurs. The Masters was not yet a tournament and the PGA Championship was not considered part of the rota.

Since World War II, Ben Hogan came the closest to winning all four grand slam events in a calendar year, with victories at the Masters, U.S. Open, and British Open in 1953. A scheduling conflict, trans-Atlantic travel, and Hogan's ailing legs prevented him from playing the PGA.

There were two other legitimate runs—by Arnold Palmer, who in 1960 won the Masters and the Open, and was second in the British Open at St. Andrews, and by Jack Nicklaus, who in 1972 won the first two legs, but was thwarted at Muirfield by Lee Trevino.

Only four golfers in history (Hogan, Nicklaus, Gary Player, and Gene Sarazen) have won the career grand slam.

The day after the Masters, Larry Dorman, golf writer for *The New York Times*, wrote that the odds of a golfer winning the modern Grand Slam have always been roughly equivalent to a baseball player hitting 70 home runs, a running back gaining 2,500 yards, or a basketball player averaging 60 points per game. In other words, possible, imaginable, but highly unlikely.

Yet, after he won the Masters, London bookmakers had dropped the odds on Tiger doing it from 5,000–1 to 100–1.

"The bigger the event, the higher he'll raise the bar," said Paul Azinger. "He's Michael Jordan in long pants."

There was talk after Augusta that the Masters Committee might have to raise the rim by either growing rough or putting in crossbunkers to make their tournament more competitive. Nick Price, Tom Kite, Jesper Parnevik, even Jack Nicklaus, agreed that something might have to be done. "If they don't make a set of Tiger tees fifty yards behind us, he'll win the next twenty jackets," Parnevik said.

Is Tiger-proofing necessary at Augusta National? Tom Watson, who once said that Tiger Woods will be the most important golfer to come along in fifty years, doesn't think so. Don't change the course for the young man who has changed the course of golf history. "Leave it alone," he says. "Let's see what the young man can do."

Jack Stephens seemed to be in agreement. "I'm not at all embarrassed that the record is broken by one shot after thirty-two years," he said. "It has stood the test of time."

Yes it had, but this is a new time in golf—Tiger Woods's time.

AFTERWORD

I hope you have a better appreciation now for Tiger Woods.
I hope you have an idea of what his life has been like, especially in those months of August, September and October
of 1996, when he transformed himself from a scholarly
economics major at Stanford to the youngest multimillion-
aire in professional golf history. Every week was a new
chapter. The Amateur. The Nike contract. The Nike commercial. The close call at Quad City. The rookie mistake at
Callaway Gardens. The win at Vegas. The win at Disney. The
Tour Championship. I think we'd all admit, the kid from
Cypress, Calif., wrote a phenomenal story. As an author, all
I wanted to do was not get in the way. I wanted to show
you things you don't see on TV, let you read things that
even magazines don't have the space to print, hear things
that you only hear with a media arm band, and feel things
that you haven't felt before about Tiger Woods.

Sure, there's material in this book that you've read before. I've written a bunch of it myself. I went back through
the clips, almost everything that was ever printed: I don't
think any 20-year-old in the world has had more words
written about him than Tiger Woods has. I said at the beginning of this book we're only getting started. I say at the end

that 20 years from now, I wouldn't be surprised if Tiger Woods lives up to his father's prediction, and wins those 14 major championships. If you count like Jack Nicklaus, he's actually only got 11 more to go. The more I researched, the more I interviewed, the more I realized that this kid really could be the Michael Jordan of golf. By that I mean the best of all time. Certainly, the golfer of the next millennium.

But on a higher level than winning golf tournaments and setting records, I've come away from this experience thinking that Tiger Woods has the potential to become to golf what Arthur Ashe was to tennis. As Michael Jordan himself says, "I admire [Tiger] for what he's done thus far because for so long it was truly a game that a lot of minorities couldn't play . . . so in that sense he's carrying an extra burden along with him, to succeed and expand and cross all racial barriers." I admire him, too, for establishing a new plateau, a higher ground, if you will. I really do believe he was put here for a bigger reason than just to play golf. I don't think he is a god, but I do believe he was sent by One.

As a parent, I've got to salute the job Earl and Tida did raising Tiger. Sure, he's been programmed for this, but I don't look at Earl as an overbearing parent at all. I look at him as a man of discipline and family values, and it's like Wally Goodwin at Stanford says, our country would be a better place if there were more parents like Earl and Tida Woods in it.

They reared a son to travel down unchartered roads, then he cut the ties, stepped back, and watched the world adopt him as their hero. Tiger Woods did indeed transcend the game, but he is not, and never pretended to be, the Jackie Robinson of golf. Those trails were blazed before Tiger Woods picked up a golf club. He is, quite simply, the new standard.

Without getting caught up in the mania, taking a step back and looking at this kid with objective eyes, it's easy to say that Tom Watson was right. That this is the most important golfer to come along in 50 years. As a golfer who plays the sport with a passion, as a writer who has covered the game since 1980, as a person who respects hard work and integrity, I'm just grateful to be around during this kid's time.

In *Heartbreak Hill,* award-winning journalist Tim Rosaforte delivers the inside story of the dramatic 1995 Ryder Cup. He captures the thrilling holes-in-one, the clutch chips, the joys, and the numbing disappointments that led to the most spectacular comeback in the tournament's sixty-eight-year history.

In addition, Rosaforte provides a thorough and insightful preview of what we can expect for the 1997 Ryder Cup tournament, including details of Tiger Woods's campaign for a space on the U.S. team, making this book a must-have for every weekend golfer and armchair fan.

HEARTBREAK HILL:
Anatomy of a Ryder Cup

TIM ROSAFORTE

Coming in September 1997
from Griffin Trade Paperbacks!

In an extraordinary book that transcends sports biography, Bob Greene takes the reader along with Jordan over two seasons with the Chicago Bulls, during glorious championship surges and trying personal moments. With rare insight, Greene reveals the person inside the icon: a man who makes millions but cannot go for a quiet walk around the block without getting mobbed, a man who competes ferociously on the court, but who performs some of his most remarkable and unexpected feats away from the limelight.

HANG TIME

BOB GREENE

"Jordan seems to open up more to Greene than anybody."
—Mike Lupica, New York *Daily News*

In April 1993, Monica Seles had been on her way to becoming the best women's player of all time. But then an obsessed fan put her life and career in mortal danger. To recover from the traumatic attack, Monica left the game she loved. Many believed she would not be able to cope with the pressure of professional tennis again.

Here is the whole truth about the rise to stardom, the terrifying assault, and the thrilling story of Monica's struggle to come back as a true champion—a woman able to handle everything life served her, and win.

RETURN OF A CHAMPION

THE
MONICA SELES STORY

JOE LAYDEN

RETURN OF A CHAMPION: THE MONICA SELES STORY
Joe Layden
_____ 96002-6 $5.99 U.S./$6.99 Can.

Since May 30, 1982, Cal Ripken, Jr. has never missed a game—a marathon performance that has brought him the 1982 Rookie of the Year Award, two American League MVP Awards, an All-Star Game MVP trophy, the much-coveted Gold Glove, and a World Series title. Now he's attained the ultimate—he's surpassed Lou Gehrig's incredible streak of 2,130 consecutive games played.

Award-winning sports biographer Harvey Rosenfeld takes us through Cal's ascent to superstardom, capturing the grit and determination of baseball's greatest living role model.

IRON MAN
THE CAL RIPKEN, JR. STORY
HARVEY ROSENFELD
WITH AN INTRODUCTION BY CAL RIPKEN, SR.
AND PHOTOS BY KEVIN ALLEN

IRON MAN: THE CAL RIPKEN, JR. STORY
Harvey Rosenfeld
_____ 95781-5 $5.99 U.S./$6.99 CAN.

They got together for their 25th high-school reunion—and came up with a crazy, enticing idea: to hop into a Ford and hit the highway for one more mellow, footloose summer in the sun.

They're headed for ball games at Wrigley Field, an old girlfriend in St. Louis, a state fair in Ohio, a convention of dental hygienists in Atlanta, Elvis Presley's old hotel suite in Las Vegas, and miles and miles of empty road beckoning to them with with the message: C'mon. It's summer. Time to remember who we were...and who we still are inside.

Hilarious and heart-stirring, *All Summer Long*, Bob Greene's first novel, brings you everything you love in his journalism—all the warm humor, sharp insights, and touching honesty, in a story you'll slurp down like a cold milkshake from the drive-in.

"Absolutely captivating." —*Los Angeles Times*

ALL SUMMER LONG

BOB GREENE

A SUPERSTAR'S TOUGHEST CHALLENGE...

Fresh off a championship season, New York Titans' quarterback Hunter Logan is on the winning streak of his life. But when he places one bet that gets traced by the Mob, ruthless don Tony Rizzo strongarms him into a point-shaving scheme that will net millions for organized crime.

IS A GAME WITH NO RULES...

Now, Hunter is trapped in a no-win situation: if he goes along with the Mob, he's risking everything he's ever played for. If he doesn't, he's risking the lives of his wife and young daughter. With the clock running out and the FBI moving in, it's up to the quarterback to make the call...and all bets are off.

TITANS

The explosive novel by
TIM GREEN

"Moves like a two-minute drill."
—*USA Today*

FIND OUT WHAT IT'S LIKE TO BE MIKE.

Sportswriter Mitchell Krugel has spent years covering the Chicago Bulls, and in that time has seen Michael Jordan mature as a player and as a person. In this fascinating biography, he provides insights that Jordan fans want to hear about their idol, including:

- Why Michael retired in the prime of his career
- How he came to grips with the tragic murder of his father
- The love/hate relationship with his teammates and coaches
- His lifelong obsession with competition and challenges

Combining excerpts from the author's interviews with Michael, as well as his close friends and the league's top players and coaches, Jordan explores the human side of a man who is arguably the greatest basketball

JORDAN
The Man, His Words, His Life

MITCHELL KRUGEL